FEMINISM AND FILM

FEMINISM AND FILM

Maggie Humm

Edinburgh University Press

Indiana University Press
Bloomington and Indianapolis

First published in the United Kingdom by
Edinburgh University Press
22 George Square, Edinburgh

and in North America by
Indiana University Press
601 North Morton Street
Bloomington, Indiana 47404-3797

Printed and bound in Great Britain by Hartnolls Limited, Bodmin, Cornwall

British Library Cataloguing in Publication Data

A CIP record for this book is available from the British Library.

ISBN 0 7486 0908 3 (cloth) (Edinburgh)
ISBN 0 7486 0900 8 (paper) (Edinburgh)

Library of Congress Cataloging-in-Publication Data

A catalog record for this book is available from the Library of Congress.

ISBN 0-253-33334-2 (cloth) (Indiana)
ISBN 0-253-21146-8 (paper) (Indiana)

1 2 3 4 5   01 00 99 98 97

CONTENTS

———◦◦———

LIST OF FIGURES

———⊂⊃———

The figures are selected from the following films; full details are given in the captions and the Acknowledgements.

The cover illustration shows a still from *Orlando* reproduced by courtesy of The Sales Company.

PREFACE

In *Adam's Rib*, Spencer Tracy tells Katharine Hepburn: 'You get cute when you get causey'. One of the many reasons I began to explore feminist theory was my very sad discovery that there is a vast discrepancy between Tracy's delight and most other men's attitudes. What such an exploration inevitably teaches is that forms of language are not simply technologies of communication but are intensely caught up in social judgements about gender. This applies equally to visual languages and thus the language of film. Yet in film studies, contemporary feminist social theories and film analysis are not usually considered together. Film studies, like much of communication studies in general, often separates its areas of inquiry from feminism's social insights. There are good historical reasons which go some way to explain why film theory is somewhat immured in racially undifferentiated psychoanalytic theory at the expense of other more general ways of thinking: for example, the institutional centrality of important, key theoretical journals like *Screen* as well as social sciences' and humanities' focus on specific theories of psychoanalysis at the expense of more racially problematised theories. But currently in a time of backlash against feminism there is a good deal at stake in extending, not curtailing, feminist critiques and in trying to use feminism's analytical tools.

Feminism and Film, then, involves a discussion both of feminist theories and of what feminist theories can help us to see and newly understand in some contemporary films. Why the linkage of feminism and film matters is because all representations, visual or otherwise, are what make gendered constructions of knowledge and subjectivity possible. Without representations we have no gender identities, and through representations we shape our gendered world.

This book derived its initial impetus from my desire to interweave film analysis with feminism more extensively for a course on feminism and film in Women's Studies at the University of East London. However, as I wrote, I realised that moments of British feminist independent film-making, feminist aesthetics and praxis have not been adequately described, nor had attention been given to, the intellectual context of Mulvey's 1975 essay 'Visual Pleasure and Narrative Cinema' or to the major feminist critics Kuhn, Kaplan and hooks. So my study underwent a similar expansion to include contemporary British intellectual history and key feminist critics (Chapter 1) as well as feminist praxis (Chapter 7).

Feminist theory has always crossed disciplinary borders to recruit the energies of autobiography, differing epistemologies and the social polemic, and has found fresh representational identities in a complex social time when identities are all too often constructed for us. Currently, feminist theory is producing some of the most exciting and intellectually challenging work in the academy. But to present the sequence of these chapters as the evolution of contemporary feminist theory over the last decades would be inaccurate. Rather, *Feminism and Film* utilises, in a provisional way, some themes and techniques from contemporary feminism (literary criticism, Black feminism, debates about pornography and so forth) in film analysis.

The risks of 'border traffic', of going beyond the usual boundaries of a discipline, mean that I can only scratch the screen's surface in an eclectic way (Humm 1991). My choice of particular feminist ideas and critics is inevitably limited by the permitted length of the book, but I use those which strike me as being applicable to a range of films not just to those films I describe here. Obviously there are other feminist critiques, perhaps most important, which are not so evidently amenable to film analysis. At this point, I am not proposing a comprehensive theory of feminism and film. Rather I hope, simply, that *Feminism and Film* will help to expand both film studies and feminist thought by bringing together, contextualising and applying some feminist ideas that have spectacularly dominated academic thinking in the past decades.

ACKNOWLEDGEMENTS

―⇒⊂―

My thanks should go first to my mother for taking me to the cinema every week from the age of 4, to both my parents for our additional weekly family visit and to the small boy in the flat below mine (whose name now escapes me) who shared my third weekly filmgoing in the Saturday morning club of Tarzan and Western shorts. Together with television reruns of old movies, my childhood was saturated in films' visual pleasures.

My students at the University of East London provided thought-provoking responses to ideas that I first tested on them, and their intelligent enthusiasms encouraged me to write *Feminism and Film*. Alan O'Shea and my colleagues in Women's Studies and Cultural Studies at UEL are a constant source of intellectual stimulation. I am grateful to Professor Judy Simons for inviting me to give a paper on *Orlando* at 'Literature: A Woman's Business', and to Margaret Drabble for her very encouraging responses to the paper at 9:30am on a cold Sheffield Saturday. Michael O'Pray kindly gave me references and journals as well as sharing his impressive film scholarship. No British film critic can survive without the tactful assistance and expertise of the library staff at the British Film Institute, St Stephen's Street. My thanks to my careful anonymous reader, to Dan for his present of the perfect pen and my major thanks to Shiona Burris for her very deft computing expertise.

Chapters 2 and 3 are vastly revised, updated and expanded versions of 'Is the Gaze Feminist? Pornography, Film and Feminism', in G. Day and C. Bloom (eds), *Perspectives on Pornography* (Macmillan, 1988) and 'Tropisms, Tape-Slide and Theory', in G. Griffin (ed.), *Changing Our Lives* (Pluto Press, 1994) respectively.

Stills from the film *Dead Ringers* are by courtesy of the Rank Organisation Plc; stills from *Orlando* courtesy of The Sales Company; still from *A Question of Silence* by Marleen Gorris, courtesy of Sigma Pictures, Maarssen, The Netherlands; reproduction of *Portrait of a Negress* by Marie-Guihelmine Benoist with permission of the Musée du Louvre; still from *Daughters of the Dust* by kind permission of Julie Dash © 1992; still from *Variety* (1984) directed by Bette Gordon, photographer Nan Goldin, courtesy of Bette Gordon.

London, December 1996

PART ONE

Chapter 1

FEMINIST THEORY, AESTHETICS
AND FILM THEORY

Mulvey, Kuhn, Kaplan and hooks

———◁▷———

INTRODUCTION

Feminism has no single vision, although it is a visionary way of seeing.
Film, on the other hand, often and anxiously envisions women stereotypically as 'good' mothers or 'bad', hysterical careerists. From Jane
Fonda's brief flirtation with independence and inevitable marriage to
Klute in the 1970s, to *Dead Ringers'* masculine appropriation of reproduction in the 1980s, to today, every Hollywood woman 'is someone
else's Other' (Gentile 1985, p. 7). Films' powerful misfiguring of the
female is what feminism seeks to disempower. The visual is therefore
a crucial visible part of any feminist theory.

This is for two reasons: first because the visual is epistemologically
privileged in Western knowledge and second because cultural images
often subtly, or not so subtly, codify and articulate 'backlash' misogyny
(Faludi 1992). It is hard not to sense that the ostentatious display in
Fatal Attraction of a hysterical career woman and the audience delight
in her murder reflects an ineffable feeling of a more deep-rooted hatred.
The goal of feminist aesthetics is to appropriate the power, if not the
privilege, of such dominant images.

Yet feminist film theory, although a sophisticated body of work,
often places mainstream cinema in a space of pure difference. Over the
past two decades, since Laura Mulvey's germinal vision of Douglas
Sirk's films, theorists drawing on psychoanalysis argue that mainstream cinema encourages an inevitably voyeuristic male gaze and

3

reproduces fetishistic stereotypes of women. By the late 1980s, feminist film theorists' insistent heterosexual model of fetishised female/mainstream male began to crumble and broadened to include issues of lesbian representation (Greer *et al* 1993; Stacey 1990). But while this newer feminist agenda, as Liz Kotz suggests, is not a closed system, its conceptualisations are often still binary: lesbian spectator/woman subject (Kotz 1993).

This concept is certainly at odds with my adolescent memories of The Globe Cinema, Newcastle-upon-Tyne in the late 1950s. A fetishising screen is not what I paid my half crown to see or saw, in *Calamity Jane*, *Adam's Rib* and my other favourite teenage movies. I saw an altogether livelier and less coherent story. And much later, as a young academic in Britain in the early 1970s, my memories of the historical moment of Laura Mulvey's essay (Mulvey 1975) are very much at odds with the later circumscriptions of film theorists. Mulvey's essay is, to me, a more original and creative engagement with that protean Zeitgeist moment of emerging visual studies than feminist scripts currently allow.

Feminism and Film comes from women's studies where media representations are the daily visual vocabulary of women's social, political and economic disadvantages. Perspectives from literary criticism, psychoanalysis, reproductive theory, postmodernism and Black feminism and feminist practice, jostle together in the more diverse tool bag which women's studies teachers need to carry. Women's Studies attends to multiple differences of race, social construction and sexual preference. It would be very inaccurate to reduce feminist film theory crudely to 'spectator theory' but I do wish to juxtapose other possible approaches.

As well as utilising more novel approaches for film study, a fundamental concern of *Feminism and Film* is to match feminism with film. In the last decade feminist studies, both inside and outside the academy, has moved on from believing that gender discriminations are always determined to not understating the different perceptions of racial and sexual identities. These perceptions visualise a wider range of cultural processes. This 'turn to culture', as Michèle Barrett argues, needs a kind of feminist film analysis which can draw eclectically on feminist theories hitherto tangential to film theory, for example reproductive theory, and connect these ideas with film styles (Barrett and Phillips

1992). In Annette Kuhn's *Women's Pictures: Feminism and Cinema* (discussed below) feminism has a subtitular role. While I wholeheartedly share Kuhn's belief that gender profoundly shapes cinema, I want at the same time to emphasise how little this process can be understood without the gravitas, the tangible vision of feminism. The subtitle is my surtitle.

FEMINIST THEORY

All variants of feminist theory tend to share three major assumptions: gender is a social construction that oppresses women more than men; 'patriarchy' (i.e., the male domination of social institutions) fashions these constructions; women's experiential knowledge best helps us to envision a future non-sexist society. These shared premises shape a double agenda: the task of critique – attacking gender stereotypes – and the task of construction, sometimes called feminist praxis – constructing new models. Feminist theory focuses particularly on women's experience of sexuality, work and the family, inevitably challenging traditional frameworks of knowledge and putting in question many assumptions such as 'universalism' – the view that there are biological universals.

Although foremothers like Mary Wollstonecraft are often claimed as feminist, the term 'feminism' only began to be used in the 1890s (Offen 1988). In this century Virginia Woolf and Simone de Beauvoir anticipate second wave feminism's attack on women's oppression (Woolf 1929; de Beauvoir 1972). In the 1960s, student and civil rights movements provided an impetus, shaping the topics and language of current feminist theory. As an identifiable area then, feminist theory dates from the 1970s with the publication of Kate Millett's *Sexual Politics* (Millett 1977).

Feminist theory is intensely interdisciplinary ranging across customary subject divisions, including history, philosophy, anthropology, and the arts among others. Certain themes recur – reproduction, representation, the sexual division of labour – while most strikingly, new concepts such as 'sexism' are created to address absences in existing knowledge as well as the social discriminations these concepts describe.

In all this, women's subjective experiences are drawn upon to enrich scholarship and scientific theories. The starting point is often consciousness raising where the personal can become political: Catharine

MacKinnon argues that feminist theory is the first theory to emerge from those whose interest it affirms (MacKinnon 1989). On the other hand, feminist psychoanalysts claim androcentric knowledge derives from masculine experiences of separation learnt in childhood.

Since feminism developed at a time when the participation of women in the work force was rising fast but discrimination still persisted, critics first focused on the sexism of language and of cultural and economic institutions. While intellectual ideas rarely present themselves in neat chronological order, the 1970s tackled the causes of women's oppression (capitalism/masculinity) describing society as a structure of oppressors (male) and oppressed (female). This moment is usually divided into forms of feminism (liberal, Marxist/socialist, cultural/radical). Liberal feminism argues that women's liberation will come with equal legal, political and economic rights, following Betty Friedan's attack on media's 'feminine mystique' which, she argues, prevented women from claiming equality (Friedan 1963). More comprehensive Marxist/socialist assessments of economic gender exploitations were made by Juliet Mitchell and others. The key questions were: did women form a distinct sex-class and how far is capitalism structured by patriarchy? (see Mitchell 1966). By widening the Marxist concept of production to include household labour and childcare ('domestic labour' debate) feminists could highlight further sexual divisions as well as women's unequal status at work ('reserve army of labour'). Startlingly, Shulamith Firestone argued that the 'material' of women's reproductive body was as much a source of oppression as material inequality (Firestone 1979).

While dual systems theory argues that both capitalism and patriarchy construct gender, requiring to combat the process, a synthesis of Marxism with feminism, MacKinnon suggests that only radical feminism counts as feminism precisely because it is post-Marxist. In opposition to a Marxist focus on production, cultural and radical feminists, for example Adrienne Rich (1976), focused on reproduction, mothering and creativity. Although the labels 'cultural' or 'radical' are often misapplied, in general radical theorists take the view that sexuality, specifically as expressed in male violence, is the cause of women's oppression and condoned by the institutionalisation of heterosexuality (see Dworkin 1981). This is the theme of Rich's milestone essay 'Compulsory Heterosexuality' which, building on de Beauvoir's premise that women are originally homosexual, proposes that lesbian-ism can be part of every woman's cultural, if not physical, experience (Rich 1980). This argument, that 'lesbian' is shaped as much by ideo-logical preferences as by explicit practice, developed from the notions of 'women identified women' and 'feminism is the theory, lesbianism is the practice' in second wave feminism.

A major rethinking of symbolic and social structures of gender dif-ference was undertaken by French feminists (*écriture féminine*). They claimed that the cultural and gendered binaries – man/woman, culture/ nature – always made 'woman' inferior (see Cixous 1976). Binaries ignore women's fluid identity and the semiotic world of mother/infant bonding. American feminists drew on object relations psychoanalysis to locate the source of male power and fear of women in men's early experience of learning to be 'not the mother' (see Chodorow 1978). These accounts of gender identity and objectification greatly enriched feminist film and media study. The notion that there is a distinctive and gendered perception (the male 'gaze') is matched by the feminist standpoint theorists who challenge false notions of rationality and universalism in the social sciences (see Harding 1991).

The 1980s saw a crucial shift in feminist theory when Black feminist writers directed attention to ethnic differences. Criticising the three-form, or three-phase, typology (liberal/Marxist/cultural) as a white women's mental map which ignored the experiences of Black women, they describe discrimination as an interlocking system based on race, class and gender (hooks 1984). They also introduced fresh theoretical arguments, suggesting, for example, that the family was not necessarily patriarchal but could be a site of resistance. Black theory derives from Afracentric history, as well as from a 'both/or' reality (the act of being simultaneously inside and outside society) and has a particular view of mothering experience (see Walker 1984 and Lorde 1984).

These critiques of white essentialism were paralleled by feminist poststructuralist and postmodern critiques of structured systems of subjectivity. Drawing on ideas from deconstruction and discourse analysis, feminists argued that gender structures are historically vari-able and not predetermined. This led, as I have argued, to what Barrett calls 'the turn to culture' and a renewed interest in cultural symbols (Barrett and Phillips 1992). Italian feminists, for example, created the term *autocoscienza* or the collective construction of new identities.

Through cultural study many of these themes were brought together in feminist peace theory which argues that violence stems from traditional gender socialisation. In opposition, pacifists created women-centred symbolic models of environmental action.

In short, feminism has a long term investment in cultural critiques. From Betty Friedan's *The Feminine Mystique* with its luxuriant plunge into the world of backlash media to the equally popular and fundamental texts of younger feminists – Naomi Wolf's *The Beauty Myth* and Susan Faludi's *Backlash* – feminists attack overvalued media myths like, for example 'infertility epidemics' and 'burnt out superwomen' (Friedan 1963; Wolf 1990; Faludi 1992). It is not surprising that the turn from deterministic models of gender discrimination would inevitably involve Barrett's 'turn to culture'. Films are conspicuous sites of social misogyny but 'women's pictures' are not necessarily symmetrically opposite to those of men. What spectatorship theory acknowledges is that media stereotypes are inextricably caught up in gendered pleasures. What feminist theory argues in addition is that the masculinity or femininity of viewing pleasures are historical, rhetorical and authored.

FEMINIST AESTHETICS

The modern concept of aesthetics, meaning a transcendence of personal experience in disinterested moments of reflection, originated with Alexander Baumgarten's *Aesthetics*, of 1750. It is a concept of disinterestedness which informs the canonic texts of Kant and Hegel (Hein 1993, p. 10). Yet visual culture reflects society, not just the individual, and it is those reflections on which feminism centres arguing that gender differences and discriminations are the common semantic of all cultures, including media cultures. The Women's Movement, at least in Britain, grew in tandem with feminist culture and aesthetics: in the autumn of 1980 there were three all-women exhibitions including the influential 'Women's Images of Men' at the Institute of Contemporary Arts, London (Parker and Pollock 1987). Further, culture creates both the ground and the impetus for feminism's creativity, thus the women's peace camp at Greenham Common generated a huge range of ecological and pacifist arts including photography, banner making and collective rituals – a compelling 'demonstration' of visual feminism.

One of the primary tasks of feminist aesthetics is to study and promote women as producers of art. The British feminist photographer Jo
Spence argues that photography should not be studied as the person-
ification of a singular and individual eye but as 'a diversity of practices,
institutions and historical conjunctures in which the photographic text
is produced, and deployed' (Spence and Holland 1991, p. 152). The aesthetic, formalist rejection of utility and the everyday was challenged
by feminists describing the rich expressiveness of women's crafts
(Mainardi 1982). The feminist playwright Michelene Wandor insistently
argues that at times of changing attitudes to women and to sexuality –
the Restoration, the Industrial revolution, the Suffrage agitation and
second wave feminism – new theatre and performance flourish, raising,
as transvestite theatre does, new questions: 'Doubts about the boundaries of what is 'masculine' and what is 'feminine' are bound to lead
to questions about the relationship between sexual appearance and
gender behaviour' (Wandor 1981, p. 19).

Film and video are not isolated from this cultural malleability,
Annette Kuhn's 'Dear Linda', an account of the making of the British
television series *Pictures of Women*, is written in an engaging feminist
epistolary form and describes how feminist aesthetic processes battled
with traditional production 'aesthetics' which in one instance, demand-
ed the acceptance of adversarial formats in studio discussions (Kuhn
1984). The interruption of this seemingly interminable gender binary
by Black and indigenous feminist art is excitingly productive as when
the American Women's Caucus for Art and feminist artists Faith
Ringgold and Ramona Sakiestewa, broaden the scope of feminist aesthetics to include rituals in which the spiritual and healing qualities
of art constitute equal grounds for value judgements alongside the
formal appearance of art objects (Touchette 1994). It seems logically
clear from these developments that the co-dependency of feminist
theory and aesthetics is a productive partnership.

What are the basic themes running through feminist aesthetics?
The assignment of a woman's signature to media products was the primary task of feminist art critics in the mid 1970s. From Linda Nochlin's
inspirational 'Why Have There Been No Great Women Artists?', Lucy
Lippard's *From the Center* (describing herself as art activist not critic)
to Judy Chicago's *The Dinner Party*, feminists tied feminist aesthetics
ostensibly to specific female experiences (Nochlin 1971; Lippard 1976;

Chicago 1979). The British feminist historian Sheila Rowbotham describes a similar need for women's creative visibility: 'In order to create an alternative an oppressed group must at once shatter the self-reflecting world which encircles it and, at the same time, project its own image onto history' (Rowbotham 1973, p. 27).

A second task was to make visible the insignia of the women's movement: the personal is political. This task, and the consequent uneasy tension of the personal and the political when it comes to art practice marks 1970s feminist aesthetics. Not only was the feminist claim that art is socially constructed at odds with a romantic concept of artistic individualism but also, and bitterly paradoxically, this claim is at odds with a fundamental feminist attachment to the lived and individual experiences of women. Further and complicating tensions were plainer in the 1980s when Afra-Americans pointed out that the white feminist focus on the body could be racist: '"Sexuality" a conceptual category that includes thinking about it as well as doing it, is something black people just don't have time for' (O'Grady 1994, p. 164). One solution was to acknowledge that artistic subjectivity simply was ambivalently 'different' from social experiences but, nevertheless, a more hopefully truthful form of knowledge. The British artist Susan Hiller calls this solution 'truth telling in art' (Hiller 1991, p. 244).

This span of thought focuses on the distinctive issue of art products. Feminist artists eagerly embraced performance, attacked the traditional concept of art as a collection of museum objects, offered some links between aesthetic and subjective epistemologies and placed all of this in a feminist cultural context responding to audience and moment. The huge task necessarily involved feminists in huge conceptual issues. For example, interrogating the Western concept of artistic individualism while at the same time affirming 'natural' and non-sequential processes of artistic construction, matching feminist theory's interrogative 'Is Female to Male as Nature is to Culture?' (Ortner 1974). Gisela Ecker, in the first essay collection of European feminist aesthetics, privileges neither artistic practice nor theory (Ecker 1985), arguing instead that feminist art itself is frequently and self-consciously theoretical. Rather than isolating specific features of art as feminist, Ecker suggests that 'feminist aesthetic theory must insist that all investigations into art have to be *thoroughly genderised*' (Ecker 1985, p. 22). Feminist aesthetics focuses on women's social subjectivity, not simply on visual imagery, and feminist art aims to transform the asocial, sexist values of traditional aesthetics.

This is clearly seen in the work of the American artist Nancy Spero who represents those images of woman historically made by men, for example, Greek iconography, wittily deflating their power with multiple images and textual over-writing, often quoting Hélène Cixous (Spero 1987). Indeed figurative feminist art of the 1970s was a tactical challenge to American abstraction: Judy Chicago's vaginal iconography similarly attempts to retrieve female images and to challenge dominant constructions (Chicago 1979). This valorization of female experience can risk essentialism so an alternative feminist approach was to foreground the social construction of femininity, for example in documentary photography as well as the psychoanalytic (Barry and Flitterman 1987). It follows that all feminist aesthetics rejects any modernist self-sufficient privileging of the visual.

In some ways this exciting, experiential multimedia, yet context-specific, aesthetic agenda reveals that feminist aesthetics was far ahead of film theory in the same decade. For example, rather than describing the visual as an intact, 'scopic field', feminist artists in the 1970s and 1980s were looking for pleasures in the gaps in visual codes (Parker and Pollock 1987). One significant result of this enterprise is Jo Spence's phototherapeutic 'restaging' of family photography (Spence 1987). Yet film theory and art theory do both scrutinise processes of symbolisation agreeing that symbols are deeply and familiarly encoded in further processes of fetishism (where a feminine image of hair or boot stands in for the female individual) and also of substitution (sexual metaphors). In addition, they record that such processes operate in tandem. Where feminist aesthetics diverges from film theory is in dismissing film theory's perception, at least of the 1970s, that such processes involve a necessary and universal objectification of women. Rather, feminist art practice continually 'revisions' representational mechanisms of sexual difference as well as subverting traditional viewing locations, by for example, establishing women's workshops and galleries. Imagining radically new mechanisms of viewing pleasure – Judy Chicago's *Dinner Party* with its admixture of dinner places, craft work and table runners – and new viewing locations – Chicago's *Birth Project* toured local health clinics and hospitals as well as galleries – went some way to subvert a patriarchal visual 'regime'.

The goal, then, of feminist aesthetics is to construct new aesthetic languages (Pollock 1989). Current examples of feminist 'theory art' which restage the body, include Marjorie Franklin's computer digital re-editing of her own image into a facsimile of Donna Haraway's feminist cyborg and Cindy Sherman's 'reconstructed' self images which mimic and mock film images and genres (Tamblyn 1994; Williamson 1983). Michele Wallace attacks the aesthetic processes of desexualisation and deprimitivisation within Afro-American studies because this denies the work of Black female artists, writers and blues singers (Wallace 1990). Clearly there is a great deal which is imaginatively creative and politically important in these projects. What helps to engender such energies is of course having a feminist audience. And here, the important projects of art and film critics do match in practice. Film screenings, like those at the London Arts Lab, contributed to many feminist activist events in the 1970s, not least because of films' 'visual pleasures'. In addition feminist film theorists worked collectively with feminist artists and activists, for example, in Berwick Street Film Collective's *The Night Cleaners* (1975). The search for new representations within feminist aesthetics, as well as new visual processes and languages, became the activity of feminist film theorists in the 1980s and 1990s.

FEMINIST FILM THEORY

By the 1970s an embryonic feminist studies was crystallising in the academy and encouraging a much sharper-eyed and theorised attention to women's filmic representations. Feminist film theory grew from four diverse intellectual formations: British Marxism's new attention to the cultural superstructure, following the impact of Louis Althusser's *Lenin and Philosophy*; the now vibrant feminist art movement; feminist psychoanalysis, for example, Juliet Mitchell's influential *Psychoanalysis and Feminism*; and feminist film *praxis* with the New York International Festival of Women's Films (1972) and a showing of women's films at the Edinburgh Film Festival in the same year organised by Laura Mulvey (Althusser 1971; Mitchell 1974).

The first feminist texts describing women's particular roles in mainstream cinema were Marjorie Rosen's *Popcorn Venus* and Molly Haskell's *From Reverence to Rape* (Rosen 1973; Haskell 1973). In addition, the journal *Women and Film* was founded in 1972. Both Rosen and

Haskell created a descriptive, emotional 'historiography' of Hollywood cinema showing how women's conventional roles, for example, as mothers or girls next door, had little representational bite on women's real identities and experiences. According to these critics, mainstream cinema did not represent women's lived experience but only stereotypes of women's social status or, indeed, lack of status. Thus, Haskell, as the title of her book suggests, argued that the frequency of rape scenes represented a general patriarchal myth that women secretly desired to be raped. In other words films reflect social power structures at large. Through semi-sociological descriptions of film content, Haskell, Rosen and Joan Mellen in her more inclusive attention to European film, hoped to reveal the sexism of such structures (Mellen 1974). A crucial theme in this 'narrative' criticism is the view that film acts largely as a social mirror.

Subsequent critics asked the obvious question: how did such patriarchal controls function? The explanatory frameworks of Marxism and semiotics gave Claire Johnston's *Notes on Women's Cinema* (1973) a new purchase on a wider continuum of women's filmic representations. Coining the term 'counter-cinema', Johnston argued that critics needed to turn from scrutinising images to interrogate the processes of film production. Images were not simply mirrors of real life but ideological signifiers. Together with Pam Cook, Johnston examined the works of Raoul Walsh in terms of unconscious and embattled masculine features:

> The task for feminist criticism must consist of a process of denaturalization: a questioning of the unity of text; of seeing it as a contradictory interplay of different codes; of tracing its 'structuring absences' and its relationship to the universal problem of symbolic castration. (Cook and Johnston 1990, p. 26)

It was this focus on gendered and signifying contradictions which was the particular contribution of British semiotic critics to feminist film theory. The lack of effectiveness of film techniques, Cook and Johnston suggest, could be just as revealing as films' intact masculinity. The task was to problematise cultural features and expose the definitional pressures of the economic and sexuality. What British semiotic critics brought to film analysis in the 1970s was the understanding that gender constructions are always fraught. Since ideological tensions are negotiated mainly through gender, women's representations are inevitably contradictory.

By the middle of the 1970s psychoanalytic theory grew generically distinct. Laura Mulvey's germinal essay 'Visual Pleasure and Narrative Cinema' (Mulvey 1975) describes a psychic context in which voyeurism, fetishism and narcissism all structure film viewing. Mulvey's essay is cited and reprinted (by myself among others), more often than any other film theory (Humm 1992). This is perhaps because Mulvey, in a hugely original gesture welds Althusserian theory, feminist aesthetics and feminist theory together with psychoanalysis. Since I discuss her writings in some detail below let me quickly here summarise her main themes and point to her impact.

Mulvey's insight, derived from study of the relationship between film techniques, spectators and viewing pleasures, is that films deliberately create masculine structures of 'looking'. It is 'the gaze', Mulvey argues, which is the main mechanism of filmic control. According to Mulvey, mainstream cinema appeals to the scopophilic instinct (a term Freud chose for the activity of looking at another as an erotic object). Mulvey concludes that this gaze is male and that cinema relies on three kinds of gaze: the camera, usually operated by a man, looking at women as objects; the look of male actors within the film which is structured to make their gaze powerful; and the gaze of the spectator, who is presumed to be male, voyeuristically identifying with the camera/actor gazing at women represented in fetishistic and stereotypical ways.

Mulvey's essay inaugurated a distinctive British and American body of work devoted to issues of spectatorship, issues which are still prominent today. Similar lines of enquiry include the work of Mary Ann Doane, who explores psychoanalytic identifications in terms of 1940s female spectatorship and masquerade (Doane 1990). Elizabeth Cowie, drawing on semiology as well as psychoanalysis argues that identification is an issue of narrative and that this involves a more complex construction of looks which may not be gender determined (Cowie 1993). Janet Bergstrom took this looser definition of identification a stage further, in her analysis of Hitchcock's films, by examining fantasy whose structure involves multiple identifications (Bergstrom 1988).

The British critic Jacqueline Rose poses a further question about women's desire for her own fetishised image in *Sexuality in the Field of Vision* and how 'to formulate in and through cinema, if one can at all, the relation between this constitution of the feminine and other forms of oppression and subjection for women, the attempt to hold the relation between the two' (Rose 1986, p. 213). Rose's argument (discussed in more detail in the last chapter) adds the further dimension that all issues of film representations are inevitably issues of women's representation. *Jacqueline Rose*

Other critics married deconstructive insights with psychoanalysis in order to explain identification and resistances. For example, Joan Copjec introduces the concept of suture, or the process of 'stitching' the spectator to the image, in her account of Marguerite Duras's films (Copjec 1988), while Kaja Silverman, in her highly original and stimulating account of identifications and subjectivity in the films of Yvonne Rainer and Liliana Cavani, adds aural signifiers to those of spectatorship (Silverman 1988). Finally, Constance Penley's major work on enunciation, the imaginary and spectatorship, contextualises many of these psychoanalytic concerns of feminist film theory (Penley 1988).

The dialogue between feminism and psychoanalysis has been hugely rewarding. Both share particular concerns: the relation between gender and identifications and issues of repression and the instability of identity. Second, both share key methods: analysing texts, whether these are films or the unconscious, in terms of codes and as if texts can represent the 'unsaid' in everyday life. What psychoanalysis offers is a reading of the feminine rooted neither entirely in the social construction of femininity (which nevertheless organises the feminine) nor entirely in biology, but, rather, seen through language and subjectivity. Psychoanalytic cases, like many films, tend to be written as narratives. Psychoanalysis tries to read the 'narrative' of each subject in terms of her or his codes of speech among other things. To do this it must focus, in particular, on syntactical forms – on distortions and on a lack of suture between subjectivity and image – which may provide access to hidden parts of a subject's personality. Film theory, similarly, confronts 'defensive' features in films. By examining condensations, ruptures and excess stereotypes in the filmic text, critics aim to reveal a hidden sub-text which may structure a film's 'identity'.

In brief, from the 1970s to the late 1980s, debates about spectatorship and identity were theory's radiant centre but such debates seemed to occlude other feminist perspectives, particularly those of Black and lesbian critics, as well as Black and lesbian creativity and theoretical entitlement. In addition feminists writing about popular culture and postmodernism were examining other identifications which purely psychoanalytic readings could not accommodate. For example, Tania Modleski argues that films such as *Three Men and A Baby* and *Gho*

very different ways, offer more multiple mothering and ethnic identifications than the simple binary male viewer/female object of spectatorship
theory (Modleski 1991). Similarly E. Ann Kaplan, as I shall describe in a
moment, untangles mothering subjectivities from Lacan's masculine
symbolic and places 'resisting' texts, such as Douglas Sirk's *Stella Dallas*,
within a more complex scenario of sentimental, melodramatic female
desires (Kaplan 1992).

By the 1990s critics involved in queer cinema's hybrid aesthetic,
combining, among other elements, autobiography, poetry and realism,
were distancing themselves from the binary heterosexism of much
psychoanalytic theory (Gever *et al.*, 1993; Wilton 1995). Black feminism, drawing on Black literary theory and Black community culture,
equally offers more pluralistic approaches than those taxonomies of
the early 1980s. Pre-eminent here is the cultural criticism of bell hooks
(discussed below), ethnographic studies of Black female audiences, as
well as introductions to post-colonial cinema (hooks 1992; Bobo 1993;
Trinh 1991). Black and lesbian feminisms are more open to newer and
formally inventive filmmaking, as testified by the films of Julie Dash.

The salient issues that excited film theorists in the 1970s and 1980s
– that 'Triple S' brand of stars, stereotypes and spectatorship – had
widened into a heightened investigation of race, sexual orientations
and culture. The following four critics, more than most, struggle to
make feminist film theory magnetically irresistible and I would like to
profile each critic's work in turn in a quasi chronological order. While
there are many introductions to the work of feminist literary critics,
feminist film critics, individually, are somewhat neglected. So my focus
is not so much on conceptual distinctions between critics but simply
on introducing the reader to key themes and techniques which are
relevant for my subsequent chapters. Laura Mulvey, Annette Kuhn,
E. Ann Kaplan and bell hooks seems to me to crystallise the variety
and the excitements of contemporary feminist film theory: the psychoanalytic (Mulvey), materialism (Kuhn), postmodernism (Kaplan) and
Black feminism (hooks).

Laura Mulvey, the 1970s and psychoanalysis

No other single essay excited and transformed contemporary film theory as much as Laura Mulvey's 'Visual Pleasure and Narrative Cinema'

(Mulvey 1975). Indeed an entire issue of *Camera Obscura* – the 'Spectatrix' – immutably fixed spectatorship as characterising 1970s film theory (*Camera Obscura* 1989). First given as a paper in 1973 in the French department of the University of Wisconsin, subsequently published in *Screen* (Mulvey 1975), and first available in soft covers two years later in Karyn Kay and Gerald Peary's influential *Women and the Cinema*, the essay maps a wide area of film spectator relations (Kay and Peary 1977). Drawing on psychoanalytic, Althusserian and feminist theories, Mulvey (describing mainstream cinema as a seamless phallocentric apparatus) took film-spectatorship analysis further than other spectator critics of that moment – like for example, Christian Metz – by going in a startling new and feminist direction (Metz 1974).

Mulvey figures cinema as irreducibly shaped by sexual difference, arguing that film is constructed around looks or gazes, which in turn shape editing and narrative, and, further, that these looks are completely and eternally those of men looking at women. As the art historian John Berger had recently and succinctly pointed out *'men act* and *women appear*. Men look at women. Women watch themselves being looked at' (Berger 1972, p. 47). Mulvey's essay marked a huge conceptual leap in film theory: a jump from the ungendered and formalistic analyses of semiotics to the understanding that film viewing always involves gendered identities.

Hugely influential as it was, critics, nevertheless did attack the essay's apparent ahistorical, totalising construction and, as a result, Mulvey went on substantially to revise her assessment in later work (Cowie 1993; Rodowick 1991; Mulvey 1989C). Yet looking back at the essay over two decades what immediately catches the eye is Mulvey's complex and certainly original typology clearly visible in the intriguing spatial organisation of the essay. Rather than subsuming Mulvy's critique into its later impact as most critics do, it is more helpful, and startling to centre 'Visual Pleasure' (historically), to ask how did Mulvey's ideas form and in relation to what: in other words briefly to explore British intellectual life of the 1970s. As Mulvey reveals much later:

[1975] was a moment when ideas about objectification and alienation which had been important to Marxist thought since the fifties met semiotics and psychoanalysis . . . it was the way that sexuality seemed to act as a currency, enabling the circulation of the female image as a consumable commodity that generated an instinctive, iconoclastic puritanism. (Mulvey 1989A, p. 251)

The Althusserian terminology of 'consumable commodity' is very instructive.

So rather than simply looking at the essay's later circulation and impact, it is perhaps more valuable to place the essay in its own historic moment. This immediately poses interesting questions: What are the specific determinates of the text? How does the text define how it is itself to be read? In 1975 I was writing a PhD thesis on anarchist criticism and the American polymath writer Paul Goodman. For me, 1970s Britain seemed to be a period of fairly radical thinking across feminism, academic disciplines and the visual arts. Nevertheless, I was merely an admiring observer not an active participant in Mulvey's exciting conjunction of Althusserian and psychoanalytic theory, feminist politics and aesthetics. In 'British Feminist Film Theory's Female Spectators: Presence and Absence' Mulvey vividly describes this moment of synthesis which came:

> Out of the Women's Liberation Workshop in which consciousness-raising, political practice and intellectual innovation were all valued and, for a time, kept in balance. Secondly . . . the 'high theory' strand of British theory was influenced by the intellectual climate created by the *New Left Review*'s break with the specific Englishness of British left culture and politics. We looked to France for our theory and to Hollywood cinema for critical raw material. In the sixties, the *New Left Review* had translated Althusser and Lacan, both of whom were to influence feminist film theory, into English for the first time. (Mulvey 1989B, pp. 68–9)

The quotation condenses a wide range of crucial influences although the 'absent sign' of Brecht is an equally important pressure. Brecht's plays were popular in British fringe theatre from the late 1960s and offered audiences a different style of spectator-text relations, one in which identifications were subordinate to Brecht's famous 'alienation effect' or 'passionate detachment' as Mulvey characterises this in 'Visual Pleasure and Narrative Cinema' (Mulvey 1975).

Mulvey goes on to point to other more specifically feminist influences:

Feminist use of the new theory and its application to popular culture grew directly out of the Women's Movement's concern with images, their contribution to fixing the connotations of gender and circulating images of women as signifying a patriarchal mythology of sexuality. (Mulvey 1989B, p. 69)

This link between feminist activism and feminist theory is clearly visible in Mulvey's career. Immediately prior to the publication of 'Visual Pleasure and Narrative Cinema' Mulvey launched a powerful attack on the British artist Allen Jones. Jones's notoriously fetishistic and misogynist images of women, are described by Mulvey as a 'narcissistic wound' and 'supremely exploitative' (Mulvey 1987, p. 127). Writing this essay encouraged Mulvey in her understanding that such fetishistic images are certainly not only the province of soft pornography but pervade mass media and the arts. Mulvey repeats her startling image of the 'narcissistic wound' in 'Visual Pleasure' (as 'bleeding').

To assess the pervasive appeal of such misogynist images or more particularly the mechanisms through which images appeal, Mulvey turned to Althusser's theories of how subjects are attracted by, or 'interpellated' into, cultural discourses (Althusser 1971). Althusser argues that individuals think about their existence as a vast network of representational systems called ISAs (Institutional State Apparatus). ISAs, one of which is cinema, offer us images of ourselves or subjectivities through a mechanism of 'recognition'. Integral to this process of the construction of individuals as subjects are particular forms of address, for example camera movements or 'interpellations'. Althusser's theory helped Mulvey clarify the systematic mechanisms by which cinematic desires might function, mechanisms which she tried to deconstruct with Brechtian techniques in her own films, particularly *Riddles of the Sphinx* (1978).

It is striking how Mulvey's 'turn to theory' spoke to that contemporary moment. The example of *Riddles of the Sphinx* is instructive. The film was first shown to, and enthusiastically discussed by, a women's group at the London art film venue, the Other Cinema, and I remember that a showing of the film was the major event at the 1978 British

Sociological Association Conference *Culture*. In her programme notes for this screening Annette Kuhn specifically highlights feminist themes, for example Mulvey's embracing of 'forgotten myths' and the portrait of mother/infant relations (Kuhn 1978, p. 12). The conference was an intriguing and summative marker of the intellectual centrality of theory with papers entitled 'Althusserian smokescreen', but it was merely a more conspicuous site of a general academic sweep into cultural theory. For example, the annual Ruskin History Workshops swiftly moved on from a 1975 scenario of 'ploughman's lunch *with beer*' and the British feminist Sheila Rowbotham's proud declaration of her non-academic affiliation as 'Dalston', to the 1979 conference where Stuart Hall's paper 'Culture in Twentieth Century Britain' and his founding of the Men Against Sexism Crèche spoke of more expansive identificatory possibilities.

As the newly founded journal *Ideology and Consciousness* made clear in its first editorial, the editors were confronted by a field that was largely unmapped. Nevertheless, the work of *Screen*, Mulvey herself and the Birmingham Centre for Contemporary Cultural Studies, were providing crucial flares (Adlam *et al.*, 1977). This was exemplified by *Working Papers in Cultural Studies*, the bi-annual papers published by the Birmingham Centre from 1972 to 1977, which shifted their attention from Lukács and Goldmann in early issues to Barthes and Althusser, claiming that even semiology was 'too materialist' and a 'materialist *psychology*' (my italics) – one describing the relation between subjectivities, activities and social formations which does not equate 'material' with 'economic' – was needed to answer the challenge of cultural politics (Chambers *et al.*, 1974, p. 3).

What is to be relished in all of this is a conspicuous general interest in the exact themes of Mulvey's essay. It is Mulvey's interweaving of these general perceptions which made 'Visual Pleasure and Narrative Cinema' a *Zeitgeist* text and explains the subsequent flood of discursive interest. Her method was first to plait Althusser inextricably with Lacan, wrapping an Althusserian strand of 'interpellation' – that a spectator's pleasure is profoundly shaped by a film's language – together with a Lacanian strand – that the unconscious is structured like a language. At a stroke she linked film techniques directly with psychoanalytic desires not only in terms of content, for example, the appeal of a strong female icon, but also in terms of similar mechanisms. In all of this we

need to remember, of course, that a 'spectator' is not Margaret Reed
(now Humm) sitting in the dark Globe Cinema in 1950s Newcastle,
but a spectator who could be 'interpellated' as a working class Geordie
girl (although this spectator is hardly a normative appellation in any
film I have seen). Without the 'mirror' of the screen, Mulvey argues, the
spectator is in a space of unknowing (Lacan 1977).

Not surprisingly subsequent feminist critics, and Mulvey herself in
'Afterthoughts', strove to 'find the lady' in order to account for women's
knowing pleasures (Mulvey 1989C). Mulvey's own solution was to
expose and reject some traditional film techniques, for example, using
360° pans rather than reverse shots in her films. Other critics, like E.
Ann Kaplan, describe different spectators: the historical spectator
(teenage Margaret Reed), the hypothetical spectator constructed or
interpellated by the film (for example *Calamity Jane*'s hypothetical
heterosexual viewer) and feminist informed readers of today (exemplified by the dyke reading of Doris Day). Yet it is startling to realise the
important switchpoint which Althusser offered emerging feminism
in the early 1970s as it was joining British intellectual main lines.
For example, Terry Eagleton's *mea culpa* plenary paper at the 1978 BSA
Culture conference openly admitted that the key problem in then current (masculine) Marxism was an absence of any theory of subjectivity.

Subjectivity was Marxism's lacuna. While most Marxists would want
to claim that any theory of the subject must be internal to social practices, Althusser (unlike Marx) did not claim that experiencing subjects
necessarily needed to be known epistemologically. Where Lukács
was preoccupied with 'wholes', Althusser introduced a Marxism which
was not shaped by specific progressive stages (Lukács 1971; Althusser
1971). Yet neither, unlike philosophic realism, did Althusser presuppose
a world independent of the subject's perception. In other words, following Althusser, representational systems became the critical object
of British cultural theory (hitherto immured in class theories) but such
systems were not seen as socially determined.

The cultural splendour of this theoretical gesture, for Mulvey and
emerging feminism, was immense. Althusser's name is not spoken in
'Visual Pleasure and Narrative Cinema' but as Mulvey suggests, his
ideas irreducibly shape the essay and, I feel, particularly shape its
organisation and rhetorical style. Curiously no one (apart from my dis-
gruntled students) has commented to date on the very odd disjointed

organisation of Mulvey's essay with its key and often quoted points all dispersed. How is the text making itself read? With some difficulty, marking my students' essays. Let me explain through quotation and close reading:

> B. An active/passive heterosexual division of labour has similarly controlled narrative structure. According to the principles of the ruling ideology and the psychical structures that back it up, the male figure cannot bear the burden of sexual objectification. Man is reluctant to gaze at his exhibitionist like. Hence the split between spectacle and narrative supports the man's role as the active one of forwarding the story, making things happen. The man controls the film phantasy and also emerges as the representative of power in a further sense: as the bearer of the look of the spectator, transferring it behind the screen to neutralize the extra diegetic tendencies represented by woman as spectacle. This is made possible through the processes set in motion by structuring the film around a main controlling figure with whom the spectator can identify. (Mulvey 1975, p. 12)

B follows A in Section III and is succeeded by C.1 and C.2. The Althusserian sentence structure matches the fabric of the essay with its ordered paragraphs. The compacting of ideas in quasi epigrammatic uncontestable sentences owes everything to Althusser as does Mulvey's constant use of alien conceptual transplants, for example, the vocabulary of vulgar Marxism with its 'division of labour', 'power' and militant 'features'. The transmutation of analogies into concepts is part of that theoretical imperialism, what E. P. Thompson once punningly identified as 'the little verbal turnstiles into the Althusserian theatre of the absurd' (Thompson 1978, p. 224). Yet, paradoxically of course, it is Mulvey's placing of gender into this categorical definitiveness which is so appealing to feminists, as if gender can be definitionally known and yet not determined. Thus, in her later, highly original *avant le temps*, account of Frida Kahlo and Tina Modotti, Mulvey argues that women's art is in dialogue with political ideologies yet can be 'innovative and explosive', overriding historical periods (Mulvey 1989C, p. 87).

To some extent Mulvey's 'Visual Pleasure and Narrative Cinema' is structuralist in the sense of her tight ordering of A, B, C1 and C2. Yet what structuralists as well as Althusser avoid is the issue of the psychic realm of language. Mulvey very precisely adds to Althusser (as if presaging Terry Eagleton's call) a psychoanalytic theory of the subject and signifying practices. What Althusser lacks and what Mulvey jumps in leaps and bounds to supply is a sense of dialogue between the subject/spectator and the mechanistic apparatus – 'the Althusserian Orrery' (Thompson 1978, p. 290). Mulvey talks about men and about women and about experience and feeling where Althusser reifies process over subject. No one who has not experienced the freezing Russian snowstorms of British left wing class debates before 1975 can truly appreciate the sheer warmth of Mulvey's essay.

'Visual Pleasure and Narrative Cinema' had great and cumulative effect and I think some significant consequences. One very good example is its impact on *Ideology and Consciousness,* a journal whose influence on British intellectual thinking in the 1970s went far beyond its seven issues (May 1977–Autumn 1980). The journal's very title betrays an indebtedness to Mulvey's linkages while the first editorial follows Mulvey's style of uncontestable sentences and paragraphs in its account of fetishism and phallocentric power (Adlam *et al.,* 1977). By laying a cloak of materialist psychology over the last puddles of the left, Mulvey established that the subject is always constituted within a set of psychical relations. To explain what precisely these relations might mean in terms of cinema Mulvey turned to Lacan.

For Lacan, the difference between the sexes is not simply biological, but takes shape in discourse and signification, for example, in cinema (Lacan 1977). Lacan develops his account of subjectivity with reference to the idea of a fiction. The acquisition of identity and hence subjectivity occurs only as we enter into the symbolic (or social production of meaning). According to Lacan, we are not born as subjects but begin by making imaginary identifications. Such identifications will always be difficult and will often be fictive. The preoedipal infant lives in a maternal world of sounds and rhythms. It is with the sight of ourselves in a mirror that we give up this bodily maternal warmth and enter social construction or the symbolic order, called the 'Law of the Father'. This is the moment of 'I' when we can create our identity as an 'I' as well as 'me'. According to Lacan, language privileges the masculine over the feminine because entry into the symbolic is oedipal. That is to say, the infant has to search for signs, figurative language, and representations as a substitute for the mother. In other words, if signifying processes create subjects then film processes, like the mirror, can encourage the viewer/subject to take on particular subjectivities. 'Visual Pleasure and Narrative Cinema' argues that narrative is the needle seamlessly stitching subject to screen. Film's stylistic agency comes from its narrative strategies which claim individuals as subjects.

An attachment to narrative strongly shapes all of Mulvey's work so that her later essay 'The Oedipus Myth: Beyond the Riddles of the Sphinx' insists on its centrality (Mulvey 1989C). The energy of Mulvey's response to narrative comes from a different source than Althusser. Mulvey's fascination with narrative, I would suggest, is another 'reality effect' of that historic 1970s moment. It is feminism which taught Mulvey about the power of stories and in her essay it is a woman who 'freezes the narrative', who disrupts the linearity and cohesion of films (Mulvey 1975, p. 11).

Narratives shaped second wave's political thinking. Women's novels such as Marge Piercy's *Small Changes* and Marilyn French's *The Women's Room* gave a sense of collective significance to women's individual experiences (Piercy 1972; French 1978). Mulvey wrote continuously for feminist journals in the 1970s and only months before writing 'Visual Pleasure and Narrative Cinema' was describing how women might enjoy the 'safety-value' of narrative melodrama watching Fassbinder's movies (see Mulvey 1989C). Reading Mulvey's early essays today what is clear is that her inventive, multidisciplinary film theory develops continually with feminist culture of the 1970s.

Losing sight of that historical moment, or not forcibly living it, many critics attack Mulvey's essay, for all that it is the seed capital of their critical careers. So, D. N. Rodowick insists that Mulvey leaves little room for historical variability (Rodowick 1991), Kaja Silverman argues that Mulvey overlooks the important semantic implications of women's voices (Silverman 1988) while gay critics argue that gay viewers share different gratifications when gazing at a male hero (Dyer 1990). Of course the questions which Mulvey did not address – questions of race and sexual preference – are now among the most compelling. But many of these accusations are themselves ahistorical in proposing that Mulvey's germinal essay be all identifications to all readers long before such questions had deeply disturbed the critical landscape. Nor do the accusations acknowledge Mulvey's own, heightened foregrounding of these very issues in her film-making and later writing: Mulvey's recouping of both the Sphinx and the hysteric anticipates Hélène Cixous and Catherine Clément's *The Newly Born Woman* (Cixous and Clément 1987).

In 'Afterthoughts' Mulvey revisits Freud to conclude that the oscillations women make between masculine and feminine identifications offer the possibility of more fluid gender identities (Mulvey 1989C). The vocabulary of this essay is fresher, more personal with confident puns 'by the scruff of the text' (Mulvey 1989C, p. 32). Its conviction of women's fluidity pervaded her films with their plural references (to the Sphinx, mothering, feminist art) which so directly influenced Sally Potter's *Thriller* and Marleen Gorris's *A Question of Silence*. *The Bad Sister*, which Mulvey made with Peter Wollen mixed documentary, home movies and interviews precisely to capture that fluidity. In 'Changes' Mulvey assesses the projectile energies of all this work and locates the point of explosion firmly in the early 1970s – a time unprecedented in its celebration of feminism and cultural theory (Mulvey 1989C).

As I have argued, much film theory of the past twenty years revisits, challenges or builds on Mulvey's ideas. Subsequent internetting covers a wide web. Mulvey's essay provides the structural co-ordinates of the first British theories of masculinity and the male spectator (Neale 1983). Mary Anne Doane reframes Mulvey's passive/active binary into an opposition between filmic proximity and distance (Doane 1990), Elizabeth Cowie adds multiple cross-gender identifications (Cowie 1984) and Linda Williams utilises Mulvey's concept in the context of pornography (Williams 1993). Even as early as the mid 1970s the Open University Media Group were introducing spectator theory into their television programmes (Thompson 1979) and currently, Black feminists construct historical spectator models (Bobo 1993). The special issue of *Camera Obscura*, 'The Spectatrix', included over fifty lengthy responses to 'Visual Pleasure and Narrative Cinema', choosing Mulvey's essay as the inaugural moment of feminist psychoanalytic theories of spectatorship (*Camera Obscura* 1989). In addition a great deal of feminist literary criticism embraces Mulvey's vision, for example, Sandra Gilbert and Susan Gubar's *No Man's Land* (Gilbert and Gubar 1988). Mulvey's configuration of Althusser, Lacan and feminism has its origin in British intellectual life of the 1970s, an as yet inadequately acknowledged

historical juncture. If Mulvey's originality lies in her paradigmatic legit-
imation of that moment, her success is visible in the way in which her
ideas have no terminus.

Annette Kuhn and materialist criticism

Annette Kuhn's *Women's Pictures* along with her other essays are
steeped in materialism and psychoanalysis. Like Mulvey, Kuhn's ideas
are very much shaped by left wing British cultural politics of the 1970s.
Trained as a sociologist in the actively Marxist red brick university world
of the 1960s, Kuhn describes driving 'forty or so miles' from Sheffield to
Nottingham in the spring of 1974 to see her first 'overtly' feminist film
(Kuhn 1994). But it was the visceral intensity of the viewing context, as
much as the films' content, which was a formative influence – an
'unpretentious setting . . . in a community centre' (Kuhn 1994, p. ix). As
a result, Kuhn specifically attacked a purely text-based critique of
cinema (Kuhn 1975). Kuhn, like Mulvey, energetically springs from the
women's movement with its enabling critique of representation but
also, and similarly, sources 'non feminist or prefeminist thinking' and
semiotics and materialism (Kuhn 1985, p. 5).

The title of Kuhn's first co-edited book *Feminism and Materialism*
flags her commitment to Marxist feminism as a 'priority' which 'as yet
is in its infancy' (Kuhn and Wolpe 1978, p. 7). In her own contribution
to the edited collection Kuhn makes a very brave attempt to take
Marxist theories of the family away from social determinism and into a
'psychoanalytic problematic' (Kuhn 1978). Cinema has more expressive
space in the subsequent and collectively edited book *Ideology and
Cultural Production*. By now Kuhn is arguing that texts such as films
may operate unconsciously in contradiction to their own conditions of
existence (Barrett *et al.* 1979). Marxism pervades all Kuhn's writing
both in her vocabulary of the 'user-value' and 'exchange-value' of films
as well as in her apologetic defence of the 'naive' pleasures of cinema
viewing (Kuhn 1985).

Kuhn's major text *Women's Pictures* (1994) is a materialist critique of
film theory and mainstream and women's films. Kuhn makes the case
for a feminist film politics based on the premise that feminism exposes
the 'socially constructed nature of knowledge' so it could be argued that
feminist film theory is itself a form of feminist cultural politics (Kuhn

1994, p. 4). Following a more orthodox approach to cinema and its economic and cultural contexts, Kuhn proceeds to review current issues in
film theory as well as feminist counter cinema, exemplified by the
documentary *Janie's Jane* and the work of the avant-garde film maker
Yvonne Rainer. It is only in the second edition of *Women's Pictures* in
1994, with its additional chapters, that Kuhn admits that feminism
might creatively function within the mainstream as in, for example,
Sally Potter's *Orlando*.

The 1994 'Postscript' is a brief and schematic but more respectful and
optimistic reading of what 'feminist' cinema might be as Kuhn argues
that such mainstream pleasures as *The Color Purple* and *Thelma and
Louise* reveal Hollywood's debt to feminism. Neither of these films,
Kuhn points out, could have been made without feminism since both
draw on specific themes of the past decades. *Women's Pictures* is a
model materialist, poststructuralist, feminist film criticism because
Kuhn attends to historical considerations describing films as cultural
agencies.

This attention to sociocultural contexts and film production informs
Kuhn's other work such as her edited collection on Ida Lupino (see
Chapter 4 below) and *The Power of the Image* which contains essays
on *The Big Sleep*, censorship, pornography and health propaganda films
(Kuhn 1985). Kuhn's account of *The Big Sleep* is an exemplary materialist reading. Her working assumption is that all films display conscious
or unconscious patterns of censorship. For example, the Hollywood
Production Code Administration vetoed any appearance of drug taking
or of gay identifications. The result, Kuhn argues, of these extra-diegesic
pressures or external controls is that they inhibit *The Big Sleep*'s narrative clarity by robbing the film of any character motivation (Carman's
drugtaking, Geiger's homosexuality). There are additional and unconscious repressions to do with the 'unspeakability' of a transgressive
sexuality. The essay, then, deftly welds the sexual politics of feminism
with a materialist history of 1940s films.

Feminist rhetoric shapes Kuhn's essay 'Women's Genres' (Kuhn
1984B), an essay which joins others of the early 1980s in grappling with
the broader visual pleasures of television soap operas and other forms
of popular culture. By concentrating on more gynocentric genres, or
genres which appeal to women, feminists countered psychoanalytic
theory's negative picture of woman as no more than the object of

man's gaze. This new angle of vision was sharpened at the turn of the decade by the impact of French feminist theory on British cultural studies. Kuhn herself translated Hélène Cixous's crucial essay 'Castration or Decapitation' for *Signs* in 1981 (Kuhn 1981). In *Women's Pictures* Kuhn, following Irigaray, tentatively posed the possibility of a feminine text as one which would have no fixed formal 'femininity' but could become feminine in the moment of reading.

Marxism's cognitive wattage shines through Kuhn's introduction to *Alien Zone*, an edited collection of essays about science fiction films (Kuhn 1990) in which she demands a film theory of 'cultural instrumentality' which will address science fiction films' mediations, repressions and cultural ideologies. Kuhn's complex articulation of materialist feminism with film has been very influential – Lucy Fischer draws substantially on Kuhn's socio-historical analysis in *Shot/Countershot* (Fischer 1989). Materialism infuses even Kuhn's autobiographical writing *Family Secrets*, where she claims that memory work continually spans 'the line between cultural criticism and cultural production' (Kuhn 1995, p. 3). Whether Marxist or non-Marxist, all feminists can gain 'visual pleasure' from watching Kuhn's inexorable arrival in feminism via the stepping stones of formalism, psychoanalysis and materialism, as if proving that a journey to feminism is the only logical and intellectually appropriate way to travel.

E. Ann Kaplan and Postmodernism

In her ambitious and patiently instructive text *Women and Film* (Kaplan 1983) E. Ann Kaplan vividly describes that pre-feminist yet generative moment of unknowing: 'I ran my first class in 1972 . . . when I began teaching the course, I was working in a void' (Kaplan 1983, p. x). Arguably, it is her own hugely prolific and eclectic concerns which filled that void. Kaplan has examined multiple representations (from family scenarios in psychoanalysis to Madonna on MTV (Music Television) and in a quasi-literary analysis of textual structures assesses how these represent women narratively.

From the beginning Kaplan criticised the élitism of British film theory. As early as 1976 in her review of Claire Johnston's 'Women's Cinema as Counter Cinema', Kaplan argues that mainstream films could circulate feminist themes (Kaplan 1976) and she sought to widen feminist spectator theory by placing this in a less determined scenario, for example, arguing that Mulvey's dominance/submission model need not be tied to gender because women, like men, can fantasise across the sexual binary.

In the first of its two parts *Women and Film* uses semiology and psychoanalytic theory to analyse Hollywood films from the 1930s to the 1970s. Kaplan's broad historical sweep allows her to argue that films from *Camille* (1936) to *Looking for Mr Goodbar* (1977), do indeed repetitively fetishise and eroticise women, and that this objectification relegates women to silence and marginality. In other words, like Mulvey and Kuhn, Kaplan focuses on representative examples of a mainstream misogyny while not losing sight of the impact of production, exhibition and distribution. But unlike Annette Kuhn, Kaplan makes women's own making of films more compulsively central. Part two of the book paints an optimistic feminist panorama ranging from experimental, documentary and avant-garde films (for example Sally Potter's *Thriller*) to the more 'mainstream' films of Margarethe von Trotta. Kaplan concludes by calling for feminists to reconstruct the figure of the mother – an act she performs magnificently herself in her later *Motherhood and Representation* (Kaplan 1992). Pluralist and comparative, *Women and Film* is immaculately embellished with terminological definitions, filmographies and a teaching appendix making the text a summative account of feminist theory, Hollywood cinema and women's film.

More plural possibilities register in Kaplan's edited collection *Women in Film Noir* (Kaplan 1980). The book emerged from a British Film Institute Summer School called in 1975 to discuss a genre 'particularly notable for its specific treatment of women' (Kaplan 1980, p. 2). *Film noir*, including *Double Indemnity* (1944), *The Postman Always Rings Twice* (1946) and *Kiss Me Deadly* (1955), Kaplan argues, attempt to restore social order 'through the exposure and then destruction of the sexual, manipulating woman' (Kaplan 1980, p. 3). The conflict between images of strong independent women and patriarchal recuperations intrigues Kaplan because this conflict enables films, Kaplan claims, to be potentially open.

The arrival of postmodernism offered Kaplan that more open space in which to explore such contradictions and possibilities. Her edited collection *Postmodernism and its Discontents* has a more political wash than other collected canvases of the postmodern (Kaplan 1988). By juxtaposing Fredric Jameson's seminal essay with Marxist historical analysis (originally the text was intended for an issue of *The Year Left*) Kaplan argues that any study of the postmodern requires a complex agenda. For example, essays offer a critique of contemporary fiction, California punk fanzines, and film, and there is her own feminist analysis of MTV. While Kaplan struggles, somewhat unsuccessfully, to distinguish 'co-opted postmodernism' from 'utopian postmodernism' (the former incorporating masculine violence and misogyny, the latter 'a challenge to the symbolic order') what is intriguing is how Kaplan makes postmodern MTV seem almost anarchically feminist. Like all of Kaplan's books, the cognitive substance of *Postmodernism* draws on an earlier and pathbreaking attention to women's television and its more inclusive representations (Kaplan 1987).

Kaplan's mapping of the maternal body is a continual focus matching other cultural feminism (Ruddick 1980; Petchesky 1987). *Motherhood and Representation* (Kaplan 1992), in best feminist fashion, grew from Kaplan's need to understand how 'on a personal level, motherhood has been one – if not the – major emotional, inter-subjective experience of my adult life to date' (Kaplan 1992, p. xi). Kaplan's theme is that mothers in particular, focus dramatic transitions in economic, political and scientific discourses, as, at the moment, in discussions about lesbian artificial insemination.

Unlike Mulvey and Kuhn, Kaplan takes a broad multi-disciplinary and historical sweep from the 1830s scrutinising novels (Stowe's *Uncle Tom's Cabin* and Gilman's *Herland*) along with contemporary film, advertising and the popular culture of Mother's Day. Most mothering representations, Kaplan argues, are melodramatic and structured into stereotypes of the angel and the witch yet they also incorporate a feature of 'resisting' domestic feminism. What emerges from Kaplan's vast scenario is how frequently mothering images reveal 'high anxiety' about social and technological change. For example, *Baby Boom* and *Fatal Attraction* try to sanctify mothering at a time when the nuclear family is no longer socially central. For this reason Kaplan concludes that feminist film theory will need to interweave feminist theories of reproduction and the postmodern with psychoanalysis.

A very similar plural approach to psychoanalysis marks Kaplan's edited *Psychoanalysis and Cinema* (Kaplan 1990) which includes studies of literary, ideological and historical narratives. In her own contribution to the volume – an analysis of *Now Voyager* and *Marnie* – Kaplan argues, following Kristeva, that although both films are Freudian schemas showing mothering traumas and instant cures (by males) the furiously stigmatised, abject mother might offer a more potent explosive figure.

Kaplan's volume does not however testify to the inexhaustible difference of all women. As bell hooks accurately and uncomfortably points out, only one of the book's essays acknowledges racial difference (hooks 1993). Constructing film theory 'along these lines enables the production of a discursive practice that need never theorise any aspect of Black female representations or spectatorship' (hooks 1993, p. 276). In some ways *Psychoanalysis and Cinema* merely mirrors other feminist film theory of that date in giving little support to conceptions of difference. Again, although *Motherhood and Representation* concludes with a short call to 'free women and minorities of their simultaneous subordination and fetishization', Kaplan's own lack of detailed attention to minority representations makes it hard to envisage what such freedoms involve (Kaplan 1992 p. 219). However, Kaplan is currently completing a volume on Black women and film. What, I think, is a great quality and strength in the circulatory energies of Kaplan's prolific work, is her vivid evocation of women 'caught in the middle of contradictory discourses' and made excitingly positive for a wide audience (Kaplan 1992, p. 219). There is no question that Kaplan's influential, interpretive projects offer film theory many strikingly heterogeneous and crucial tools.

bell hooks (Gloria Watkins)

The absence of Black women in white film theory of the 1970s and 1980s is very transparent: *Screen*, often saluted as the ensign of progressive film theory, effectively 'screened out' Black and Third World cinema in the 1970s (Mercer 1994). By the 1990s more representative and multiple identities were at last appearing in feminist and other criticisms and Black film-making, for example, the films of Spike Lee and John Singleton, itself became popularly mainstream. The fact that Black experience has a less marginal authority in both film practice and in film theory is due in part to the extensive work of artists and writers like bell hooks.

In the opening chapter of *Yearning*, hooks carefully positions herself as a cultural critic. Cultural criticism is a daily event in Black life, hooks points out citing as an example the deconstructive humour of Black folks watching *Amos n' Andy* (hooks 1991). She suggests that this criticism is a form of resistance, a means of subverting dominant representations. Equally well informed about British cultural theories of the 1970s hooks pays attention to the work of the Birmingham Centre, John Berger and Laura Mulvey. However she swiftly moves from that safe space of cultural studies which made 'writing about non-white culture more acceptable, particularly in the humanities' into a much more thoroughgoing political critique (hooks 1991, p. 9).

Yearning builds on the social theories of *Ain't I A Woman?* and *Feminist Theory* to give full attention to Black culture, Black masculinity, whiteness and postmodernism. 'Unlike other chi-chi collections' hooks refuses to isolate cultural criticism from theories of race and gender and her essay 'An Aesthetic of Blackness: Strange and Oppositional' is an urgent and productive model of that more qualitatively political theory, making an incisive plunge into Black aesthetics from the springboard of autobiography. The essay begins in the house of her grandmother (hooks took the name of her maternal great-grand-mother) 'a quiltmaker, she teaches me about color . . . and learning how to belong in space' (hooks 1991, p. 103). In a revealing use of present tense rather than past perfect hooks argues that Baba teaches her 'to see'. The home, hooks's base image, helps her to visualise aesthetics not simply as philosophy but more as a 'way of inhabiting space' (hooks 1991, p. 104). Black aesthetics is historical, political and communal, based on the belief that beauty, especially beauty created collectively, is an integral feature of everyday life. In other words Black aesthetics should not be prescriptive (as it was in the Black Arts Movement) nor transcend the everyday. hooks's interdisciplinary, communal standpoint informs those essays which are directly about cinema: her analysis of Stephen Frears/Hanif Kureishi's *Sammy and Rosie Get Laid*, Wim Wenders' *Wings of Desire* and Spike Lee's *Do The Right Thing*. hooks argues that, in very different ways, each film mirrors the social exploita-tions and misrepresentations of Black women. In Wenders' films 'whiteness is sign and symbol' but even Black independent films are not, in fact, independent if they 'reinforce stereotypes and repressive structures of domination' (hooks 1991, p. 171). While praising Spike Lee's films as 'political art', hooks bravely takes issue with Lee's debt to the outmoded sexist construction of Black masculinity that was a central dynamic in the 1960s Black power movement (hooks 1991, p. 181).

Amplifying, but not qualifying, her critique of Lee in *Outlaw Culture*, hooks goes on to argue that it is Lee's material position which shapes his misogyny. In other words hooks, with the explanatory aegis of materialism, argues that *Malcolm X's* white production values and necessary appeal to a cross over audience created a patriarchal and fictional version of Malcolm while ignoring the crucial influence of Ella, Malcolm's politically progressive sister.'Lee's work cannot be revolutionary and generate wealth at the same time' (hooks 1994, p. 150).

hooks expertly supports her courageous and clear sighted argument with reflective close reading in collaboration with family, students and friends. One of the striking and delightful features of her style is a range of vivid conversations (even if these might be invented). hooks frequently adopts the Woolfian interrogative, subtly and accessibly defining postmodernism or German angst with the inspirational gesture of a white feminist companion who expectedly 'didn't get it' (hooks 1991, p. 115). The personal vivifies all hooks's writing. As she suggests in *Outlaw Culture*: 'I think that a lot of what's going on in my work is a kind of *theorizing through autobiography* or story telling. My work is almost a psychoanalytic project that also takes place in the realm of what one might call "performance"' (hooks 1994, p. 208). This autobiographical story telling hooks calls 'stepping out'.

Black Looks scans popular music, advertising, television, literature and film creating a Black aesthetic. What distinguishes hooks's ambitious work is her resolute attention to the personal and to the collective. hooks argues that the conscious masculinity of Black films made by men, as well as the psychoanalytic theories of many white feminists cannot give pleasure to Black female spectators. If the Black female body needs to be rescued from a masculine gaze, it needs at the same time, to be seen by white feminist critics. For this reason hooks suggests that the first task of Black feminist criticism is to attack mainstream cinema's objectification of Black women which, as in Cathy Tyson's lesbian prostitute character in *Mona Lisa*, constantly equates Black female identity with sexuality.

hooks's essay 'The Oppositional Gaze' is the subsequent and more complex response in which she actively confronts Mulvey's 'Visual Pleasure and Narrative Cinema' and other white feminist criticism.

Why is it, hooks asks, that feminist film criticism is aggressively silent on the subject of Blackness and specifically silent about Black women (hooks 1992, p. 123)? Feminist film theory is 'rooted in an ahistorical psychoanalytic framework that privileges sexual difference, actively suppresses recognition of race, while re-enacting and mirroring the very erasure of black womanhood that occurs in films' (hooks 1992, p. 123).

Black women, hooks explains, write little about spectatorship precisely because Black women are not included in cultural critiques. A Black woman's oppositional gaze derives, not from psychoanalysis or semiology, but from 'the capacity of black women to construct ourselves as subjects in daily life' (hooks 1992, p. 127). Black women participate, as hooks does so luxuriously herself 'in a broad range of looking relations, contest, resist, revision, interrogate, and invent on multiple levels' (hooks 1992, p. 128). hooks celebrates Julie Dash's films as 'subversively claiming that space' (hooks 1992, p. 128), as does the gay British film maker Isaac Julien. Julien's film *Looking for Langston* portrays 'transgressive desire' and embodies and re-enacts 'a transgression we witness and watch' (hooks 1991, p. 194). To hooks, the cinema is not a place of escape but a space of confrontation and collectivity. Hence, she finds a rich source of cultural authority in sharing film viewing with 'one of my black sisters' and from 'talking with black spectators' who are always syntactically pre-eminent in hooks's essays (hooks 1992, p. 127). Unlike white feminist film theory, hooks creates tutelary spaces, performative encounters of the personal with the academic.

What are hooks's other themes? The first is that recovery work needs to be inextricably bound to analysis of racist and sexist conventions, for example, Michele Wallace's account of 1940s Hollywood (Wallace 1993). Second, that Black women artists should embody the specific resistant, aesthetic values of Black communities; Wallace's mother, the New York artist Faith Ringgold, mixes community sewing and painting while Alice Walker uses the vernacular in her writing. Patricia Hill Collins agrees that African-American women are 'cultural workers', transmitting folkways and creating Black female spheres of influence in a 'culture of resistance' (Collins 1990, p. 147).

These everyday cultural resistances are matched by films' strategic inflections such as Julie Dash's use of a secretive mutual gaze between the two Black women in *Illusions*. Another resistance is obvious intervention as in directly incorporating Black speaking voices in Jacqueline

Bobo's ethnography, or using 'call and response' to test ideas in connection with kin and community (Bobo 1993). Thus, *Yearning* has none of the customary distancing academic baggage of footnotes and hooks contributes to many non-academic outlets in order to speak more directly to Black women outside the academy. hooks is a dialogic critic, like Alice Walker, writing in an 'engaged dialogue with friends, colleagues and students' (hooks 1991, p. 10).

Black aesthetics' most consistent concern is with contradictory, rather than essentialist experiences, embracing diaspora and displaced identities. hooks's account of Euzan Palcy's *A Dry White Season* is one good example. hooks praises Palcy's representation of displaced whiteness when 'Ben transgresses the boundaries of white supremacy by the seemingly unimportant gesture of publicly embracing Emily, the black wife of the murdered gardener' (hooks 1991, p. 188). Palcy reveals at this moment, hooks suggests, a 'radical critical consciousness to be a learned standpoint' (hooks 1991, p. 188). hooks's attention to 'whiteness' is equally radical since it is rarely addressed directly in either mainstream cinema or theory (Pajaczkowska and Young 1992).

Film theory is indispensable to any Black aesthetic because, as hooks points out, 'more than any other media [film] experience determines how blackness and black people are seen' (hooks 1992, p. 5). Creating a vivid constructionist, not essentialist, film theory, *Yearning, Black Looks* and *Outlaw Culture* cut across the customary discrete divide between experimental, mainstream and popular cultures magnificently constructing Black identities 'not outside but within representation' (hooks 1992, p. 131).

SUMMARY AND STRUCTURE OF THE BOOK

It is striking how often feminist film theory abandons feminism. One vivid example is the way in which critics idealise avant-garde or experimental films while ignoring feminist documentaries (Juhasz 1994). What is also occluded is a reservoir of dynamic techniques in the deeper waters of contemporary feminist theory. Much of the rest of this book, although not all, draws on conceptual frameworks which to date have been largely extrinsic to film theory: second wave feminism, literary theory, reproductive theories, postmodernism and Black feminism, as well as feminist praxis. My aim is not to describe a discrete, new or additive feminist film theory but rather to introduce a range of ideas from areas of feminist thinking and apply these to films. My purpose in interrelating feminism with film is to look differently, with different visual pleasures than, I think, has been possible to date.

The steady growth of feminist scholarship, feminist publishing and, not least, women's studies from the 1970s has created a number of new disciplinary perspectives as well as categories including the 'abject mother' of psychoanalysis and the 'sexual harassment' of the psycho-analytically disturbed. *Feminism and Film* is written as a testing site where readers and students can engage with film and feminism. Of course any selection of films and theories appears to legitimate a particular narrative but *Feminism and Film* hopefully might offer more flexible explanatory tools.

Chapter Two: Sight and Sound

This is an historical chapter absorbing itself in well constituted feminist theories about pornography and the visual in an account of Alan J. Pakula's film *Klute*. I try to dam the flood of discursive attention to the inevitable controlling gaze by listening to women's voices in Bette Gordon's *Variety*. In some ways the spoken can disrupt the specular. My aim is to show, by reviewing and utilising pre-postmodern feminist theories as well as more recent ones, specifically those centring on pornography, how feminism is not a monolithic formation but a highly complex and continuously changing set of ideas.

Chapter Three: Cronenberg's films and feminist theories of mothering

This chapter is the meeting place of film and feminist theories about reproductive technology, the body, and mothering about which David Cronenberg's films reveal both panic and a desire to absorb the gynae-cological into masculinity. To date critics have tended to follow Julia Kristeva, and characterise such masculine anxieties as castration fears. While Kristeva's theories certainly have a place, the chapter argues that a more feasible framing of Cronenberg's fears can be found in Melanie Klein's scenarios.

Chapter Four: Author/auteur: Feminist theory and feminist film

From the late 1960s and throughout the 1970s the notion of a work's origin, of the significance of a male or female signature, indispensably occupied feminist literary criticism. At the same time auteur theory in film studies argued that film organisation and the meanings films produce depended on a director's world view. While auteurship reached a point of stasis in late 1970s film theory with the impact of poststructuralism's 'death of the author', feminist literary theories about authorship grew ever more diverse and exciting. For example, Sandra Gilbert and Susan Gubar, Elaine Showalter and Nancy Miller describe the energies of 'double voice', 'inflections' and 'gender crossings'. Turning to these newer gender effects I hope sharpens my reading of Marleen Gorris's films *A Question of Silence* and *Broken Mirrors*.

Chapter Five: Black feminisms:
Julie Dash's Daughters of the Dust

The absence of any focus on Black differences in mainstream film theory from the 1970s excluded a major and creative source of spirituality, mothering and community culture which had shaped the writing of Alice Walker and Audre Lorde among others. This apartheid is at last being challenged and affirmatively surmounted by Black film critics – bell hooks, Michele Wallace and Jacqueline Bobo. There is no question that Julie Dash's *Daughters of the Dust* answers spectacularly to these new identifications and the new celebrations of Black feminist theory.

Chapter Six: Postmodernism and Orlando

While not abandoning history, postmodernism eclectically juxtaposes high art and popular culture and challenges boundaries between public and private selves. This chapter scrutinises the main theories of postmodernism – from Fredric Jameson, Charles Jencks, and Meaghan Morris – applying these to Virginia Woolf and Sally Potter's *Orlando*. Although the invention of the cinema took place in tandem with cultural changes now labelled modernist, Virginia Woolf's *Orlando* together with her essay on cinema challenge modernism's assumptions about gender and historical narratives. Potter's reworking of *Orlando* shares

Woolf's passion for parody, her address to the reader/viewer as a self conscious participant, and her subversion of *his*tory – all definitional features of postmodernism.

Chapter Seven: Practising feminist theory:
a media case study of the 'Personal is Political'

The last chapter connects feminist theory to feminist media practice. It asks the question: to what extent can feminist praxis create non-hegemonic, non-determined representations? One answer lies in the margins by looking at feminist community photographic practices whose visual transformations have been little theorised. Two feminist critics – Jacqueline Rose and Avtar Brah offer alternative angles of vision to issues of difference. Tracing their ideas the chapter focuses in depth on one case study: tape slide's audio visual strategies. Because publishing costs restricted the number of book illustrations, I have not been able to include my tape slide prints here and therefore describe the work in detail. Since one of the motives of *Feminism and Film* is to show how theories of feminism are exemplary for understanding the intimate functioning of the visual, one intensive study at a bedrock, quotidian level is, I hope, a highly appropriate and positive conclusion. I have luckily witnessed in teaching how tape slides' application of montage, sound overlay and fissured spectatorship, to issues of mothering, the body and autobiography, can purchase the political through new visual representations of the personal.

The disparate feminist theories I draw together focus on similar issues: racial, maternal, lesbian and linguistic differences and all strikingly agree that such differences function saliently on a visual level. To make more sense of the increasing range of cinema's gendered rhetorics requires looking continually for new ideas and new paradigms. While feminist theories never satisfy all the needs of feminists I hope that my friction of feminism with film might strike a few bright sparks.

Chapter 2

SIGHT AND SOUND

Pornography, The Gaze, *Klute* and *Variety*

———⟶∘⟵———

It is a commonplace of cultural theory that contemporary culture privileges 'sight' as a primary mechanism of knowledge and as a primary medium of communication (Jenks 1995). Indeed the power of vision has been an organising principle of epistemology since the Greeks. Following Michel Foucault's influential model of visualisation and surveillance in *Discipline and Punish*, where he describes how the Panopticon prison replaced physical force with a regime of observation, of surveillance, it is frequently claimed that contemporary culture operates similar scopic regimes (Foucault 1977; Jay 1993). Thus, Simon Watney in *Policing Desire* draws on Foucault's concepts coherently to theorise a long history of gay discriminations and photographic surveillance (Watney 1987). The gaze, as Jean-Paul Sartre suggests in his chapter on *le regard* in *Being and Nothingness*, is a key instrument of social control (Sartre 1944).

In Chapter 1 above I described feminist film theory's argument that women are inevitably reduced to the objects of a male gaze in mainstream cinema. We are excluded from our own 'looks' not only by film techniques – in shot-reverse-shot or the implied exchange of looks between characters – but also in narrative. The work of Laura Mulvey, Annette Kuhn, E. Ann Kaplan and bell hooks, I suggest, describes how the eroticisation of women on the screen comes about through the way in which film assumes the spectator to be a white male and encourages his voyeurism through specific camera and narrative techniques (Mulvey 1975; Kuhn 1985; Kaplan 1980; hooks 1992).

The gaze is both a metaphoric concept in film criticism and an integral part of film construction. Laura Mulvey first introduced the idea that men look at women in film with a sadistic voyeurism which is assisted by dominating male characters and a symbolic fetishisation of women's sexuality (Mulvey 1975). Mulvey argues that classic cinema creates the illusion, through a complicated system of point-of-view, that the male spectator is sharing the gaze of the male character thus women become objectified erotic objects existing in film simply as recipients of the male gaze.

The urgent task of feminist film theory has been to theorise the gendered features of visual desires. For these reasons film theory was caught up in the task of theorising the relation between spectator and screen as an issue of sexual difference. For example, Mulvey explains films' erotic violation of women by revealing filmic systems of voyeuristic pleasure. She suggests that feminist directors can create new images of female sexuality by using avant-garde practices of spectator film relationships which deconstruct the scopic gaze. As Teresa de Lauretis argues 'the project of feminist cinema . . . is to construct another (object of) vision and the conditions of visibility for a different social subject' (de Lauretis 1984, p. 68).

While Mulvey's essay opened up the question of gendered spectatorship, it nevertheless derives from Oedipal psychoanalytic theories of subject formation, and so allows little scope for analysing female objectifications in other cinematic processes. Just as spectators may have shifting and mobile identifications it seems likely that sexual difference might be constructed in multiple ways. So Constance Penley suggests that film theory could pay more attention to 'the perpetually changing configurations of the characters' (Penley 1989, p. 80).

Similarly, while the effect of sound on spectators is loudly acknowledged in television criticism about viewing experiences, such as in analysis of how children can simultaneously play and watch, most film theories, by contrast, do not call attention to sound (Ellis 1982; Morley 1995). In addition, feminists rarely trace the ways in which women in mainstream films often lack independent vocal energies as well as independent images. Yet film is no longer a silent medium.

In *The Acoustic Mirror*, however, Kaja Silverman does speculate about the importance of the voice in her feminist critique of mainstream cinema's representation of women. Silverman claims that because synchronisation functions as a 'virtual imperative' in mainstream cinema which synchronises voices of both men and women with their bodies, the female subject inevitably has a 'receptivity' to the male voice as well as to his gaze (Silverman 1988, p. 310). *The Acoustic Mirror* is a very positive account of how feminist film-makers can make what Silverman calls a 'phallic divestiture' by focusing attention on the female voice. And she cites a range of subversive techniques including letter reading devices, the alignment of the female voice with a male body as in Marjorie Keller's *Misconception*, and Yvonne Rainer's *Journeys from Berlin/71* all of which free up the female voice from its obsessive and exclusive reference to the female body. Silverman's insight into strategies of filmic subversion follows Michel Foucault's understanding that male subjects control the unfolding of discourse by 'owning' discursive practices which women need to subvert (Foucault 1972).

In Silverman's reading there are no positive female voices in mainstream cinema. As she affirms in her essay 'Dis-Embodying the Female Voice', classic cinema's female subject 'is associated with unreliable, thwarted, or acquiescent speech' (Silverman 1990, p. 309). Rather than suggesting that cinema does not find it easy to assimilate an independent female voice, as I shall go on to argue in relation to *Klute*, Silverman believes that female voices exist only in a 'trance like state' in mainstream cinema (Silverman 1988, p. 31), and that a 'true' female subjectivity can only appear when, for example, Yvonne Rainer replaces synchronisation with counterpoint.

This view of the submissive relation between word and image in mainstream cinema is common to other avant-garde feminist film makers. Trinh T. Minh-ha also values 'freeing' the voice from the image and like Marguerite Duras, breaking away 'from the habit of "screwing" [as she puts it] the voices to the mouths in realist cinema practices' (Trinh 1995, p. 57). Silverman's is a sophisticated and fascinating analysis while Trinh's rejection both of a homogenous voice and close up in her own films produces often stunning images. There is, then, no necessity in filmic terms for the tying of voice to image. Still, there is no question that mainstream cinema protects what is an artificial unity of identities by collapsing the activities of hearing and seeing. On the other hand, it also seems urgent not to write off mainstream cinema as a violently repressive artifice. For these readings muffle the affirmative female voices which often do have a place in classic cinema (only of course to fall silent by the end of the film). Silverman's negativity dampens any need to analyse mainstream cinema at all if it were true that women are continually and systematically denied sight and voice. It seems urgent to find an alternative approach from which it might be possible to hear some resistant speech.

In order to raise questions about possible resistances I intend to juxtapose readings of *Klute* and *Variety* to test the utility of combining linguistic with film criticism. Both films animatedly represent a woman's body and her voice within the context of pornography. Hence before analysing them in detail I need to address that context of pornography by examining the ideas which now shape both general feminist theory about pornography and in particular feminist media analysis. It would be schematically gratifying to be able to make clear distinctions between kinds of pornography: soft porn, hard porn, erotica, Hollywood cinema and so forth, but it seems crucial to me that mainstream cinema's sexual representations should not be studied as if other sexual representations, often defined as pornographic, are radically different. That way we lose ourselves again in questions of what is, or is not, pornography. I will purposefully avoid entering into the complex debates about legislation and gay and lesbian pornography, all of which is outside the focus of this chapter, and instead describe and juxtapose those issues of relevance to film studies. Pornography is too easily regarded by both anti-pornography and anti-censorship feminists as a privileged form of representation. This view was particularly current in the liberal sixties and clearly visible in Susan Sontag's path-breaking essay 'The Pornographic Imagination' in which she claims not only that pornography has a 'peculiar' access to truth but that it can be shared when it projects itself into art (Sontag 1966). This image of an intellectual, 'cultured' uncontaminated spectator continues until the end of the decade in other texts such as Morse Peckham's *Art and Pornography* (Peckham 1969).

Alternatively there was a great deal of work in the social sciences about the visual effects of pornography. Feminist sociologists working within the broad area of sexual theory found that male spectators watching films make stronger links than women between what they see and what they want to be. In an extensive survey of 668 respondents answering a 42-item questionnaire Pauline Bart provides convincing evidence that, at least in laboratory conditions, viewing pornography can desensitise males not only to sexual violence but also to pornography itself (Bart 1985). These issues of gender identity and spectatorship are, I shall show, part of *Klute's* appeal, triggered by Pakula's use of generic *film noir* codes and specific camera movements.

Feminist theories about pornography take hugely divergent approaches to this issue of visual objectification while agreeing that pornography can represent male sexual attitudes. Indeed it is the very binary representation/reality which is so hotly debated in feminist work. Feminist theories of the 1980s and 1990s can be characterised as bipolar, forming two opposed groups: anti-pornography and anti-censorship feminists. This divergence stems, in part, from the historical moment of second wave feminism and its double task, the first part of which is to understand and eliminate violence against women. Susan Brownmiller's *Against Our Will* argued that sexual violence (specifically rape and the threat of rape) enables men to control women. The second part is to prove that cultural products are important examples of sexual politics, requiring the kind of response exemplified by the Miss America demonstrations in the early 1970s (Brownmiller 1975).

Pornography is usually described as that form of verbal or pictorial material describing sexual behaviour which is degrading or abusive and structured by gender and power relations (Cowie 1992; Goodman 1992). Although, as Elizabeth Cowie points out, the use of the term 'pornography' to describe obscene representations is comparatively recent, dating, as it does, from the mid-nineteenth century. Susan Brownmiller argued that pornography was a visual expression of timeless patriarchal and misogynist myths about women's sexuality and the dehumanisation of women which often results (Brownmiller 1975). However, a later and divergent view is that of anti-censorship feminists who claim that such descriptions are too sweeping. Drawing on more recent interdisciplinary and psychoanalytic work, these feminists argue that pornography involves issues of fantasy and fetishism too complex to be reduced to any possible effects; and that pornographic representations could be an important, even creative, part of women's – not just men's – sexual pleasure (Segal and McIntosh 1992; Williams 1993). As the film critic Linda Williams suggests, anti-pornographers have gone too far in defining pornography as the graphic, sexually explicit subordination of women (Williams 1993). Andrea Dworkin's claim that pornography has triggered many forms of brutality throughout history is equally sweeping (Dworkin 1981). Yet it is also true, as Black feminists argue, that pornography does re-inforce notions of biological determinism through its portraying of Black women as animals (Collins 1995).

My analysis of *Klute* and *Variety* is placed on the border between these two opposed positions, hence my need fully to rehearse both sets of views. By contrast, I want to argue that *Variety* displaces the typically misogynistic visual portraits of pornography in cinema with women's vivid sexual stories but that women's stories, or a woman's stories (Bree/Jane Fonda), are also a potentially subversive part of mainstream films like *Klute*, hence the 'silencing' of Fonda.

While feminists against censorship are right to fear any anti-pornography alliance with the New Right and its anti-feminism, it is also true that the meaning, and therefore effect of pornographic images is never clear. In turn, as Katie King suggests, the Sex Wars are themselves fluctuating and unclear:

> White heterosexual socialist feminists find themselves aligning with white lesbian s/m people to critique the anti-porn movement and a consolidated radical/cultural feminism, Black feminist les-bians find themselves aligning with white self-proclaimed radical feminists to critique the symbolic and erotic uses of the para-phernalia of domination/domination. A different group of white self-proclaimed radical feminists align with the anti-porn critique and draw distinctions between an early radical feminism and a later developing cultural feminism. Lesbian s/m people point out that they have most in common in terms of legal criminalisation and street bashing with gay men, especially s/m gay men, s/m heterosexuals, and other visible and/or ostracised sex perverts. (King 1994, p. 141)

What is to be relished here, is the forcible linkage of political positions with cultural representations and the urge to match sexual identities with sexual significations. Hence feminist debates about pornography are a crucial source of ideas about visual objectification which are of particular relevance to the study of films like *Klute* and *Variety*. My own view is that while there is no question that any increase in legislation necessarily incurs an increase in State taxonomic repressions, still the work of anti-pornographers and in particular that of Catharine

MacKinnon are often inaccurately stigmatised. Certainly it is true that MacKinnon tends to equate representations with reality, for example, in her explicit comment that pornography is 'not a distortion, reflection, projection, expression, fantasy, representation or symbol either. It is sexual reality' (MacKinnon 1989, p. 198). MacKinnon argues that pornography enables men to have whatever men want sexually because pornography connects visual with sexual objectifications and presents itself as fantasy while it actually 'distributes' power (MacKinnon 1995, p. 214). However, MacKinnon does frequently and very interestingly separate sexuality from pornography and suggests that, while pornography is clearly an industrial product, pornography also involves issues of epistemology. It is MacKinnon's focus on ways of knowing which answers spectacularly to feminist film theory. Indeed MacKinnon precisely does not argue that the effects of pornography can be empirically demonstrated. Because 'pornography chills woman's expression it is difficult to demonstrate empirically because silence is not eloquent' (MacKinnon 1989, p. 206). Pornography, to MacKinnon, dispossesses women of the power of sexual definition or speech, '*the power to tell who one is*' (MacKinnon 1989, p. 209).

In other words MacKinnon, like Foucault intriguingly, suggests that pornography is an example of a social regime of truth where power lies not only in visual and social objectifications but in the subjugation of sexed subjects in discourse. Behind MacKinnon's apparent anti-masculinity lurks a more complex philosophical argument about seeing, knowing and representations. It is precisely this denial of women's speech, not simply her visual objectifications, which I want to take up in my account of both women's stories and women's visual portraits in *Klute* and *Variety*. Following MacKinnon, feminist film analysis needs to go beyond issues of visual content, *mise en scène* and narrative, into coincidences of the organisation of erotic visibilities with discursive rhetorics. Feminist film criticism to date, is avowedly anti-repressive. Linda Williams has made a study of pornography her major theoretical work. In *Hard Core* and other essays Williams analyses pornography's erotic impact. Yet, while Williams clarifies a range of gay and bisexual representations and resistances, her attention is still to 'the gaze': 'Bisexual porn which makes a point of articulating a female gaze at male couples, is even more confounding of heterosexual presumptions of the workings of desire' (Williams 1992, p. 56). More usefully for my analysis, Mandy Merck, for example, defines pornography as 'a mode of address' in terms of the images it creates for particular audiences (Merck 1992, p. 226).

Pornography may include other regimes of knowledge than simply the visual. In other words while pornography's organisation of the visual is its most obvious and spectacular success – consider the way in which advertising draws on pornographic postures and costumes – it is also possible to speak of a connection between sexual representations and more multiple identifications than those of the visual. Critics too often direct their energetic gaze to visual pornography and exclude pornography's verbal modalities. Rather than focusing on 'good' or 'bad' images a more reflexive approach might be to look at relationships between sight and sound. Such an approach is already common in psychology; Robert Jensen examines men's stories about their experience of pornography in order to assess how pornography is implicated in a wider system of 'women hating' (Jensen 1995, p. 302).

My own teaching provided a case that illustrates, for me, the impossibility of isolating a technical analysis of camera positions, however sophisticated, from the contextual discourse in which these occur. My Women's Studies class were watching *Not a Love Story* armed with Ruby Rich's attack on the film (Rich 1990). *Not A Love Story* is a documentary about pornography directed by Bonnie Klein which includes interviews with porn moguls and the feminist critics Susan Griffin, Kate Millett, Margaret Atwood, Kathleen Barry and Robin Morgan. Because Klein deployed traditional cinematic practices, Rich claims that the film cannot be feminist since it uses a camera 'gaze' which simulates, through intimate zooms, the typical vantage point of a male consumer of pornography. Rich deplores Klein's use of a male cameraman and shots which turn the 'viewer into a male customer normally occupying that vantage point' (Rich 1990, p. 408). In addition Rich points out that 'at no point does the camera offer a shot from the point of view of the women up on the stage' (Rich 1990, p. 408).

My class largely rejected Rich's reading, not because they disagreed with her technical deconstruction, but because, for them, the film's meaning was lodged in the moving stories told by the women interviewed as much as in camera movements. A purely visual reading, in other words, did not satisfy these women students. The voices of fascinating and independent women (however problematically presented) won out over the visual construction of spectator relations. The problem, then, for feminist criticism is that cinema identifications are not so easily and simply defined. Any attempt simply to deny that viewers are moved by what they hear, as well as by what they see, will create an imbalance.

Cinema's mechanics of exclusion are more complex than those of visual sexual fetishisation alone and required detailed attention. Of course it could be argued that discourse analysis is inappropriate for pornographic/erotic films, since the visual objectification of women is so overwhelmingly marked. But feminist criticism, from the work of Dale Spender on, argues that the absent woman in patriarchal language is a violent repression (Spender 1980). Since the rapid transferring between media of discursive as well as visual representations point to the speed at which symbolic slippage occurs from film to everyday culture, feminist criticism needs a more complex approach to understand the meaning and diversity of differing sexual representations.

I want to place alongside existing critiques of *Klute*, which focus in the main on issues of spectatorship, an account of what that spectator hears or does not hear. As we have seen in Chapter 1, feminist analysis of spectator identifications concentrated on mainstream cinema, in particular on *film noir* and within that, on shot organisation. Identifications are described in terms of the look, and films are read as constructing a series of looks involving the spectator through techniques of shot-reverse-shot. Since these are thirty per cent of all shots in a film there is good evidence to support these readings and to conclude that cinema is self-evidently voyeuristic. It is not surprising that cinematic voyeurism should involve problematic identifications for women. But, if one of the most important areas of feminist film theory is the critique of the 'gaze', an equally crucial aspect of the relationship between women and cinema, it seems to me, concerns the representation of the voice.

Much of pornography denies a dimorphism of verbal and visual eroticisms – the idea that the verbal and visual are distinct. One vivid example is *Penthouse* magazine, whose letters page and long 'autobiographical' articles represent more explicit sexual desires than is permissible in soft-porn photography. *Penthouse* includes articles about consumer products such as cars, film and music reviews, and interviews with celebrities as well as the letters and sexual confessions.

Founded in 1969 by Bob Guccione, the magazine deliberately set out to compete with *Playboy* from its first issue and now has a circulation of over one million (Dines 1995).

Unlike *Playboy*, *Penthouse* creates strong juxtapositions between language and image enabling more violent sexual energies to emerge in print. Readers' letters describe sexual experiences in great detail and are often constructed in realistic narratives using a more explicit vocabulary ('cock', 'clit' and the like) than the subtitled picture-sequence stories can use. Comparing two issues spanning the past decade (from 1985 to 1995) two startling features jump out: photographic representations are amazingly similar in the two chronologically distant editions, both of which rely on soft focus and artistic settings, but locutionary positions in 1995 are uncontestably more violent and much more deeply misogynist than in 1985 (*Penthouse* 1985; 1995). In the 1995 example I examined, many correspondents were exact about physical excitations even though they may have shared what Angela Carter in *The Sadeian Woman* calls the 'timeless, locationless area outside of history' (Carter 1979, p. 12). Carter had prefaced her account of de Sade's career with polemical ruminations about the nature and status of pornography in general, concluding that de Sade's writing is of 'particular significance to women' because of 'the problems he raises about the culturally determined nature of women' (Carter 1979, p. 1). A key example of these 'cultural determinations' is the six column letter from Graeme D. Lincoln which describes in precise chronological order the memorable moments of arousal from the huge exactitude of 'stiff nipples' to the obligatory and richly valued cum-scene 'quite a lot of it flew straight over the crumpled Kleenex and spattered against my shirt' (*Penthouse* 1995, pp. 12–13). Elsewhere in the magazine other autobiographical reveries of 'my hard nail' describe the excitements of sex in car parks or on traffic islands, an oddly popular sexual location. More disturbingly the interviews with 'real' wives are full of gang-rape fantasies and the fantasy of enjoying 'horny men pulling themselves off on me' (*Penthouse* 1995, p. 80).

If the letters relied on a predictable vocabulary in which penis strokes were always 'deep and furious' or body perfume always 'light', they do have a sensuality denaturalised in the visual imagery of the rest of the magazine. The graphic actions of sexuality are markedly absent in *Penthouse*'s picture sequences with the weak innuendo of their sub-titles. Discussing Goldie's blond hair the editors agree that'anyone who owns a good treasure understands the need to guard it' (*Penthouse* 1995, p. 71). Photographic interiors resemble nothing more than Habitat catalogues with stripped (*sic*) pine furniture and plants and are further distanced by the mediation of a 'constructed' editorial/camera crew devoted to archaisms:'also, if we may be so forward, Goldie possessed a pair of the perkiest, prettiest breasts we have seen in quite a while' (*Penthouse* 1995, p. 72). There are also clear stylistic correspondences between the soft porn magazine visuals and more 'acceptable' main-stream photographic representations of women, since *Penthouse* offers free calendars photographed by Helmut Newton, a one time house photographer of *Vogue* magazine, as well as placing its tightly framed erotic tableaux in'arty' studio settings. The more circuitous route of the verbal to the pleasurable clearly offers greater sexual stimulations than the more static visual.

I hope I have been able to demonstrate by rehearsing feminist theories about pornography as well as extra-cinematic examples such as *Penthouse* that the distributive pressure of the verbal in both pornog-raphy and cinematic objectifications of women is complex. My sense is that there are some distinctive gains to be won in tracing the linkages between linguistic and visual sexual objectifications even in those films which appear to be only dramatic examples of visual misogyny.

Klute is a film in which the gaze imposes itself with particular force, through a continuous series of camera oppositions and strategic points of view which identify a (male) spectator with male characters. Directed by Alan Pakula in 1971, it is one of a cycle of such films, including *Dressed to Kill* and *Looking for Mr Goodbar*, which show women being hunted down and physically assaulted. The narrative of *Klute* involves the gradual exposing of Bree Daniel's career of prostitution by Klute, an ex-policeman hired by Cable (finally revealed to be the psychopathic killer), in order to solve a mutual friend's murder. On one level *Klute*, like many *film noir*, shows, step by step, how men are free to violate those women who have placed themselves outside conventional family life, and finally impose on them a heterosexual monogamous sterility where patriarchal control is more certain.

Using a series of narrative oppositions between Bree's own investi-gation into her sexuality in psychoanalysis and Klute's increasing sexual control over Bree through *his* investigation, the film homogenises camera movements with this patriarchal agenda. The opening shot focuses on Klute sitting centrally at a family meal using his gaze like a horizontal camera pan, so that his character is our ingress to the film's narrative. The murderer, like Klute, is allowed the freedom of sweeping horizontals as he masturbates while listening to a tape of Bree's recorded voice, as he sits at a long boardroom table. Pakula himself has acknowledged that he fully intended to immobilise women in a series of narrow verticals, using camera 'tunnels' and framing women in doorways in opposition to the masculine horizontal (Ciment 1972).

Pakula's misogyny is a constant and consistent pressure in all his films even in those he made later in the 1990s. Greta Scacchi vividly describes Pakula's camera technique in *Presumed Innocent* (1990) 'it wasn't until I saw the film that I realised the camera which was there had tracked back and looked up my arsehole – sorry to use this foul language, but I'm angry, you see. They were *stealing it from me* (my italics). I was thrilled to work with Alan Pakula. Now I don't want to see the fuckwit again' (Billen 1995, p. 8).

Not surprisingly, critical response to *Klute* revolves around the question of the gaze. Whether critics adopt an iconographic, a structuralist or semiotic approach, most have felt compelled to read the film mainly in terms of the physical/perceptual control of female sexuality. In an interesting and detailed reading Christine Gledhill focuses specifically on 'the two apparently contradictory film making traditions' – *Klute*'s modernity which, Gledhill claims, places the film within a humanist realist tradition of European art cinema along with the stylistic appeal of the *film noir* (Gledhill 1980, p. 6). Like many essays written in the late 1970s (see the section on Kuhn in the opening chapter above) Gledhill finds it necessary to justify her film analysis as politically correct since it decodes a 'socially produced reality of which signifying systems are part' by looking at the 'ideological requirements' of the two genres and how films might aesthetically subvert generic requirements (Gledhill 1980, p. 6).

Gledhill's work marks an important development from the 'images of women' approach of the early 1970s particularly in the way in which her '*progressive or subversive reading*' clarifies 'structured determinants' (Gledhill 1980, p. 12). While Gledhill does occasionally use linguistics terminology for example '*what is being said about women here*', she uses this terminology analogically not directly. Gledhill, in her analysis of *Klute*, broaches the issue of Bree's voice 'that speaks of a struggle for control' but argues that Bree is never independent and concludes that 'words are shown in this film to be deceptive, not adequate to the truth, and eventually dangerous' (Gledhill 1980, p. 123). This is because both murderer and Klute 'bear towards her [Bree] an intense and ambiguous staring gaze' (Gledhill 1980, p. 121).

Terry Lovell, from the different direction of semiology, also draws attention to the gendered identification of the protagonist Klute and a male spectator. Lovell reads *Klute* solely in terms of visual signifiers, concluding that the presumed statement, *énoncé*, of the film equates a visual diminution of Bree with her diminished sexuality (Lovell 1980).

It is possible, along with Lovell, to read *Klute* iconographically, watching Bree's sassiness, signified by her hippie clothing, submit to the moral authority Klute brings with him from the opening country scene. A semiological examination would involve other oppositions all equally visual: Bree's attempt to gain an independent sexuality through a modelling career is correlated with deformity, since the models are inspected while sitting under wall-hung masks of burnt faces. And Klute's owning a 'phallic' key to Bree's apartment means he can 'redecorate' to eradicate Bree's feminine colour 'keys' of purple and red with a masculine blue and grey. Structurally, the film displaces Bree's brief recounting of her childhood in the warm setting of her psychiatrist's wall-mounted photographs of children with longer temporal sequences illustrating her increasing childlike dependence on Klute.

Klute might seem to rely, then, only on scenic visual codes. But this visual tightness of fit is too exact. The film's more complex narrative of male misogyny involves an eclipse of the female voice as much as the female-punishing visual structure. Equally concerned to constrain Bree from speaking the film simultaneously excludes her from control over her own sexuality. *Klute* resorts to a number of devices to signify male power over female speech. One is the opposition between Bree's 'story' scenes (which develop chronologically but not, of course, heuristically), with the visual scenes of prostitution. The psychiatric interviews are the prime examples of this device. In the first interview Bree, if not confident, nevertheless gives an intelligent, even witty account of her behaviour and *mores* as a prostitute. Knowing more than her clients, she can deliberately control their sexuality by creating any appropriate sexual narrative. This verbal recounting is supported by a scene dramatising Bree's call-girl success. Together the two scenes create an ambience of realism with their revealing attention to the necessary and attractive details of Bree's everyday preparations. Bree, as female subject, refuses to hear herself from the place of patriarchy, and insists, instead, on a disjunction between her self-image and that projected for her in the 'social discourse' of prostitution.

Bree's independent discursive sexual narratives cannot be sustained. Witness another interview she has with her psychiatrist after Klute begins to render her self control inoperative. In the second interview Bree speaks less coherently and, in particular, cannot now recount, or account for, the physical sensations of her sexual relationships. The sound-track seems merely a sequence of distancing 'subtitles' which replace her own former vivid sexual similes. The film's placing of Bree's voice as the foundation of Klute's investigation evidences a masculine fear of women's assertive speech. The tape of Bree narrating her self-created and pleasure-arousing sexual 'therapy' is stolen by Cable and held by Klute. Both murderer and investigator use Bree's voice to stimulate themselves, as it were. The stealing of Bree's voice is duplicated by another tape recording of the orgasmic killing of Bree's friend Arlyn.

In other words, in these cases it is the tape recording not the camera, which is the apparatus which controls, manipulates and objectifies women. Through depriving Bree of access to her own erotic language Klute is able, finally, to relegate her to suburban closure, taking her away from her last telephoned encounter as he has already stripped her apartment bare of visual imagery. The intimate stories of sex which Bree creates for her clients – for example, the fascinating account of aristocrat sexuality – are denied any circulatory energy just as Bree could not perform an Irish voice with Klute as spectator.

The mutilated female voice is a vital character in *Klute* which has a clear semantic sub-code alongside the codes of the visual. The film cannot be reduced to the level of its visual signifiers alone, since we must say that its complexity is best understood through deconstructing the two codes of 'voice' and 'gaze'. It is these two codes together that produce a thematics of sexual violence. In fact, if Pakula had wished us only to see Bree's mutilation he would have made a very different film. I would argue that *Klute* horrifies female spectators not only because we are 'framed' in Bree's journey from prostitution to monogamous suburbia but also because in her silenced voice we hear her sexuality repressed.

If taken seriously, these significant cinematic issues will involve a reconfigured theoretical project, one which can address both viewing and listening pleasures. So it is by questioning a rigid distinction between verbal and visual sexual representations, that director Bette Gordon gives women an independent sexuality in her film *Variety* (see Figure 1). Speaking of *Variety*, Gordon says that although she became interested in pornography 'out of film theory as opposed to feminist social issues' still one of the problems from a feminist perspective is that the 'pleasure of looking in the cinema has been connected with the centrality of the image of the female figure' (Gordon and Kay 1993, p. 92). Gordon suggests that one of her central projects in *Variety* is to raise 'various questions: How does the camera produce and construct certain prescribed positions and marginalise others' (Gordon 1990, p. 419).

The film shows how the voice has a particular stake in the reconstitution of that more diverse female sexuality. As we have seen from the controversy over *Not a Love Story*, feminists are suspicious of films about pornography because such films often utilise 'pornographic' points of view. *Variety* tries to escape the dilemma by showing that a more adequate representation of female sexuality needs different semantic as well as visual codes. As Gordon explains in conversation with the film-maker Karyn King 'I think that in our work we have both been struggling to tell the *story* of sexuality [my italics] in a conversational way' (Gordon and Kay 1993, p. 97). As a result of this intent there is no visual representation in the film of the central character, Christine, having sex. Gordon fulfils Angela Carter's call for a moral pornographer who would use pornography as a critique of current relations between the sexes. Like *Klute*, *Variety* consciously structures two codes into its text, but sets up a power struggle between the saying and the selling of sexuality. Through this double perspective, Gordon ensures that the active spectator will question pornographic representations.

Christine wants to be a writer, a coiner of words, but instead coins money working as a ticket-taker in a pornographic movie theatre (Fig. 1). Her boyfriend is an investigative reporter trying to establish Mafia involvement in a local fish market. However, it is Christine who 'tells' the story of that connection through trailing a client of the theatre to the market and to his other business assignments. Further, Christine

Figure 1 Bette Gordon's *Variety* (1983)

tells elaborate stories of sexuality, recounting her reaction to the pornography she sees (which we never see in full but only overhear) and she collects fresh fantasies of imaginary sexual encounters. For example, Christine tells her lover her fantasy about a woman who takes a hitchhiker home. In the dream the hitchhiker watches Christine have sex with a snake then with a tiger. Christine's voice is juxtaposed with the face of her lover now mute and angry from his felt inadequacy.

Gordon, then, is trying to evoke and dismiss the visual manipulation of female sexuality by balancing this with the power of speech, pornography offering her a vantage point for analysing sexual objectifications. Through Christine's stories we sense the presence of what else could be – but isn't being – said or shown. As Shklovsky says, we can 'make strange' a genre, which is what Gordon does, by avoiding a certain logical resolution to her thriller, since both female protagonist and male victim slip away from the final frame (see Humm 1991).

Of course, like *Klute*, *Variety* is concerned with the visual in several different ways. Gordon's choice of pornography as subject is not haphazard. She appeals to an audience of 'knowing' viewers who enjoy allusions to thrillers, *film noir* and blue movies. *Variety* exploits the genre of the classic *film noir* to draw us into its story. Yet by replacing a male with a female investigator Gordon ensures that attributes of the *noir* genre, in particular the central character's function as the only source of morality, can shift to the female. In addition, Gordon denies her viewers the satisfaction of a male voyeur by creating an active female voyeur in Christine's obsessive tracking of her anonymous client. Christine actively enjoys watching men playing sports and reading porn, and watches herself being seduced by her client in a fantasy sequence.

Gordon works continually to turn around our expectations of appropriate feminine sexual behaviour. In the opening sequence Christine dresses alongside a girlfriend, using the camera as her mirror. Mirrors are not the narcissistic Lacanian nightmare they are in, say, *The Eyes of Laura Mars*. Here, Christine 'controls' the camera gaze, confronting men in sleazy porn bookstores and creating male anxiety by mirroring their voyeurism. In addition Christine aggressively manipulates audience viewpoint by opening and closing curtains in the motel to limit our gaze at the man she pursues, who, in any case, never sees his pursuer. Gordon jokes continually about 'looks'. Christine promises to 'look out' for her client's favourite porn film as if it was an everyday television programme; she arrives at the ball game to hear only a moment of the Anthem 'Look, can you see by the dawn's fading light'; she parodies blue movies by wearing a blue sweater and a blue waspie or bustier and enjoys the traditional iconography of *film noir* flicking away her cigarette under the only street lamp.

Gordon wants us to attend to the visual but also wants us to be conscious of its alternative by means of excess and open parody. She encourages a dual consciousness, an active questioning of the typical 'way of seeing' female sexuality. It is the voice which marks a shift and a realignment of the traditional genre. The insertion of verbal fantasy challenges the stability of a sexuality fixed by the visual and Gordon forces us into the gap between verbal fantasy and visual identity.

Bette Gordon uses the tape recorder to introduce this split subjectivity into her film. In her apartment Christine listens to her answering machine, continually switching it on and off and replaying significant moments. The voices are those of her mother, her boyfriend and a dirty phone caller. They are disembodied traces of social life which do not mesh with Christine's own activity in control of the machine and her authoritative speeches elsewhere in the film. Our cues to her emotions and to those of other characters are always located semantically. The fantasy stories (which are written by the novelist Kathy Acker) are a kind of Hitchhiker's Guide to a Sexual Galaxy and spoken in a deliberately unrealistic and discontinuous way. To begin with, the voice is monotonous, contrasting markedly with a standard thriller. Christine incorporates long pauses, and stresses connectives – for example, 'to' – rather than nouns. They become what Luce Irigaray calls an italicised version of what passes for the neutral – a way of evoking and dismissing the usual male pornographic narrative of violent sex (Irigaray 1985). Gordon's is a significant statement about the inappropriate matching of female voice and female image in mainstream cinema. She interrupts *film noir*'s generic representations of women to suggest a more unstable female sexuality.

The most consistent aural device that Gordon uses is perhaps her most important statement about the social context of female speech and the significance of that context to women. In one scene, call-girls, waitresses and out-of-work actresses meet with Christine in a bar, enjoying telling stories about prostitution. They encourage each other to talk and share subversive strategies. The stories are funny but engage us as much through the intimate connection Gordon makes between content (a verbal efflorescence of sexual activity) and social context (the spoken catalogues of daily finances or fetishisms). The message is simple but convincing. Only women together can *speak* porn in order subjectively/objectively to analyse their sexuality. Gordon's depiction of prostitution focuses not on the visual violent relation of male client and female victim but rather on women's collective recounting of their experiences. Women vividly perform responses to their own performances. Where Mulvey speaks of the freezing of a fetishised image of female sexuality, Gordon uses an erotic female voice to freeze the male gaze. As she suggests 'I try to intervene with the way in which the dominant culture presents ideas. My work is in the mainstream, but I insert questions and discomfort into images, narratives and stories (Gordon 1990, p. 420). There are, then, a number of devices with which Gordon plays her film images off against her film voices, encouraging us to question our understanding of the visual, refusing to represent female sexuality as a site of male violence and instead generating a more complex picture. As Juliet Mitchell suggests in *Psychoanalysis and Feminism*, sexuality is like a language only brought into being through the process of learning (Mitchell 1974).

It is important, therefore, not to isolate particular kinds of visual representations but to look at the context of representation which includes the voice, in a fuller discourse of sexuality. Only then can we see the extent of cinematic misogyny visual and verbal. From Scheherezade on, women have always known how to utilise the power of speech to save their sexuality as well as themselves. Still, part of the problem of dealing with speech in film has, no doubt, to do with a domination of explicit sexual imagery. But it is articulation which must be stressed, not simply representation. The emphasis then shifts from describing films' visual sexism to an examination of how sexism operates within a fuller regime of representations. The eye of the beholder has been under a feminist optometrics but his ear has escaped attention.

Moving on into the field of feminist theory this chapter offers some tentative counter-arguments about cinema's sexual representations and, within that, about the place of women's imagery and language. There is no solution to the mechanisms by which masculinity excludes women from playing an active part in narratives, but we can attempt to engage with this better, I think, by regarding film as a series of inter-connected visual and verbal discourses.

Chapter 3

CRONENBERG'S FILMS AND
FEMINIST THEORIES OF MOTHERING

———— ◦◦ ————

Refiguring the body is a central activity of contemporary culture. Questions about the body's appropriate shape, age, sexual practices and desires are the constant topics of magazines, television programmes, and health books, as well as popular science and psychoanalysis. These questions about body fallibility and bodily reproductions lead directly to questions about gendering, about women's differences from men and their consequent subordination. For these reasons the trope of the body is at the centre of current feminist theory. In the contemporary world it is women's bodies in particular which are bounded by common misconceptions about sexual differences and the reproductive technologies which keep such differences in place and in which feminist theory has a fundamental interest (Haraway 1989).

Popular culture, particularly film, frequently portrays women's bodies as at best fallible and at worst corrupting or diseased — as metaphors for larger social problems (Douglas 1975). Currently feminist theories of science, psychoanalysis and postmodernism focus on the body as an object of gendered knowledge in order to understand the connections between gendering, the maternal, body imagery and the psychic (Grosz 1994; Butler 1990; Kristeva 1983).

Many contemporary films resonate with fears of women's bodies (*Alien*) and pathologise women's reproductive power (*Carrie*). Films also portray modern medicine as obsessed, like the spectator, with issues of body control and reconstruction (*Coma*). For these reasons critics frequently assign David Cronenberg's films, particularly *Rabid* (1977), *The Brood* (1979) and *Dead Ringers* (1988) to this apocalyptic visionary genre of physical disease and women's monstrosity (Nguyen 1990). There is no question that Cronenberg's films do indeed address issues of gender power and reproductive technology. But my feeling is that Cronenberg's films testify to the desires of the male psyche as much as they represent the horrors of women's reproductive bodies. Rather than assigning Cronenberg to sci-fi or horror, I feel that his particular struggle, in film, with a masculine gender identity and its own reproduction is more readily understood through the wider frameworks of explanation provided by feminist theories of reproductive technology and by key thinkers such as Mary Douglas, Julia Kristeva, Bracha Lichtenberg-Ettinger and Melanie Klein (Douglas 1975; Kristeva 1983; Lichtenberg-Ettinger 1995; Klein 1993). All these writers crucially affirm the linkage of masculine gender identity to the maternal and the tensions they describe in this relationship are, I believe, analogous to the tensions about masculinity in Cronenberg's films.

For this reason the present chapter will concentrate more on a web of theory interweaving points about Cronenberg's films to illustrate feminism's cluster of ideas. Cronenberg's films are popular and very well known and it seems worthwhile to focus less on their narrative detail and reflect more on the crucial, creative issues they raise. Engaging with filmic fantasies of the maternal – which, in 1997, is very much in question – is crucial for feminist theory because all images of motherhood are conflictual, phantasmic and political. For example, in Melanie Klein's theory of artistic creation, the mother's body functions as a 'beautiful land' to be explored and films, like all the arts, can similarly be a means of recreating the maternal body. This is the key theme of Cronenberg's *Dead Ringers* (Suleiman 1985).

Cronenberg's films, particularly the incestuous and homosocial *Dead Ringers*, call out for more complex critiques than either those applied to date or even the initial thoughts about bodies in second wave feminist theory. While the writings of Simone de Beauvoir, Kate Millett and other second wave feminists, raised critical questions about the constraints of social gender constructions, both de Beauvoir and Millett initially argued that women's revolutionary goals could be achieved only at the expense of biological differences and with the civic enfranchisement of our productive, not reproductive, abilities (de Beauvoir 1972; Millett 1977). Second-wave feminists, keen to down play the biological in favour of women's social and political advancement, figured the perfect body as the eradication of the feminine/maternal (Firestone 1979).

In Cronenberg's films the body is not transcended by the social meanings attached to it. Masculinity is positioned in tension both with its own horrific construction of the feminine and also with its psychic desire for the maternal feminine, particularly for the reproductive body. In *Dead Ringers* the mothering body is not simply a fetishised object of the male gaze but the very source of male desire and identity, the matrix through which male subjectivity is established. Bev and Elly's masculinity is incomplete without the maternal so that maternal fetishes such as their surgical copes are there to promote cohesion with the maternal rather than simply the objectification of women.

Because, for Cronenberg, this masculine subjectivity always involves the agency of abjection, desiring the phallic within the maternal, his films inevitably end in violence or paranoia. *Dead Ringers* ends as Bev and Elly try to impose, on a male anatomy, female reproductive organs. The result is death since this new material body is, at least in terms of contemporary scientific possibilities, unlivable. Nevertheless, its psychic power is legitimised by the film's symbolic identifications. Cronenberg crucially images masculinity as inclusionary rather than exclusionary like the othering practice of socially constructed masculinity. Although misogynist characterisations of women do emerge in *Dead Ringers* and indeed, in his other films, masculinity is more a matter of interconnectedness between masculine desire and the maternal/feminine rather than the dyadic difference described by Nancy Chodorow in *The Reproduction of Mothering* (Chodorow 1978). What Chodorow's term 'reproduction of mothering' describes is the sexual division of labour which encourages women to 'mother' and the way in which this in turn has different effects on the psychological development of girls and boys. Given female parenting, girls develop relational capacities by internalising the role of caring and 'reproduce' their mothers; while boys learn to reject the female aspects of themselves such as nurturing and empathy in order to adopt a masculine gender identity (to be not the mother). In opposition to this, Cronenberg's mobilisation of masculinity involves man's desire for, and subsequent re-entry into the maternal. And this is what the power of Cronenberg's symbolic depends on.

Cronenberg's films raise important questions about masculinity,

about the symbolic boundaries of gender and about the force of abjection. At stake is the issue of the materiality of bodies and what Judith
Butler terms the 'performativity' of gender. For Butler the body is not a
passive receptor of social norms but a signifying, performing system of
meanings (Butler 1990). Cronenberg's bodies are never normative. In
The Brood Nola gives birth to hideous mutants, the physicalisation of
her psychic desires. In *Scanners* bodies are controlled and destroyed
with awesome psychic powers, while in *Dead Ringers* Bev gives his twin
brother Elly a bisexual anatomy. This recasting of women's bodies
constitutes a powerful and abject materiality as well as a new psychic
domain.

Such an attack on sex gender distinctions and on dichotomised
anatomical sexualities suggests a deconstructive if apocalyptic challenge
to essentialism. I am not arguing that Cronenberg is either prototypi-
cally feminist or even politically thoughtful but the sheer power of his
bodies to seep across gender boundaries suggests that a new set of
feminist perspectives needs to be explored. His films make clear that
universal representations of men and women can be challenged, if not
always in ways we might desire to see literally embodied.

Cronenberg's films bring the interrelation of bodies, technology and
the subsequent creation of a new body aesthetic one step nearer. What
makes his work so fascinating is his constant visceral attention to the
materiality of the body, to the precise anatomical details which are the
tangible effects of his own psychic needs and desires. On the visual
plane, Cronenberg's bodies go through several physical transformations.
Never simply gratuitous metaphors of social fears they are figurative
representations of deep psychic states. In *Shivers* (1976), originally
called 'Orgy of the Blood Parasites', Dr Hobbs creates parasites to
substitute for failing body organs which then infect the world through
aphrodisiac qualities. *Rabid* further extends Cronenberg's theme of the
relation of science, sexuality and gender mutations with Dr Keloid's
radical surgery creating a rabid woman who spreads disease epidemi-
cally, while in *The Brood* Dr Raglan's Psychoplasmics are mechanisms
by which psychic disorders can take physical shape resulting in the
reproduction of mutant children. Other creative expressions of new
bodily processes occupy *Scanners* where telepathic powers enable
scanners to break through body boundaries with violent and destructive effects.

Genetic transformation is the central motif of Cronenberg's remake *The Fly*; scientist Seth Brundle mistakenly recasts his body into 'Brundle Fly', in a womb-like teleportation machine, by amalgamating the genetic structure of a fly with his own genetic composition. In *Dead Ringers* the Mantle twin gynaecologists, operate with the 'mutant', Mantle Retractor and finally 'feminise' their incestuous longings in Bev's anatomical suture of Elly. While the mere repetition of artistic motifs is not enough to indicate a filmic obsession – financing, production and distribution, and reputation also count – Cronenberg's constant transposition of mothering to the realm of fantasy suggests that the maternal dimension does shape his work. Women's bodies are not, for him, Freud's dark continent and certainly never Irigaray's lesbian libidinal dark continent of the dark continent. Still, as Cronenberg himself argues, his films are crucially relevant to feminism: 'As horror films are so primal, and deal with such primal issues – particularly death and therefore also sexuality – they are automatically in the arena that has become the feminist arena. It's a natural genre for the discussion of these issues' (Cronenberg 1992, p. 57).

It could be argued that Cronenberg's films are strikingly misogynist since women characters are either presented as rabid sexual parasites or breeders of mutants or they have their reproductive capacities eliminated. Indeed, this misogyny has been categorised as an example of the dread of women and male castration anxiety (Creed 1990B). Yet Cronenberg's anxiety is not represented dyadically: male anxiety versus castrating, abject woman. Rather his films set out the process of identity construction as involving a return to primal desires as much as to primal fears.

Dead Ringers was based on a real life case of identical drug dependent New York gynaecologists Stewart and Cyril Marcus who died of barbiturate withdrawal in 1975. Cronenberg drew on newspaper accounts of the twins' lives, on a fictionalised best seller *Twins* by Bari Wood and Jack Geasland as well as on the intriguing headline: 'Twin Docs Found Dead in Posh Pad' (Gleiberman 1988, p. 45).

Concerns about women's reproductive needs was a key social theme at the time of inception of the film in the 1970s. Following Kate Millett's *Sexual Politics*, a new calculus of gay and feminist thinking asked men to rethink masculinity which became as a result, both in theory and in historical practice, a more troubled identity. Cronenberg's film is certainly marked by a grappling with the implications of these new gender ideas. The feminist movement of the 1960s and 1970s had attacked the medical establishment in particular, calling for new practices of healthcare and childbirth and moving issues of reproduction out of the private sphere into public visibility. Inevitably all new rhetorics of the female body raise social fears. For example, the nineteenth century's medical obsession with women's uteri can only be fully understood in terms of class concerns about a diminishing middle class birthrate (Jacobus *et al.*, 1990). Similarly *Dead Ringers'* obsession with opening and and correcting the female reproductive body matches contemporary masculine anxieties about feminism's reproductive rights campaign.

Susan Faludi argues that the portrayal of women in Hollywood films in the 1970s is marked by a backlash against feminism: 'In typical themes, women were set against women; women's anger was depoliticised and displayed as personal depression instead; and women's lives were framed as morality tales in which the "good mother" wins and the independent woman gets punished' (Faludi 1992, p. 141). Cronenberg's male scientists are examples of that backlash. The Mantle twin gynaecologists join a catalogue of Cronenberg's paternal scientists – Hobbes (*Shivers*), Keloid (*Rabid*), Raglan (*The Brood*), Ruth (*Scanners*), Antoine Rouge in *Crimes of the Future* – who experiment on women with deadly consequences. Triggering Rouge's Malady, a disease from cosmetics, Rouge causes the deaths of hundreds of thousands of women. In this sense Cronenberg's films both parody the dominant norms of medical science while acting as a vehicle for more transgressive male psychic fears. Although many critics take Cronenberg's films to be merely exploiting the popular and disturbing imagery of surgery and biomedical research, to me his films suggest that this masculine terrain is haunted by idealisations of gender and of phantasmatic pleasures which are not reducible to a simple opposition between mad male scientists and women victims.

Analysis of Cronenberg's films can only adequately proceed by addressing other psychic issues, specifically the relationship between the construction of masculinity, infant anxieties, and abject and mothering discourses. At the heart of Cronenberg's enterprise is male infant anxiety and the tensions between male gender identity and the maternal. Representations of reproductive technology simply situate that tension, they are the site of the 'performativity' of masculine fears rather than their cause or symptom. We witness and even come to identify with the symbolic constitution of the male subjects. Yet it is a subject who enacts the psychic excess of the masculine symbolic and its sanctioned misogyny while at the same time delegitimating that symbolic by his desire for the maternal.

This doubled desire is what makes Cronenberg's films, I would argue, powerfully attractive to female as much as to male viewers. As Cronenberg suggests in an interview with Mitch Tuchman as early as 1984 when comparing his films with those of Stephen King: 'My morality plays are set in the realm of science and technology. King's are unabashedly Christian but my battles are not between good and evil but between body and mind' (Tuchman 1984, p. 192). Yet am I right to want to link psychoanalytic theories of infantile fantasy with Cronenberg's themes and to seek in his films evidence of an obsession with the infantile? One way to find out is to isolate features which have not previously been explained by Cronenberg's critics or which cannot easily be accounted for in the kinds of analysis which have so far been applied to his films.

CRITICISM OF CRONENBERG

There is a great deal in common among the more than one hundred reviews, interviews and essays about Cronenberg's work. In general, most readings identify his gender representations with generic horror motifs, with mythology or with sheer misogynism, while ignoring the films' often complex psychoanalytic and philosophical dimensions. Thus there are those critics like Pete Boss, who argue that Cronenberg shares the horror movie's fascination with bodily degeneracy and disease. In 'Vile Bodies and Bad Medicine' Boss explicitly states that Cronenberg's films are about the ruination of the physical subject (Boss 1986), thus evading the implications of Cronenberg's psychic desires for the female body interior by focusing on Cronenberg's black humour, for example, the hideously disfigured cancer patient in *The Brood* who remarks 'I've got a small revolution on my hands and I'm not putting it down very successfully' (Boss 1986, p. 17). While it is true that Cronenberg's fascination with disease is hardly a secondary feature, Boss ignores his intimate marking of disease with gender inflections.

Other critics suggest that such metabolic breakdowns occur in relation to the postmodern condition of our society, a society marked by the extraordinary possibilities offered by technological advance. Shelley Kay's 'Double or Nothing' draws attention to issues of cloning, biocybernetics and artificial intelligence which have a special place in contemporary thinking. Yet while a trope of the body as a self-determining system of mechanistic biology does attract Cronenberg, his films do not figure the alienation of postmodern subject (Jameson 1988). Rather than postmodernism's obsession with surface, Cronenberg traverses interiority thereby encouraging his male characters into intimacy with the feminine.

Kay joins other critics immured in mythology and fantasy by arguing that *Dead Ringers'* twins are mythological archetypes. 'The archetypal pair of twins Castor and Pollux, the astrological Gemini, were born out of an egg from the union of a woman and a god disguised as a swan. The twins featured in *Dead Ringers* and *A Zed and Two Noughts* are the result of the union of myth (the swan) and genetics (the god)' (Kay 1989, p. 35). Kay characterises the double suicide in *Dead Ringers* as Nietschean Apollonianism – or the urge to individuate self from other – without examining any of the propulsive characteristics of twins.

It is undoubtedly true that twins are charged with powerful meanings in most societies, sometimes representing the human polarities of good and evil. And it is also true that the Mantle twins have their counterparts in Indian mythology – the twin gods Asvin credited like them with removing infertility (Mittler 1971). But look beyond myth to science. The scientific study of twins may be a relatively recent phenomenon – usually dated from Sir Francis Galton in the late nineteenth century – but it reveals that not only are twins biologically rare (one in eighty births in Britain), undergo a hazardous pre-natal life, but they often achieve below average scores on intelligence and language tests and are more prone to depressive psychoses (Gedda 1961; Kallmann 1953). Psychoanalytic writers suggest that each twin suffers problems of differentiation. That is, the process of differentiation from the mother is complicated by the lack of a satisfactory body autonomy (Burlingham 1952). These vital tropes of reproductive powers, rarity and psychosis which would contribute to a livelier and more coherent story of the 'fabulous' Mantles are obstinately ignored by Kay and other critics.

Melanie Klein's speculations, as we shall see in a moment, invite us to ask as Kay's do not, about the importance of 'twins' as a psychic issue. In *Envy and Gratitude* Klein offers the arresting and pertinent thought that the twin 'represents an entirely reliable, in fact, *idealized internal* object' – perhaps one to be retrieved with the Mantle retractor (Klein 1993, p. 302). The Mantle twins are split affectively and relationally into good (gentle Bev) and bad (narcissistic Elly). *Dead Ringers* focuses heavily on anxieties of splitting, enacting Klein's key motif of all masculine development – the desire to retract the omnipotent phallus from the mother. The writings of Julia Kristeva, Bracha Lichtenberg-Ettinger and Melanie Klein, as I hope to show, are much more open to these concerns than Kay's superficial glossings of mythology.

Spectatorship readings inform other critical attacks on Cronenberg's apparent misogyny. For example, Dan Thu Nguyen draws on Mary Ann Doane's analysis of medical films of the 1940s, to argue that Cronenberg's films 'operate' a similar misogyny. The move from 'symptom on the surface of the woman's body into the inner recesses of her being has as its ultimate aim the restoration of the specularity of women' (Nguyen 1990, p. 50). According to Nguyen, Claire Niveau's 'female anatomy' in *Dead Ringers* is 'monstrous' while Beverly Mantle's desire to penetrate her is a desperate attempt to 'respecularise' the female figure. In Nguyen's view the film offers two clear images of the female body: as 'site of reproduction' and as 'dark continent'. Neither can serve as the embodiment of Mantle needs. Nguyen claims that Claire is the only female figure in *Dead Ringers* ignoring the crucial triangulation scene between the Mantle twins and Elly's girlfriend Cary. By sharing her body the Mantle twins can enjoy an incestuous homoeroticism, thus male psychic desires are figured in a more complex form (Nguyen 1990, p. 49).

A more sustained discussion of *Dead Ringer*'s attention to physical embodiment is in Florence Jacobowitz and Richard Lippe's 'Dead Ringers: The Joke's on Us' (Jacobowitz and Lippe 1989). Taking an opposite tack to Nguyen, Jacobowitz and Lippe focus on an important distinction which has formed one of the mainstays of feminist film criticism – that between a film as a critique of misogyny and as complicit with a misogynist position (Jacobowitz and Lippe 1989, p. 65). They assert that the contemporary reappraisal of Cronenberg's work is due to an increasing concern about AIDS and ecological decay. Fears and anxieties about traumatic disease, they claim, are fundamental to current critical consciousness. Like Nguyen, Jacobowitz and Lippe assert that Cronenberg depicts a voyeuristic male fantasy 'with which Claire is complicit' (Jacobowitz and Lippe 1989, p. 66).

Jacobowitz and Lippe are ultimately concerned with character relationships at the expense of *mise-en-scène* and narrative and hence discuss only the issue of women as victims rather than what is to me the centre of *Dead Ringers'* diegesis: Cronenberg's sophisticated exploration of the male psyche. Not surprisingly Jacobowitz and Lippe are forced to conclude that Elly and Bev's emotional and physical breakdown has no 'critical placement for the viewer' (Jacobowitz and Lippe 1989, p. 68). And yet, Cronenberg has frequently and strongly identified with Bev Mantle, for example, in his acceptance speech at the Genie Awards. Such an identification might raise intriguing issues of male gender identity, but rather than considering this, Jacobowitz and Lippe argue only that the final scenes of the film 'do not allow for a coherent reading' while the film itself is underpinned by a facile romanticism 'reminiscent of *Tristan and Isolde*' (Jacobowitz and Lippe 1989, pp. 67–8). This collapses *Dead Ringers* into a battle of sexual politics.

Several critics have attempted to locate Cronenberg within a Canadian cultural context. Discussing generic criticism of the director, Gaile McGregor in 'Grounding the Countertext: David Cronenberg and the Ethnospecificity of Horror' argues that an adequate account of *Dead Ringers* from a Canadian perspective not only reveals that 'the other is self' but that in Canadian literature protagonists frequently relinquish excessive masculinity by symbolic subordination to woman (McGregor 1992).

Certainly Cronenberg himself frequently draws attention to his Canadian roots and his films are usually shot in Canada. He also seems to identify masculinity's symbolic subordination to women with a colony's actual subordination to the Imperial power implying that if independence is granted rather than fought for the personality may stay dangerously unresolved. In an interview with George Hickenlooper, he suggested 'We [Canadians] are much more like Bev and Elly in *Dead Ringers*. It all begins with our past. We didn't have a revolution. We got our independence from England diplomatically and politically' (Hickenlooper 1989, p. 7). Margaret Atwood hints at something similar. Canada's leading writer has pointed out that Canadian literature involves 'archaeology, necrophilia or resurrection, depending on your viewpoint' (Atwood 1982, p. 231). In 'Canadian Monsters: Some Aspects of the Supernatural in Canadian Fiction' Atwood describes fictional *wendigos* (werewolves) and *wabenos* (monsters) as metaphors of destructive internal environments. She suggests that this mixture of semi-human and magic protagonists represents a mass of dark intimations in the Canadian soul (Atwood 1982), concluding, with interesting implications for any analysis of *Dead Ringers*, that contemporary Canadian monster figures are now much more concerned with man's relationship to himself as opposed to his relationship with a natural environment.

In other words, following Atwood and McGregor, we could read *Dead Ringers* as a symbolic unification of a dependent Canada with the displaced male. Yet this is hardly the day-to-day currency of masculinity that my students seem to enjoy when watching *Dead Ringers*. By locating Cronenberg only in a Canadian concern with social and geographic boundaries, McGregor ignores that more crucial boundary of the psychoanalytic.

Critical readings, then, of Cronenberg have tended to trace and affirm his embodiments solely in terms of violence and victimisation, though one critic who has attended to the psychoanalytic, Barbara Creed, does conclude that Cronenberg's films are characterised by sexual disgust (Creed 1990B). I will return to Creed's essay later but I would like to emphasise how distant we are in these critiques, from a psychoanalytic understanding of male introjections.

My intention is to explore representations of reproductive technology and the male psyche in *Dead Ringers* specifically in relation to the theories of Klein to argue that Cronenberg offers a vital angle of vision on masculinity. The film opens up the issue of male infant anxieties challenging a specularity in which film viewing pleasures are tied to the gender of the spectator. In trying to make sense of this discourse of masculinity I will outline contemporary feminist theories of reproductive technology since I see this work as exemplary for understanding Cronenberg's reproductive obsessions.

FEMINIST REPRODUCTIVE THEORIES

The past two decades have brought issues of reproduction and the body to the centre of contemporary feminist thought. Feminists ask critical questions about how female and male bodies are made differentially intelligible in social and medical discourses and about the discriminations, exclusions and maltreatments which result. Feminist theories have altered the terms with which we understand the body and the impact of such understandings on popular culture. Barbara Ehrenreich and Deirdre English's *For Her Own Good* was a germinal account of the misogynist history of American obstetrics (Ehrenreich and English 1978). In brief, what Ehrenreich and English describe is the bias toward surgical interventions which characterised this rapidly developing speciality. The nineteenth century eagerness to dissect women created a new technology of gynaecological instruments (Showalter 1992) and even today, half the hysterectomies performed each year are estimated to be medically unnecessary. In response to this objectification, feminists called for women's control over reproduction not least the American psychologist Mary Sherfey who turned to ideas of parthenogenesis (self-reproduction) (Sherfey 1976). Cronenberg's films respond to, and condense, many of these issues. In *The Fly* and *The Brood* protagonists parthenogenetically give birth but, as if to focus Cronenberg's belief in male agency, their offspring are only mutants or metamorphised foetuses. Part of the interest of popular culture like the cinema is that it renders more visible the relation between gender constructions and social misogyny.

Feminist theory put this relation tellingly in question. Evelyn Fox Keller and Donna Haraway, in particular, argue that new representations of bodies emerge at the intersection of cultural metaphors and visualisation technologies (Fox Keller 1990; Haraway 1989). Fox Keller accurately describes how metaphors of a masculine appropriation of reproduction – 'Oppenheimer's Baby' – characterised American bomb construction (Fox Keller 1990). Indeed it is obstetrical technologies of visualisation such as ultrasound which have disrupted the 'very definition, as traditionally understood, of "inside" and "outside" a woman's body' (Petchesky 1987, p. 272). This prevalence of the male gaze, or 'the privileging of the visual', feminists argue, is a primary feature of Western medicine. What results from this 'panoptic of the womb' is masculine control over reproduction linked to a 'masculine quest for immortality' (Petchesky 1987, p. 278). Reproductive technologies have played a major part in this patriarchal quest, from Nazi obstetrics and the sex hormone research of Adolf Butenandt and the pharmaceutical company Schering-Kahlbaum A G, through to contemporary science's focus on fetal surgery at the expense of vaginal delivery (Kaupen-Haas 1988).

No issue is more fraught in contemporary feminist theory than the issue of the reproductive woman and her discursive victimised figure. However, other feminist scholars argue that this axis of masculine power and woman victim is too rigid and that while reproductive discourses may depend on a rhetoric of mechanisation, visualisation and a male panoptic gaze, representations of reproduction in popular culture reveal deeper psychoanalytic dilemmas (Kaplan 1988). Following Kaplan, a recasting of reproductive representations and gender as a more dynamic interrelation might uncover some of the fantasies on which Cronenberg's films draw. As Cronenberg himself suggests, 'I'm really saying that the inside of the body must have a completely different aesthetic. You take the most beautiful women in the world and you cut her open – is she as beautiful on the *inside*? Is there an aesthetic for the inside of the human body?' (Billson 1989, p. 5).

CRONENBERG'S REPRODUCTIONS

An intense interest in gynaecology and a specialist medical knowledge consistently mark Cronenberg's work. He claims to be Dr Antoine Rouge of *Crimes of the Future* and Martin Scorsese's description of his first meeting with Cronenberg is frequently quoted: 'the man who showed up at my apartment in New York looked like a gynaecologist from Beverly Hills' (Jaehne 1988, p. 20). Cronenberg played the role of the psychoanalyst, Decker, in Clive Barker's *Nightbreed* and Barker describes Cronenberg's addiction to the psychoanalyst's dual personality and how he persisted in 'freaking out the film's crew by remarking how comfortable the Buttonhead mask became after a while and keeping it on during the sometimes lengthy breaks between scenes' (Floyd 1990, p. 23). In homicidal mode Decker becomes a monstrous alter ego. Cronenberg played a similar cameo role as a gynaecologist in *The Fly*, and he made the twins anatomical representations in *Dead Ringers* obsessively accurate. For example, in the earlier dream sequences and in the final scene the twins are transformed into an exact anatomical match of the real life Siamese twins Chang and Eng with their connecting tissues (the chest) and common vital organs (the liver).

Cronenberg has never hidden his belief that 'it's in men's nature to try to take control of his environment away from chance. So in a sense my doctors and scientists are all heroes', the feminine is positioned more ambiguously in relation to that masculine appropriation (Jaehne 1988, p. 24). Masculinity in Cronenberg's films is a troubled terrain:

> I remember when I was in school that gynaecologists had a lot of trouble with the ladies. It was obvious to me that gynaecology meant a very well established relationship with the opposite sex, with the doctor having the upper hand . . . they know more about the woman's body than she does. On a technical level. But it's possible to develop an aesthetic point of view about this, which is what I'm trying to explore. It is gynaecology that provides the whole environment for the twins; it is an extension of their *very inception*. They form as children *a complete unit*, in the way a man and woman might, that excludes everyone else. *Not just women*. They're utterly into themselves . . . the Mantle twins are mated halves of one organic unit (my italics) (Jaehne 1988, pp. 20–2).

Gynaecology and psychoanalytic desires rub in uneasy tension here and suggest that feminist reproductive theories, film theories of the gaze and horror genres alone, cannot capture and explain all the viewing pleasures of *Dead Ringers*.

One critic who has grappled with a more complex appreciation of Cronenberg is Barbara Creed. In her article directly about *Dead Ringers* – 'Phallic Panic' – Creed makes a detailed analysis of Cronenberg's iconography in relation to psychoanalytic themes arguing that the mythical status of woman (as the name Claire Niveau implies) is 'clearly alluded to in the film's opening credits' (Creed 1990B, p. 127). Creed importantly focuses on Cronenberg's themes of doubleness, male hysteria and castration anxiety to argue that the film is a major representation of male hysteria. However, she reads Cronenberg's hysteria as a defence against castration rather than as a desire to enter the maternal. By relying heavily on Freud, Creed inevitably searches for castration anxieties and even when she turns to Kristeva's *Powers of Horror* along with her account of other anxieties, draws only on Kristeva's theory of narcissism in which male narcissism is a defence against the mother, a 'looking away'. Creed's central argument, as her title suggests, is that *Dead Ringers* is a 'phallic panic of male anxieties about symbolic castration' (Creed 1990B, p. 145).

Creed's reading, while it does justice to the vibrant male anxieties at work, nonetheless, by describing these anxieties only as castration fears, ignores the film's more complex images of desired interdependency with the maternal. Unlike other critics, I cannot agree that Cronenberg's films enact and reinforce deeply embedded stereotypes of the feminine but, rather, believe his films more problematically demonstrate the tenuousness of the symbolic. It is the tight fit between representations of the abject mother and the male psyche which goes some way to explain Cronenberg's difficulty in clearing gender boundaries. To me, the materiality of Cronenberg's bodies are more distinct from the social power relations which customarily encode the body. Cronenberg associates the mutuality of the Mantle twins with a primal desire for the maternal/sexual and the film drives towards mergence not separation or objectification. I am not arguing that stereotypes of women do not exist in Cronenberg's films but that their presence is not a result of male hysteria but of a male desire for the maternal. As Homi Bhabha suggests in relation to race, the excess of colonial discourse reveals both a dualistic fear of, but also desire for, the Other (Bhabha 1983). In *The Enigma of Woman*, Sarah Kofman characterises Freud's 'panic' about women in similar terms. 'Why did he seem panic-stricken?' (Kofman 1985, p. 65). Kofman answers that it is the excess in Freud's exaggerated account of femininity which he uses to reveal the alleged instability of women which, in a vicious circularity, engenders panic. Similarly it is the excess of reproductive imagery in *Dead Ringers* which allows us to think otherwise about gender. A fundamental theme in the film is the masculine infantile desire of the Mantle twins to return to the feminine, to the maternal, in order to retract the phallic – most obviously shown in the significant name bestowed on the Mantle *Retractor*.

MARY DOUGLAS

Mary Douglas's *Purity and Danger* provides some preliminary ideas for an analysis of how such psychic anxieties are etched onto body representations (Douglas 1966). Douglas argues that anxieties about the body – cultural taboos about diet, dirt and the pollution of bodily orifices – are connected symbolically to assumed threats to social order. A detailed examination of Douglas's theories is outside the scope of this chapter but in general Douglas argues that all cultures depend on boundaries between animal and human and that such boundaries are intimately connected with gender, power and the body. Working from Douglas's theme, it is clear that Cronenberg's films do address body disintegration processes and map these processes onto gender instabilities. For example, Seth Brundle in *The Fly* transgresses male/female boundaries as well as human/animal boundaries by reproducing himself as 'Brundle Fly'. *Dead Ringers* shares this scenario anatomically with the feminising of Elly by Bev. Twins in particular, Douglas argues, break cultural boundaries. Among the Lele of the Kasai, Africa, 'when a human couple produce twins or triplets they have been able to break through the normal human limitations. In a way they are anomalous, but in the most auspicious possible way' (Douglas 1966, p. 168). *Dead Ringers* illustrates this potency of anomaly: it is Claire Niveau's abnormal triple cervix which triggers the twins into more perverse pleasures.

JULIA KRISTEVA

In *Powers of Horror* Kristeva, like Douglas, charts how cultures create body boundary rituals in order to stabilise gender. The Bible, Kristeva points out, has three main categories of abomination: food taboos, corporeal alterations and the feminine body and incest (Kristeva 1983, p. 83). *Powers of Horror* is the first of a triad of works in which Kristeva examines the three key attributes of subjectivity: horror, love and melancholy. Whereas Douglas rejects the subjective dimension Kristeva embraces subjectivity. The 'abject' mother marks the first differentiation of subjectivity, Kristeva argues, by ritualistically differentiating proper-clean from improper-dirty. Unlike Lacan, Kristeva suggests that cultural representations reveal the recovery of the maternal body not its suppression. The repressed maternal authority is likely to reappear in images representing our deep unconscious fears and desires in much of literature, art and popular culture. 'Why does *corporeal waste*, menstrual blood and excrement, or everything that is assimilated to them, from nail-parings to decay, represent – like a metaphor that would have become incarnate – the objective frailty of the symbolic order?' (Kristeva 1983, p. 70). Kristeva answers that because the maternal body is our first site of desire and of prohibition, mothers represent the in-between, the realm of the abject which must be struggled against to enter the symbolic, hence the maternal body becomes a phobic object and therefore, evil. Films which centre on the horrific maternal, like the abnormal triple cervix of Claire Niveau, allow us to experience cathartically our deep psychic feelings. The abject – in *Dead Ringers*, Claire Niveau – both attracts and repels but also illustrates the fragility of symbolic body boundaries.

Cronenberg's 'maximal stylistic intensity' which, to date, directly 'follows' Kristeva, is his film of William Burroughs' *The Naked Lunch* (Kristeva 1983, p. 141). Both film and novel bring into view those features of apocalypse and abjection described by Kristeva. *The Naked Lunch* has its abject characters: Willy eating holes through the floor and the Buyer who sucks people into himself like a boa constrictor, by means of drugged assaults on individual subjectivities. Bodies leak fluids and vomit as *The Naked Lunch* intimates a deep fear of the maternal through its hospital bedpans full of 'blood and Kotex and nameless female substances, enough to pollute a continent' (Burroughs 1969, p. 81). Cronenberg captures these resonant features in his film images of addiction and loss of bodily control. Very suggestively for my argument, Cronenberg created fictional drugs for the movie so that they 'would have internal, metaphorical connections' attached to them, rather than 'external, social ones' (Cronenberg 1992, p. 164). Cronenberg describes *The Naked Lunch* in terms of abjection as a play on the inside/outside distinctions of cultural authority and his own consistent desire to exteriorise the abjected interior. 'You have to be outrageous. You have to turn it inside out and make it physical and exterior' (Cronenberg 1992, p. 165). As Kristeva suggests, any hierarchy of inside/outside depends on the symbolic exclusionary prohibition of the abject coded as maternal: 'The obsession of the leprous and decaying body' [like the Mugwumps and Sex Blobs of *The Naked Lunch*] 'would thus be the fantasy of a self-birth on the part of a subject who has not introjected his mother but has incorporated a devouring mother' (Kristeva 1983, p. 102).

Devotees of the abject like Cronenberg do not cease looking, Kristeva suggests, for the desirable, terrifying inside of the maternal body. The ultimate moment of abjection is the birth-giving scene representing the door to the invisible parts of the mother's body. The mutant off-spring of *The Brood* and the womb monstrosity of *The Fly* have a counterpart in *Dead Ringers'* devouring mother – Bev's nightmare vision of Claire separating the twins with her teeth. The excess of Cronenberg's maternal matches Kristeva's claim in 'Motherhood According to Giovanni Bellini' that poetic language, in which we could include film language, verges on the psychotic because the maternal body signifies excess (Kristeva 1980).

What is crucially relevant to the cinematic in all of this, is that Kristeva consistently represents the maternal as spatial and as material. Judith Butler in *Bodies that Matter* pushes Kristeva's concept of the abject a little further by arguing that the abject/maternal is neither prior nor opposite to intelligibility, but part of the zone of the social; for example, heterosexuality simultaneously abjects homosexuality while identifying with that disavowal (Butler 1993). As Butler suggests 'normality' depends on, and is articulated through abjection. In order to understand how the abject maternal is not external but becomes a crucial incarnation of the masculine we need to draw on other formulations of masculine anxiety. Because what is at stake in Cronenberg's films is not a refusal of the abject maternal. Mother Nola in *The Brood* may produce monstrosities and horrific female flesh but the power of the maternal is not thereby invalidated but rather, at one level confirmed.

BRACHA LICHTENBERG-ETTINGER

A great deal of the most exciting recent feminist thinking about identity and the maternal takes the maternal into psychoanalytic dimensions that cannot be captured by images of the abject or castrated mothers at all. Bracha Lichtenberg-Ettinger does a new kind of justice to the power of the maternal, not its horror. As she points out in *The Matrixial Gaze*, whereas for Lacan castration anxieties shape human drives, Lichtenberg-Ettinger returns to Freud to find another way: a 'beyond-the-phallus feminine field' (Lichtenberg-Ettinger 1995, p. 22). Freud, she claims, did *separate* the *castration complex* and the *maternal womb/intra-uterine complex* and this enables Lichtenberg-Ettinger to give psychoanalytic force to uterine mother/infant relations (Lichtenberg-Ettinger 1995, p. 7). While Lichtenberg-Ettinger's focus carries silent assumptions about foetal identity (which she is careful to disclaim, at least in footnotes: 'I believe in the full rights of women over their bodies') it does open up the possibility of finding that film and artistic representations might draw on 'intra-uterine fantasies' – a whole new layer of masculine and feminine identity (Lichtenberg-Ettinger 1995, p. 24). In intra-uterine fantasies there can be no passive object and active distancing subject, no opposition between subjectivity and objectivity, indeed no concept of specularity, of maternal 'lack' at all, for this is a feminine world of total interaction, of fluid and shared, albeit singular, experiences.

Lichtenberg-Ettinger's speculations invite us to ask about the importance of maternal, uterine features, of the intricacies of interactive maternal experiences and how these might be identity constituting. *The Matrixial Gaze* deconstructs and disempowers all those patriarchal psychoanalytic histories of maternal exclusion and abjection by theorising identity through, not in spite of, or recoiling in horror from, the maternal. Lichtenberg-Ettinger's theories are immensely fertile for helping us turn from Lacanian specularity to the psychoanalytic writing which has most thoroughly acknowledged these intense infantile drives: the work of Melanie Klein. The maternal theories which Klein arrived at are valuable and crucial to readings of male infantile anxieties like Cronenberg's. Klein's thinking (before Lichtenberg-Ettinger's) helps us unfold maternal meanings not contaminated by the Oedipal.

MELANIE KLEIN AND *DEAD RINGERS*

Melanie Klein persuasively points to maternal bodies and to the anxieties and conflicts which these bodies arouse. In her analysis of very young children, Klein noted how fantasies of projection and introjection played out by the child represent the mother's body as both a threatening and desirable object. Like Cronenberg, Klein is more intrigued by the person projecting/introjecting than the maternal into whom he projects. In a child's fantasy the mother's body contains a number of desirable features: milk, magic faeces/babies and the father's penis, all of which the child powerfully desires but also envies and hates.

Famously, Klein first discovered the infant's desire to project into, and retract from, the mothering body in analysis of her own child, Erich. Her son's loss of interest in play, Klein attributed to his unconscious interest in her own pregnancy. Erich described his phantasies of Klein in very Cronenberg-like cinematographic terms 'I would like to see your stomach too and the picture that is in your stomach' (Klein 1991, p. 33). Erich revealed a deep desire to enter his mother's womb which he equated with his faeces ('Kakis') and his father's penis, claiming that he 'would beat his "kaki" because it came so slowly and was so hard. After Papa puts his wiwi into mamma's wiwi . . . the seed runs in deeper into her body . . . and it becomes a child . . . I would so much like to see how a child is made inside like that' (Klein 1991, pp. 33–4). *Dead Ringers* centres on this phallic in the maternal, and shares Klein's presumption that the maternal controls the processes of separation and identity, as it does with the surgical sutures of Elly.

Klein's basic theme is that infants are born with two conflicting impulses: love and hate and therefore learn to introject a good mother (her feeding and reproductive power) but also learn to come to terms with the destructive mother, or symbol of authority represented as the 'good' and 'bad' breasts. In 'A Contribution to the Theory of Intellectual Inhibition' (1931) Klein describes her analysis of a seven-year-old boy with strong aggressive phantasies of attacking his little brother inside his pregnant mother. The phantasies included the child's dreams about fish, crabs and a joint of meat which looked like a house. Klein interprets this 'meat-house' as representing the body of the mother into which the boy wishes to insert his faeces (the crab) and poison both her and his father's penis (Klein 1991, p. 238). It was the boy's inability to read the word *poisson* which triggered the dream and allowed Klein to conclude that the mother's body is the first object in a desire for knowledge. Reading, indeed any epistemological search or creativity, represents the taking of knowledge from the mother's body.

Klein's theory matches Bev's obsessional taking in of knowledge in *Dead Ringers* – a taking in impaired by his sexual relationship with the mothering body of Claire Niveau. If, as Klein claimed, a key infant phobia is the fear of the father's 'bad' penis in the mother then to be a successful gynaecologist means coming to terms with the phallic-retaining mother. In a much later essay 'The Psycho-Analytic Play Technique' (1955), describing her work with three-year-old Peter and other children, Klein links this anxiety with male gender identity and specifically with anxiety about attacks on the inside of the body: 'The oral-sadistic relation to the mother', Klein claims, 'is the prototype of all internal persecutors' (Klein 1991B, p. 50). One way in which the infant copes with such anxiety and fear is to project the persecutory fear onto the maternal body and onto the father's penis as a part object within the maternal body. Peter's 'strong fixation on his mother' involved smashing toy cars which 'stood in his unconscious for smashing his father's genital in the mother' (Klein 1991B, p. 44). Cronenberg often describes his own fascination with smashing cars. Making his film about drag racers *Fast Company* (1979), was like looking into body interiors 'into the brain of the people who designed it' (Cronenberg 1992, p. 12).

If the mothering body creates great anxiety then the boy may develop hypochondriacal anxieties about his own body in identifying with hers (Segal 1979). A boy's feminine phase is marked by fears of being scooped out and having his insides annihilated. In her classic analysis of little Dick, 'The Importance of Symbol Formation' (Klein (1930) 1991), Klein discovered Dick's double projective identification from watching him play in an empty cupboard representing his wish to re-enter the mother. Turning to *Dead Ringers* Bev's hypochondriacal anxieties and drugged 'play activities' represent a similar feeling of enslavement. Bev's breakdown in object control is triggered when his excessive idealisation of his twin brother Elly, as well as the self esteem underpinning his own experimental research, cease to function. As Cronenberg argues about his films 'if you want to tap into the collective unconscious . . . part of that is becoming very childlike. It seems natural to go where the primal energies and concerns are' (Hickenlooper 1989, p. 4). The appeal of horror, Cronenberg claims, stems precisely from its ability to project infantile anxieties, 'things much more primordial – those old standbys, death and separation' (Cronenberg 1992, p. 60).

The direct 'appropriation' of the mother's body, according to Klein, derives from the anal-sadistic in which those bodily excretions so beloved of horror films – blood and faeces – are equated with the desire to steal or retract the child/faeces and the father's penis/faeces. Klein's equation of faeces/child, mother/retraction is hugely relevant both to the depiction of uterine imagery in *Dead Ringers* but more importantly to the name of the famous Mantle invention: the Mantle

Retractor so far overlooked by critics of the film. I will come to the specifics of the term 'retractor' in a moment, but first we need to grapple with the implications of Klein's work in order fully to understand the significance of Cronenberg's choice of the term. Klein argues that art repeats the experience of separating from the mother. Artistic illusion repeats the infantile play with part objects which 'stand in' for the mother, for example, a child's toys. Art (or film) is not then, as Freud had claimed, the sublimation of instinct but stems from a desire to repair relations with the mother.

Klein, in a key footnote to her major essay 'Envy and Gratitude', draws attention to the visual. 'The etymological root of envy in the Latin *invidia*, which comes from *invideo* to look once at, to look maliciously or spitefully into' (Klein 1993, p. 181). This emphasises the projective nature of anxiety. Just as in her unpublished essay on Citizen Kane Klein describes Kane's dying words 'Rosebud' as a projective fantasy of the breast. Rather than a Freudian model of scopophilia in which visual pleasures derive from looking, from spectatorship, Klein's theories offer a far wider range of infantile and psychic symbolism. Her concepts of the anal, the abject and the mother are intensely illuminating in relation to *Dead Ringers*, a film in which the abject but desired maternal is so evidently a major preoccupation.

Many of Cronenberg's themes would appear to illustrate Klein's ideas in several ways. First Cronenberg is himself deeply attracted to the concept of play, Klein's major and innovative psychoanalytic technique. Klein felt that the transference relationship which allowed the therapist to work with more primal primitive forms of the unconscious – projections and introjections – was best expressed in play. Children's fantasy games with little figures, cars, bricks and so forth represented the psychic content of the infantile mind. Similarly Cronenberg continually cites 'the seriousness of play; the necessity to have that fantasy. For me, it's the reason for returning again and again to certain themes' (Cronenberg 1992, p. 19). *The Brood* corresponded to Cronenberg's other concern with childhood and his then current personal concern with custody battles for his daughter Cassandra which he translated into the 'horrific inner life' which reminded the actress Samantha Eggar 'of her own childhood' (Cronenberg 1992, p. 76).

Cronenberg describes his outrage at cuts to *The Brood* and *Videodrome* made by the Toronto Censor Board, in infantile anxiety terms: 'The experience was so unexpectedly personal and intimate, it really shocked me: pain, anguish, the sense of humiliation, degradation, violation' (Cronenberg 1992, p. 105), Cronenberg's image of censorship is 'like sending your beautiful kid to school and he comes back with one hand missing. Just a bandaged stump. You phone the school and they say that they really thought, all things considered, the child would be more socially acceptable without that hand, which was rather a naughty hand' (Cronenberg 1992, p. 105). In terms of Klein's theory of infantile anxiety, Cronenberg is working through the infantile depressive position evident in his emphasis on masculine signifiers 'he' (although his own child is female), where his film is a privileged means of relating to persecutory fears and castration anxieties.

Second, Cronenberg is intensively and self evidently body conscious. Monstrous body anatomies are predominant in his films. Anxieties are metaphorically represented by mutants, parasites and other creatures involving the phallic and the excretory. For example, in *Shivers* (1975) parasites grow internally but emerge as excretions through mouths or vaginas. They are both sexual and excremental in their genesis and turd-like appearance. Rather than reading Nola's birthing of a penis-like object as a Freudian substitute phallus, Klein's theory illustrates how Nola's parasites represent the result of fantasised attacks on part objects, and the desire to retract the father's penis and introject the mother's breast. Cronenberg describes his films anatomically as 'integral, organic, living things' (Cronenberg 1992, p. 68). Similarly Cronenberg's class analysis (such as it is) is couched in visceral terms 'the middle class . . . is more like an amoeba. It can absorb anything' (Cronenberg 1992, p. 65). Scripts resemble internalised phallic objects or, in the case of *Dead Ringers*, an 'aborted foetus' (Cronenberg 1992, p. 138). The script of *The Brood*, he tells us, 'insisted on getting written. It pushed its way right up through the typewriter' (Cronenberg 1992, p. 75). Rejecting any connection between *The Fly*'s symbolism and a historically specific disease such as AIDS, Cronenberg reached for more archetypal and psychic representations in relation to his father's death from cancer (Cronenberg 1992, p. 129).

The gynaecological setting of *Dead Ringers* allowed Cronenberg to weld his association of the phallic and the excretory more closely with the abject mother. 'Gynaecology is such a beautiful metaphor for the mind/body split. Here it is: the mind of men – or women – trying to understand sexual organs . . . the young twins operate by dissection, can we dissect out of the essence of femaleness? . . . It's a very potent metaphor, such a perfect core' (Cronenberg 1992, p. 145). The phallic, identified with faeces, must be retracted and to do that it is necessary to 'dissect out of the essence of femaleness'.

This quotation reveals the third way in which Cronenberg's films illustrate Klein's theories through his fascination with 'absorbing' femaleness. In many interviews Cronenberg talks in infantile terms about the sexuality of 'someone living inside you' (Cronenberg 1992, p. 45), and during the making of *Shivers* he economised by living in his special effects workroom, sleeping – in a distorted image of a foetus' environment – 'in a bed slimy with fake blood and there were parasites taped to my windows and leeches in the fridge' (Cronenberg 1992, p. 47). Cronenberg delights in negotiating gender: in *Rabid*, Marilyn Chambers is of indeterminate gender, and character names are not gender specific, for example, Dr Ruth in *Scanners*. Further, he referred to the gender creativity of *The Brood* as 'human beings swapping sexual organs' (Cronenberg 1992, p. 52). In *Dead Ringers* Cronenberg experienced working with 'the female part of myself' in 'the least macho movie I've ever done' (Cronenberg 1992, p. 147).

Klein worked with similar maternal transferences in her analysis of Richard, a little boy she treated in Scotland during the war. Klein argues that transference involves a desire to introject the idealised female part of the mother, that is, greedily to incorporate the content of the mother's body while simultaneously and psychically being shaped by envy of the maternal breast. The beneficent and destructive aspects of the mother fantasised as the good and bad breasts are part of all infantile symbolism. One key scene in *Dead Ringers* reproduces this fantasy. When Elly visits Claire on location in her trailer she is shown in right profile being made up in left profile. Turning to Elly, Claire's face reveals the split image of the good/bad mother: the 'good' attractive right profile and the 'bad' bruised and badly beaten left profile created by cosmetic special effects.

In her analysis of Richard, 'The Oedipus Complex in the Light of Early Anxieties', Klein introduced colour symbolism to express such infantile anxieties. Richard longed to take his father's place with his mother and fight 'the bad men and their dangerous genitals' transferring them to a blue crayon in play (representing himself and his brother) with red crayons representing his mother (Klein (1945) 1991, p. 381). *Dead Ringers* makes use of similar, sexualised colour contrasts between the blue male Mantle apartment and the baroque red garments and rooms of the gynaecological work. When Bev 'feminises' he wears a red tee shirt to play squash in contrast to the apartment's blue dressing gowns. As Cronenberg suggests, his films aim to introject the female into the male with 'the idea that female sexuality is invented by men' (Cronenberg 1992, p. 184).

The arrested desire for the mother, which is the central theme of Melanie Klein's work, floods *Dead Ringers*. The desires and expressions of the male psyche are the dominant and informing feature of the film. Elliot and Beverly Mantle, the brilliant and successful twin gynaecologists return to an originating infantile relation with the mother by sharing Claire Niveau. The narrative is structured by their opposing characteristics (arrogant Elly is 'the shit' and Bev is the sympathetic, social inadequate), by their desire for each other and by a need for separation. Claire Niveau's 'fabulously rare' triple cervix attracts both men into a triadic sexual relationship involving the interdependence of masochism/desire or lust/hate in Kleinian terms. The cinematographer Lee Wilson's optical effects, his 'invisible soft split-screens' enabled Cronenberg to overlap figures and suggestively represent interdependence (Lee 1988). In addition Jeremy Irons, playing both twins, always played his role 'with a bug in his ear so he could listen to his own voice in playback' (Lee 1988, p. 39). Randy Balsmeyer and Mimi Everett's real time portable motion control system allowed Cronenberg to reproduce 'precisely repeatable moves at, high speed' further contributing to the integrative, rather than binary, shooting of Irons. This ingenious, metaphoric organisation of camera moves is hinted at in the opening credits shot by Balsmeyer and Everett with the same format of camera bi-pack matts so that images combined on the negative (Shay 1988).

The zygotic tightness of fit between the film's technology and its theme of a psychic incestuous twinning with the mother, is suggestive: Cronenberg discarded one major special effect – a quarter size parasitic figure of Bev growing out of his own abdomen – in order to reinforce the triangular focus. From the thirty-five filmed twin shots, Cronenberg selected only nineteen. Rather than a dyadic, homosocial attraction, Cronenberg claims the twin's desire 'is platonic. It allows them the freedom to relate to other bodies' and that he himself 'learned a lot about my "feminine" side' (Jaehne 1988, p. 27). The original source for the film – the New York gynaecologists Cyril and Stewart Marcus – shared a similar, insular dependence leading ultimately to their drugged deaths rather than independent selfhood. The inability to separate and the interweaving of emotional identities which informs *Dead Ringers* is a feature of the infantile paranoid which is the focus of Melanie Klein's work. As Michael O'Pray suggests 'Cronenberg's men are victims of their inability to resolve internal dilemmas' (O'Pray 1992, p. 10).

Klein's main themes – the identification with projected parts of the mother and the desire for her phallic introjected part object – could be said to be themes reaching far back in Cronenberg's career. Max Renn the protagonist of *Videodrome* (1982) has both a vaginal slit in his abdomen and a penile flash gun. Transsexual mutations appear with penis-like probosci, and it is not insignificant that Cronenberg's favourite film director Brian de Palma chose the name Dr Elliott (the name 'Elliot' is given to one of the Mantle twins) for his schizophrenic transvestite killer in *Dressed to Kill* made eight years before *Dead Ringers*. As Cronenberg suggested in interview with Mary Gaitskill he is hugely attracted to 'a sexuality that's beyond bisexuality, that is primordial and almost *infantile*' (my italics) (Gaitskill 1992, p. 81). Triangulation, as Eve Sedgwick points out, balances the destabilising threat of homosexuality (Sedgwick 1985). In English literature, Sedgwick suggests, male homosocial desire is often mediated by desire for a woman. The triangular *mise-en-scène* is a crucial moment in *Dead Ringers*. The dance sequence in the Mantle apartment erotically unites Bev and Elly via the body of Elly's girlfriend Cary. The scene has an interpretive composition inflected by an unusual (for Cronenberg) intimately revolving camera.

Dead Ringers matches Klein's image of the mothering body as a simultaneously 'good' and 'bad' "container' for the phallic, with infertile Claire – wearing the obvious signifier of a witch-like black dress – who is 'bad' and needing 'to be punished'. As a 'bad' mother Claire introduces Bev to drugs, feminises him and invites him to 'play'. As a good, active sexual mother with Elly, Claire wears a confirmation-like broderie anglaise nightshirt and later, hearing Bev's 'confession' wears a high collared Victorian white shirt while lighting candles in a ritualised Marian iconography. It is Claire's thirst for knowledge of the twins which encourages Bev to child-like dependence, forcing him into her world of drugs precisely to avoid revealing that he and Elly are separate people. By the time of the trailer scene Elly openly states his desire to fuse with Bev and Claire in a shared triangulation. Yet triangulation is not an easy embodiment. For example, Elly cannot allow his girlfriend Cary to give mouth-to-mouth resuscitation to Bev: 'don't touch him, he's my brother'. In Bev's separation nightmare Claire both bites the twins apart and drags forth a phallic object from the excrescence. Claire offers the maternal security of a warm fire-lit apartment while simultaneously abandoning Bev for her film career. Rejection by the mother leads to Bev's abjection. *Dead Ringers* closes with Bev and Elly's entry into the pre-Oedipal world of infantile eating desires: for cake, 'pop' and ice-cream which 'mummy forgot to buy'. The film's thematic enactment of Klein's description of infantile psychic reality with its destructive yet succouring mother is summarised in Bev's account of the disparity between the inner and outer world of women who reproduce. Women's interiors are, to Bev, 'all wrong'. The patients are getting 'strange', Bev claims 'they look all right on the outside but are deformed on the inside'.

Dead Ringers, then, reinforces the theme of infant/maternal interdependence in three ways: through shot construction, with imagery, and with its major and crucial signifier, the Mantle Retractor. In general, mainstream cinema privileges shot-reverse-shot or angle-reverse-angle cutting. This is frequently described by film theorists as a 'sutured discourse' one in which the reverse shot triggers the spectator into completing the 'sutured' hole or absence in the filmic field (Heath 1977/8, p. 64). This classic cinematic process is reinforced by a narrative system where causal links between fictional events are made clear by continuity editing in order to bridge temporary pauses with a high degree of narrative closure (Cook 1993). While Cronenberg customarily avoids art cinema's unconventional continuity and violations of shot sequence, *Dead Ringers* does not rely on classic cinema processes. There is an absence of point of view shots and a constantly distanced camera. For example, in each new scene the camera pulls back from a central frame: a blank sheet, a glass door, the arched room of the award ceremony or a sculpted Italian chair. Without question the effect forces spectator identification with the twins. The film is distant – there are no zooms or telephoto shots or hand held cameras – nothing which could offer alternative identifications to the Bev/Elly/Claire triad.

Further, *Dead Ringers'* imagery, particularly water/pool imagery, reinforces the theme of infantile anxiety and interdependence. Scenes are flooded with blue light like amniotic fluid, for example, in the scene of Bev's nightmare and separation anxiety. Cronenberg wanted the Mantle apartment to feel 'like an aquarium . . . that's why I wanted their apartment to be purply and blue and sub-marine' (Cronenberg 1992, p. 144). Pool metaphors are applied both to women and to disease, for example, in media accounts of prostitution or AIDS, where the intention is to convey the thought that bodily fluids are noxious and the product of moral or physical disorders. In *Crimes of the Future* (1970) Rouge's Malady involves the eating of body fluids exuded from the multiple orifices of post-pubertal women. In *Dead Ringers*, Cronenberg frequently counterposes scenes shared by Claire and one or other of the twins with the sound of rain or running water. The final descent into the pre-Oedipal is matched by shots of exterior rain and an interior shower.

Finally, the Mantle Retractor is the exemplary sign of *Dead Ringers'* exploration of an infantile psychic desire to enter the maternal body and, in Kleinian terms, retract the father's penis. Barbara Creed argues that Bev's anatomical tools, modelled as they are on Andreas Vesalius and Ambroise Pare's scientific and monstrous illustrations are an example of mythic fetishism (Creed 1990b). While undoubtedly the fetishisation of technology is a Cronenberg obsession, the Mantle Retractor haunts *Dead Ringers* with a more infantile totemic force. The crucial opening scene shows the twins as young children initiating the violently repressive energy of the infantile and its conclusion in reproductive technology.

The purpose of introductory scenes is presumably to introduce. Perhaps it was Cronenberg's undergraduate training in literature which encourages his cinematic desire for supremely inclusive introductions to his films. All the themes of *Dead Ringers* are scrupulously present in the opening depiction of the young twins' biological obsessions and desire to explore the sexual interior of a neighbouring girl. The scene's images and events represent those of the film as a whole and focus on the significance of anatomical instruments. The female/water imagery dyad is floridly expressive in the twins' 'humans have to internalise water' in order to reproduce 'because we don't live under water' and 'women are so different from us'. The distant, stylised camera synchronically framing the twins turning their backs to the girl hints at the later synchronised tracking shot of Bev and Elly shooting drugs in the final scene. Most telling, the opening ends with the twins'"inter-ovular surgery" and precise dissection of an anatomical model.

Initially disparaged in medical school, the Retractor is emblematised in gold like an Oscar when it becomes the 'standard of the industry' and it is visible at all moments of crisis and anxiety in the film. For example, as Elly attempts to de-tox Bev, Bev himself feverishly 're-designs' the instrument. Claire herself, and very significantly, holds up one of the Retractor's hand-crafted steel supporting tools to camera in close-up (see Figure 2), and Bev's devotion to his personally-designed 'gynaecological instruments for operating on mutant women' is signi-fied after Bev's anatomical dissection of Elly, by matching the positions of his shaver (itself often commercially known as a Retractor) to the preceding close up of one of the instruments in emphatic slow motion.

A retractor presumably retracts implying that Bev and Elly wish to bring back something from the mothering uterus; they are not simply suffering fear of castration from a *vagina dentata*. As Elly says to Bev, the Retractor 'is not for internals but for surgical retractions'. Clearly the Retractor is neither a dissecting instrument nor a version of conven-tional forceps. Of course non-pregnant uteruses are much smaller than many women imagine (about the size of a fist) and investigations may need a complex tool. In addition, cervixes do change position during the menstrual cycle and the os or entrance is often small (Boston Women's Health Book Collective 1973). But although there are many varieties of obstetric forceps all are designed in some double-bladed fashion to fit a baby's head. None are designed to retract since tauto-logically a baby emerges once only.

The Retractor's name embodies its iconic psychic nature and its moment of genesis. It was during Cronenberg's 'aborted' work in Rome for *Total Recall* creating the penis-like steel earthworms – 'Sandsubs' – and mutations – 'Ganzibulls' – that an exhibition of ancient torture instruments stimulated his interest (Florence 1991). The Retractor is a brilliant visual metaphor for Cronenberg's complex psychic desires. As Cronenberg suggests in interview with Nigel Floyd: 'Bev has made something very physical that represents his state of mind, just as I have in making the film' (Floyd 1988, p. 20). It seems patent to me (and here I disagree with Creed) that Cronenberg has little effective investment in the mythic quality of the instrument in the main because *Dead*

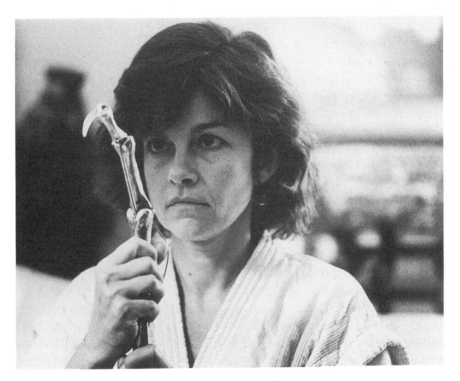

Figure 2   Geneviève Bujold as Claire Niveau, with one of
the gynaecological instruments in *Dead Ringers* (1988)

Ringers clearly avoids the moralisations that are a concomitant part of
the mythic. Nor can the Retractor function only as a metaphor for the
way in which masculine technology dominates reproductive medicine.
Rather the psychic coherence of the name comes from its function:
retraction.

Melanie Klein describes how the infant construes the mother's
sexual relationship with the father as involving the retention of the
penis inside her body. According to Klein, it is not the castrated mother
of Freud's theories which arouses male anxiety but envy of the mother
fantasised as penis retainer (Sayers 1989). A desire to retract the penis
informs all infant desires. Realisation of this desire in infant play is
what Klein describes as the acting out of anal and oral attacks on part
objects such as dolls. The pathological persecutory and depressive
anxieties that result when experience of good external relationships is

denied consists of a hallucinatory lack of boundary between self and other, for example, Bev and Elly. The exploitation of the Retractor name in *Dead Ringers* alludes to these psychic issues: Bev's dream of Claire's membrane attack, the recurrent story of Chang and Eng, the Siamese twins who could not live without each other, and the Mantle twins refusal to treat male patients 'we don't do husbands'. Cronenberg invokes, and gives a powerful structural authority to, his psychic 'retracting desire' by filming the final scene of Bev's incisions in 'real time'. The closing foetal *pietà* of Bev holding Elly is not a nihilistic closure but a very precise metaphorical realisation of Kleinian infant desire as well, of course, an indication that no such subjectivity is attainable.

The inability to stabilise a gendered subjectivity is a continuous theme throughout the film most obviously in the naming of Elliot and Beverly as Elly and Bev, simultaneously masculine and feminine. The lack of a firm symbolic name marks the failure of the social pact psychoanalytically. The names Elly and Bev carry no stable social legitimacy or precise gender. Claire, Cary and others joke about the lack of precise gender referentiality and, as I have suggested, Elliot may be named after de Palma's dual personality and transvestite Dr Elliott. Since Elly and Bev lack effective patronyms, the pre-Oedipal, the semiotic, inevitably structures their identities. The feminisation of both names positions the masculine as subordinate. Inevitably the maternal is the only guarantor of psychic identity. The feminising hysteria which floods *Dead Ringers* is narratively and patronymically predictable and stresses the importance of naming as a way of calling individuals into being as subjects. Cronenberg's films all emphasise the importance of naming: the optometrist in *Videodrome* is Barry Convex, the sado-masochist is Nicki Brand, while in *Shivers* Dr Emil Hobbes is concerned with Hobbesian population control. Cronenberg's unprecedented punning mocks the function of naming as a way of inserting the individual into the symbolic. Rather than constructing believable social backgrounds for his characters which would augment the social, Cronenberg's puns avoid socially differentiated individuality in favour of the psychic.

As Klein argues, names are an essential part of the magic formula of identity creation. Klein describes the story 'If I Were You' by the French novelist Julian Green whose protagonist Fabian Especial is a minor official unable to relate to others, particularly to his mother, so enters into other identities to gain a richer life. Klein points out that with Fabian's use of pseudonyms 'Poujars' and 'Elise' he 'literally leaves his self and enters into his victim' and that this is a key example of projective identification' (Klein 1993, p. 166). Patients who do not know where these projected parts of themselves have gone to, experience great anxiety and insecurity. The process of reintrojecting a projected part of the self or retracting an identification includes internalising a part of the object. In *Dead Ringers* this would be introjecting from women's anatomy.

Dead Ringers is more richly steeped in the thematics and aesthetics of a male psychic desire for introjection than Cronenberg's earlier films. For example, while Dr Keloid's skin grafting in *Rabid* is, like Bev's anatomical surgery in *Dead Ringers*, similarly described as 'radical', *Rabid*'s world is haunted more by the social, with its World Health Organisation vaccinating 'safe' people with plastic IDs, than *Dead Ringers*' obsessive interiority. To make any sense of how an infantile psychology involving the good/bad mother so actively dominates *Dead Ringers* virtually requires that film theory turns away from spectatorship to those more complex explanations available in feminist theory and particularly in the work of Melanie Klein.

From a Kleinian perspective, *Dead Ringers* is a fascinating, far more complex film than one which merely represents the misogyny of masculine reproductive medicine. *Dead Ringers* is an exemplary, potent fantasmatic of male anxieties not simply a film about phallic panic and castration fears. Rather, *Dead Ringers* is a hugely accurate depiction of male infantile anxieties and desires. These anxieties and desires function especially saliently at the level of imagery (water/red/blue), camera movements and signifiers (the Retractor). *Dead Ringers*' real achievement is to create psychic portraits which act the plot of our contemporary gender concerns.

Chapter 4

AUTHOR/AUTEUR: FEMINIST LITERARY
THEORY AND FEMINIST FILM

If there has been one trait most markedly characteristic of women's cinema, I would say that it has been *the project to work with and against narrative*, shifting the place of the look, playing with genre/gender crossing and reversal, image-voice disjunctures, and other codes of narrative construction . . .

The importance of narrative cinema as a mode of working through the relations of female subjectivity, identity and desire cannot be understated. (de Lauretis 1990, 25)

While more than half of all commercial films have literary origins, the coupling of author/auteur or literature/film is continually contested. So, to discuss some of the ways in which literary criticism, specifically feminist literary criticism, offers possible tools for film study might seem to add further problems and complications. Yet two relevant events suggest that the marriage of literature and film is one unlikely to be easily dissolved even if it is always in crisis. The South Bank Centre in London chose to celebrate the centenary of British cinema in 1996 not by creating a mediatheque but with *Writing in Light*, a series of Voice Box lectures looking at 'the ways in which the language of film has influenced poetry and fiction and how they share technique, construction and form' (South Bank Centre 1996, p. 1). While in America in 1996, the annual conference on Literature and Film has reached number twenty-one with *Genre and Gender in Film and Literature*.

But to begin with, what is usually meant by literature/film study? While there is no exact critical method the term has served for some time as a general umbrella for criticism about the relationship between cinematic and literary forms and I need briefly to mark out my own exact concerns before assessing the precise contributions of feminist literary criticism. My concern is not with literary works transferred to film, neither the current popularity of Jane Austen novels nor the use of assertive literary syntax in film voice overs, for example, in *Trainspotting* – what Alfred Hitchcock might have dismissed as photographs of people talking. Nor is my concern the impact of literary techniques on film, though that is undeniable: Sergei Eisenstein argues in 'Dickens, Griffith and the Film' that W. D. Griffith came to montage from Dickens's fictional use of parallel action. It was not only that 'literature has contributed so much', according to Eisenstein, but more significantly literature is 'the act of viewing – not only the *eye*, but *viewing'* (Eisenstein 1992, p. 395). Though, as Patricia Mellencamp argues citing this essay, Eisenstein describes an 'inner unity'; topography not narrative (Mellencamp 1995, p. 58).

The late 1920s and 1930s, with the impact of Eisenstein's earlier films and writing, witnessed a vivid cross-fertilisation of literature and film, like Macpherson's Pool Group of writers and film makers, but by the 1960s literary paradigms were less in fashion. A very influential text – George Bluestone's *Novels into Film* – speaks to that historic critical moment in which criticism stood on the threshold between Leavisite humanism and poststructuralism. That is to say, the critical task changed from establishing the moral value of great texts to theorising their structures. Unlike earlier critics, Bluestone argues that novels and films are very different from each other: a difference conditioned by different origins, audiences and modes of production. Examining case studies of film treatments of 'classical' novels – *The Informer, Wuthering Heights,* and *Pride and Prejudice* among others – Bluestone argues that films, unable to render linguistic tropes, inevitably abandon language characteristics, supplying in their stead spatial variations and montage (Bluestone 1966).

So it may seem paradoxical to utilise literary criticism for *auteur* study since that flourished partly in reaction to film criticism's literary past; obviously it would be too sweeping to suggest that a critical analysis created for one narrative form (literature) can be readily and unproblematically applied to another (film) (Cook 1993). My intention is to look at some linguistic markers chosen by feminist critics and how these might be similar to film tropes but, to be further exact, I am not talking about theories of film language which have a long history in film studies, the obvious example being Christian Metz's translation of film into linguistic sign systems in which shot sequence is structurally equivalent to semantic sentences (Metz 1974). Rather, I want to explore specific literary tropes and apply these to film techniques. As Duncan Petrie points out in his introduction to the British Film Institute research of Marina Warner:

> one tends to forget that the history of cinema is relatively short and that the modes of narration and codes of representation which distinguish the medium are prefigured by a vast and extensive history of cultural production and transmission which have been hugely influential on the new medium (Petrie 1993, p. 1).

My sense is that there is, currently, a fresh and sophisticated span of feminist literary thought which can be broadly useful for film study. In the 1990s, feminist literary theory is extensive and reflective, receptive to all those nuances of framing, inflection and particularly authorial viewpoint which intensively concern critics of women's films. No concept of gendered media representation can function without a concept of authorship.

This chapter focuses on the work of Marleen Gorris, the first woman director to win an Oscar. Marleen Gorris's films have distinctively gendered preoccupations and styles, her first two films – A *Question of Silence* and *Broken Mirrors* – being elaborately women-centred films about women's experiences of sexual exploitation, violence, the everyday domestic 'abuses' of heterosexuality and the sexual division of labour. Both films structurally connect female friendship and women's subsequent psychic liberation. In the prizewinning A *Question of Silence* (1982) the plot centres on the murder of a male boutique manager by three women, the determination of whose sanity is the court-appointed task of a psychiatrist, Janine. In a series of sympathetic but differently focused interviews, Janine questions the instigator of the murder, Christine, a catatonic housewife immured in domestic isolation with her children, Annie the bawdy, large, diner owner and Andrea an intelligent secretary whose business expertise is appropriated by her employer. Through a succession of flashbacks, combined with the women's responses to Janine and scenes of Janine's own married life, we witness the psychiatrist herself growing into a women-centred consciousness.

Broken Mirrors, with a budget of over a million guilders (£250,000), was the biggest Dutch domestic hit of 1985 and was awarded best feature film at the International Gay Film Festival, San Francisco. Here the focus divides between the daily interactions of prostitutes in a brothel and the abduction, torture and murder of Bea, a housewife and mother, by a serial killer. Again, Gorris aligns these two kinds of sexual abuse. The growing friendship between Diane, a new prostitute and young mother with a junkie husband, and the experienced Dora, who similarly 'mothers' an elderly neighbourly male squatter, encourages both women, after a horrific, violent attack on another brothel member, to leave prostitution. *Broken Mirrors* ends with a potentially important move to 'lesbian experience' building on the 'lesbian continuum' of *A Question of Silence*. These two terms 'lesbian existence' and 'lesbian continuum' were coined by Adrienne Rich in her hugely influential essay 'Compulsory Heterosexuality and Lesbian Existence', to describe how lesbianism can be a part of every woman's emotional if not physical, experience (Rich 1980). 'Lesbian continuum' is the exploration of lesbian history and culture in which every woman can engage while 'lesbian experience' includes the specifically sexual component of lesbian identity. As contemporary reviews of Gorris's films make clear, her films seem remarkably 'closed' to male viewers. The critic Philip French's comment that *A Question of Silence* is 'the unacceptable face of feminism' was not an isolated opinion (Root 1986).

The bigger budget film *The Last Island*, was made with a Dutch production crew but with a different producer, director of photography and composer. The film's action is set in a Pacific island (actually Tobago) with five male and two female survivors of a plane crash. The film is an adult *Lord of the Flies* with discontent simmering between the men: a French scientist, a gay business man and his new lover, a religious fanatic of a British army officer, and Jack a young American. At first resourceful and co-operative in boat and shelter building, the men soon become violent both towards each other and towards Joanne, the younger woman. Unlike *Broken Mirrors*, in this film religious belief triggers death and havoc and a denouement where the men murder each other. Only Joanne and the elderly wise woman are left alive on what we are told is the last island on earth. The men represent a range of nationalities and politics and their deaths at the hands of each other suggests Gorris's move towards a more mystical/mythical belief that only women can survive contemporary masculine destructions.

Antonia's Line, Gorris's fourth film is the logical outcome of this conviction. Winner of the Academy Award for Best Foreign Language Film of 1995, *Antonia's Line* chronicles almost fifty years of Dutch village life, in which gifted intelligent women willingly choose and enjoy a constant cycle of birth and creativity. Antonia and her daughter, grandchild and great-grandchild transform the masculine culture of the village from one of casual sexual harassment combined with religiosity to one of communal support.

The structure of the film – a mixture of Antonia's memories and the voice of Sarah, her great-granddaughter – is engendered by women to reflect the way women have power over their lives and particularly over their sexuality. So, in the episode in which Daniëlle visits the city to become impregnated, she, with the assistance of the earthy, continually pregnant Letta, quickly chooses a man, enjoys a half-hour of passionate sex in a fairytale hotel while Antonia and Letta, waiting below, have time for only one drink. All three women, Gorris's favourite triad, quickly leave both man and venue, laughing uproariously.

Yet Gorris has so far been remarkably 'silent' autobiographically in interviews. There are none of the customary detailed embellishments of physical appearance, family history, or the typical *Bildungsroman* of unknown writer to famous director. In only one interview to date is there any mention of her appearance 'tall, with pale shoulder-length hair and black expensive looking boots and jeans' (Dickenson 1985, p. 12). As she pointed out in 1984 'I find it extremely difficult to talk about my own films, I don't like to explain things that I have already explored in the film' (*Screen International* 1984, p. 156). Gorris's imprint is much more subtly autobiographical and marks framing and camera movements. For these reasons the authorial project of feminist literary criticism with its attention to subtle discursive formations of gender might be powerfully truth telling. Rather than representing Gorris as some exemplary auteur, feminist literary criticism would make instructively explicit those minute textual places where authorial energies surface.

What are the telling representational effects which current feminist literary criticism explores and how useful are these for Gorris's films? In her essay 'Toward a Women's Poetics' (Donovan 1987) Josephine

Donovan calls for a feminist aesthetic which directly addresses the experience of women. One of the central features of this aesthetic will be 'gynocriticism', a term Donovan takes from the work of Elaine Showalter. 'Gynocriticism is part of the process, of the praxis, through which the voices of the silenced are becoming heard' (Donovan 1987, p. 107).

'Gynocriticism' is a way of assessing works of art specifically in relation to the interests and desires of women. As Donovan points out it involves a separate female way of thinking, and a recognition that women's experience has been effectively silenced by a masculine culture. This response to that silencing, is a new epistemology which creates or uncovers a 'newly visible world of female culture' opening up and sharing this world with women readers/viewers.

One good example of gynocriticism, which is relevant to cinema, is what Donovan calls 'a collective social construction of reality' (Donovan 1987, p. 101). This is the process experienced in consciousness raising (CR) groups where peer support and a shared political perspective enable women to construct a women's epistemology. Marleen Gorris achieved this by working with the same small handful of actresses who share her background in theatre rather than film, and with the same producer, cameraman and editor on both *A Question of Silence* and *Broken Mirrors*. Since neither film is simply one woman's story, there are a plurality of psychic and social differences represented both by the women characters themselves (*A Question of Silence* has middle class, educated and working class, Black and white women; *Broken Mirrors*, in addition, has women of different nationalities) and textually in narrative mixtures (*Broken Mirrors*' fairy tales and *film noir*). Also, many of the actresses in *Antonia's Line*'s epic, fairytale saga of different generations of women are better known for their stage careers, notably Wimie Wilhelm who plays Lette. In addition the film has the same art director (Harry Ammerlaan) and costume designer (Jany Temime) as Gorris's first two films.

The second feature of women's experience which Donovan finds to be a nearly universal determinant of women's consciousness, and therefore impacting on representation, is domestic labour which, she argues, is both contingent and immediately physical. The routine, repetitive tasks of housework, for example, are unending and cyclical, a reality captured in *Broken Mirrors* explicitly ending as it began with a cleaning woman clearing away the bloody detritus of the brothel. The

sights to be relished and enjoyed in *Broken Mirrors* are not the displayed and sexualised bodies of prostitutes but women's shared,
understated domesticity of towel giving and hygiene rituals. In other
words, Gorris rejects a major convention of traditional *film noir* in
Broken Mirrors' thriller format by displacing the moral certitude of a
centred male detective in favour of an ethic grounded in the daily
reality of the brothel; in what Sara Ruddick calls 'preservative love'
(Ruddick 1980, p. 342). *Antonia's Line* is a detailed portrait of women's
farm work in postwar Holland. Willeke van Ammelrooy who plays
Antonia, prepared for her performance of Antonia's ageing body (from
forty to eighty years) by 'tying lead plates to her arms, shoulders and
legs which get progressively heavier the older I get in the film'. These
made a 'huge difference to even the smallest of movements like lifting
a cup' (Guild Entertainment Press Release).

Could existing film auteur theory, if reconsidered, provide sufficient
conceptual tools to deconstruct feminist films? 'Auteurism' developed
in the 1950s from the critical ideas of the French journal *Cahiers du
Cinéma* and its main contributors, Godard, Truffaut and Rohmer, who
argued that, although social contexts shape film processes, it was the
director who authored a film. In Alexandre Astruc's now classic essay
'the birth of a new avant-garde: la *caméra-stylo*' (1948), it was as the
title suggests, the camera which Astruc identifies as a writer's pen, or
metaphorical penis, and as the mechanism with which directors
inscribe their ideas onto film (Astruc 1968). Andrew Sarris, the coiner
of the term 'auteur' in his column in *The Village Voice* and creator of the
critical method, argued against the exact interest in social representations which could be said to inform Gorris's films (Sarris 1968). Sarris
edited translations of *Cahiers du Cinéma*, and in *The American Cinema*
describes the history of that cinema as the self-expressive signatures
of Hollywood directors rather than a collection of ideas to which these
signatures were signed. A move towards the notion that a film's
structure produces the author's viewpoint was taken by Peter Wollen in
Signs and Meaning in the Cinema, particularly in the second edition
(Wollen 1969 and 1972). The principal directors whose work is often
cited in auteur theory are Nicholas Ray and the exiled German film
director Douglas Sirk, whose films made use of experimental theatre
techniques which Sirk himself had pioneered in collaboration with
Bertolt Brecht: the use of 'staged' scenes which comment on, undercut

or distance the overall linear narrative. Indeed the term *mise-en-scène* originated in the theatre where it refers to a similar arrangement of stage scenes, although in film criticism the term now encompasses all camera 'events'.

For Marleen Gorris, like Sirk, the theatre and the thriller have both been important sources of ideas. Gorris studied first in Dutch theatre then transferred to pursue an MA in Theatre Studies at the University of Birmingham. Gorris uses *mise-en-scène* in *A Question of Silence, Broken Mirrors* and *Antonia's Line* to make a coherent artistic statement about women's subordination. The café scenes of Annie's sexual harassment in *A Question of Silence* are exactly paralleled in *Antonia's Line* in which the 'backward' Deedee is displayed for men in a scene reminiscent of the wife sale in Hardy's *Mayor of Casterbridge*. In other ways Gorris' films do not match existing auteur criteria. For example auteur art films, a category in which Gorris's films were originally introduced to Britain although not marketed as such, deliberately address their audiences as knowledgeable cinemagoers – that is to say, those who understand film techniques – or frequently play with difficult expressive codes such as sharp breaks with story lines. Auteurism lost critical leverage during the seventies with an epidemic of poststructuralist, Lacanian and discourse studies of 'cinematic apparatuses' and spectator reception of and resistance to, such apparatuses. I am not alone in pointing out that it is hardly surprising that the auteur ceased to be a central issue in film theory just at the moment of the burgeoning of feminist literary criticism in the 1970s. The timing is no coincidence. One year before *A Question of Silence* appeared, Rosalind Petchesky was arguing that the women's liberation movement was the most dynamic force for social change (Petchesky 1981). The largest demonstration for women's rights in history – the 1970 Women's Strike for Equality – had inspired a huge growth in feminist organisations and important legal changes. Congress approved the ERA (Equal Rights Amendment) in 1972, legalised abortion in 1973 and, in one decade, passed over seventy other women's rights bills (nearly forty per cent of all American women's rights' legislation passed this century).

There was similar and substantial progress in Europe and Australia including Equal Pay Acts in 1972. Nor were these changes confined to political and social spheres but had a heavy impact on popular culture. Even soap operas, including the US prime-time television series *The*

Mary Tyler Moore Show, tackled a range of feminist issues (Faludi 1992). By the time *A Question of Silence* came out in 1982 a marked gender voting gap was visible and in that year white men, for the first time, became less than fifty per cent of the American work force. Such huge shifts in ways of thinking and in social and economic behaviour would inevitably impact on what women might desire as media consumers and on what questions they might ask about media constructs.

In response, feminist media critics have struggled to create a space within auteur theory for more appreciative interpretations of women's sexual experience and desires, as for example, Tania Modleski did in her study of voyeurism and sexual difference in the films of Alfred Hitchcock (Modleski 1988).

Kaja Silverman's *The Acoustic Mirror* marks what is potentially an even more significant shift in auteur thinking. Silverman focuses on the ways in which an author is '*one* of the speakers of his or her films' (Silverman 1988, p. 202). Rather than arguing that particular characters act as an author's stand-ins, Silverman suggests that the author as 'speaking subject' is 'any representation or network of representations' (ibid., p. 202). Thus, following Silverman it could be argued that in *Broken Mirrors*, Gorris's 'voice' becomes a fundamental element of Diane's sense of self as she becomes the author of her own life by breaking the brothel mirrors. In *Antonia's Line*, Danielle 'voices' her artistic creativity by falling in love with Lara, her daughter's teacher. Yet while Silverman's concept might help her to a more complex reading of authorial differences, Silverman herself is surprisingly pessimistic and literal (*sic*) about the value of literary theory to the work of film deconstruction. Rather obviously Silverman points out that cinema is not a linguistic medium: 'What is the filmic equivalent of the first-person pronoun' (ibid., p. 200). By assuming that authorial literary criticism concerns itself only with first person narratives, Silverman glosses over literary criticism's other more sophisticated interrogations.

Work on female authorship in feminist film criticism of the 1990s has tended to focus on avant-garde film directors (apart from Judith Mayne's *Directed by Dorothy Arzner* which looks at the Hollywood industry). Sandy Flitterman-Lewis's *To Desire Differently: Feminism and the French Cinema* compares the films and careers of Germaine Dulac, Marie Epstein and Agnes Varda (Flitterman 1990). Flitterman-Lewis was editor of *Women and Film*, the first magazine devoted specifically to feminist film criticism and in 1974 she helped to found *Camera Obscura*. *To Desire Differently* draws on her doctoral dissertation in which she argues that these women film makers' connections with alternative film practice – 1920s avant-garde (Dulec), 1930s Poetic Realism (Epstein) and the 1960s and New Wave (Varda) – allowed them to explore female subjectivity in experimental ways as Epstein does using experimental sound production techniques in *La Maternelle*.

Lauren Rabinovitz's *Points of Resistance: Women, Power and Politics in the New York Avant-garde Cinema 1943–71* examines, as the title suggests, how independent cinema offered women greater opportunities for artistic success (Rabinovitz 1991). The book has an engaging style with its dramatic opening account of Maya Deren's famous bohemian 'shower-party', which reminded me of Adrienne Rich's story of 50s suburban housewives in *Of Woman Born*. Rabinovitz makes an excellent historical survey of avant-garde Greenwich village with its alternative film venues, organisations and particularly the warm and key relationships between the women film-makers themselves. Judith Mayne's *Directed by Dorothy Arzner* (1994) is equally vivid as a portrait in the 'literal and figurative senses of the term' (Mayne 1994, p. 6). The book examines Arzner's career, her relationship with Marion Morgan and the thematic and stylistic preoccupations in her work as well as how her image has been assessed and appropriated. Mayne's argument is that Adrienne Rich's concept 'lesbian continuum' or women-identified experience, precisely describes Arzner's career in which the contribution of women's friendships and communities is its most 'consistent and important feature' (Mayne 1994, p. 131). Finally Annette Kuhn has edited a collection of other critics' essays on Ida Lupino – *Queen of the 'B' s* – again to redress critics' misogynist view of women directors (Kuhn 1995B).

While very valuable, in some ways these texts do not consider the textual specificities of authorship in the kind of details described by feminist literary theorists. For example, Sandra Gilbert and Susan Gubar's germinal *The Madwoman in the Attic* focuses on some of culture's most serious exclusions – women's subcultures and anxieties of femininity – represented in motifs of the domestic and the madwoman (Gilbert and Gubar 1988). This is basically a revisionist history taking an existing model – Harold Bloom's androcentric paradigm in *The Anxiety of Influence* that literary sons suffer an anxiety of authorship and

Oedipal struggle with male precursors – to show that women confront culture with an author's double: the madwoman a 'maddened double functioning as a social surrogate for a docile self' (Gilbert and Gubar 1979, p. x). The central question addressed in *Madwoman* is a crucial question for readings of women's films: how do women authors manage 'the difficult task of achieving true female literary authority by simultaneously conforming to and subverting patriarchal literary standards' (Gilbert and Gubar 1988, p. 73). Gilbert and Gubar's answer is to trace and affirm the more extensive features of female authorship: the vivication of anxieties of authorship in characters writers detest, an 'oddity' and 'eccentricity' of style, for example, a revision of genres, as well as linking aspects of female sexuality with textuality.

Following Gilbert and Gubar, Elaine Showalter's account of the differences of women's writing was an important breakthrough in authorship criticism. Showalter alights on four models of women's literary differences: biological, linguistic, psychoanalytic and cultural. Biological difference can be highlighted by deconstructing literary symbols of the body. Linguistic difference shows in a woman's use of multiple registers. Psychoanalytic difference is visible in a difference of theme, for example mother/daughter affiliations, and the cultural is represented by women's muted groups often occupying what Showalter calls 'wild zones' (Showalter 1986). This last difference – the wild zone of women's subcultures – has been taken up by one of the few film essays marrying literary and film approaches to Gorris: 'A Jury of Their Peers: Marleen Gorris's *A Question of Silence*' (by Linda Williams). Williams suggests that Gorris's feminism is displayed in her use of an alternative and passionate women's wild zone, for example, the women's disruptive laughter in the courtroom, which Williams mythologises as an 'unknown world of matriarchal Shadow' (Williams 1988, p. 113).

While Williams' analysis does usefully allow her to argue that Gorris clearly problematises conventional film shot structure with subversive laughter, Williams does not pay attention to other exciting and productive examples of Gorris's signature which Showalter's ideas could make tangibly available. Showalter's more radical notion of women's double voice, which is a simultaneously muted and dominant literary presence, is much more relevant for our purposes.

Finally Nancy Miller's fascinating work on authorial representations offers many productive insights. In 'Changing the Subject' and *Getting*

Personal Miller writes about the visibility of signatures and the politics of authorship. Rejecting Roland Barthes's reductively invisible author, Miller argues that women are not burdened by 'too much self, ego, cogito' (Miller 1991, p. 106). In her account of subjectivity in Adrienne Rich's 'When We Dead Awaken' (Rich 1980) Miller asks: on what grounds can we refigure the relation of female subject to social text? – a question which seems to crystallise the concerns of feminist film criticism. Miller's solution, matching Showalter's, is that women writers often assume the signifiers of masculinity in addition to our women's garb. Miller draws on Barthes's term *'biographeme'* to describe authorial inflections as well as on Mary Ann Caws's term 'personal criticism' which describes a similar stylistic intensity in the lending of oneself (Barthes 1977; Caws 1990). Concepts of 'inflection', 'intensity' and 'double voice' can help to identify those authorial features in film texts which are less obvious, perhaps more deliberately oblique, than traditional marks of authorship in mainstream cinema such as a director playing a leading or subsidiary character as Woody Allen does.

Gorris argues that with *A Question of Silence* she 'started writing something which turned out in the end to be a film script . . . I just started writing for myself' (Rowe 1982, p. 10). Women's social reality provides Gorris with luscious material: 'One day sitting in a bookshop', Gorris read 'a small news item which described a couple of women attacking a shop owner'. This becomes the linchpin in *A Question of Silence* (Mackintosh 1983, p. 13). Although the news item read that two women were 'beating to death a *woman*', Gorris spectacularly refuses to consider this anti-feminist possibility in *A Question of Silence* giving voice to this through Andrea the secretary claiming that none of the three women could murder another woman.

Gorris's authorship is clear first in her tight directorial control of the production process, as she insists on an unusual final cut format in which editing is 'an exploring expedition'. In addition Gorris writes all her scripts and directs them herself largely because other directors 'all wanted to change the structure, which I thought was about the most important thing in the film' (Rowe 1982, p. 10).

Gorris's films fit comfortably within the consolidations of authorship chosen by feminist literary critics. That is, her films are double voiced following Showalter's model of muted and dominant languages. In addition there is a marked intensity of camera identification, a lending of herself in the scenes with Janine, Dora/Diane, and the mother/ daughter dyads of *The Last Island* and *Antonia's Line*. Gilbert and Gubar's 'anxiety of authorship' reveals itself in Gorris's generic subversions and in her less than satisfactory 'Othering' of the Black prostitute Tessa in *Broken Mirrors*. Finally there are recurrent signatures, a quieter authorial voice, in Gorris's repetitive use of particular elements: a constant focus on hands; on the red boutique bags and Bea's red coat; her choice of *pietà* iconography in *Broken Mirrors* and of Botticelli's *Birth of Venus* in *Antonia's Line*. These tiny moments of authorial emotion recall Nancy Miller's concept of inflection.

Gorris creates her muted and dominant double voice in *Broken Mirrors* by filming the scenes where the serial killer captures and tortures Bea in 'dominant' objectified documentary style. This involves deep focus and grainy faded film stock as Gorris denies viewer engagement with the killer by occluding his face. In contrast the brothel scenes share an intimate camera. In the scenes where the murderer selects and then captures Bea, the camera is at waist height, the murderer shot from behind, sometimes headless and in deep focus. When he leaves his office, faceless, having identified himself only by a mechanically exact placing of pen and notebook in close up, the camera tracks but does not even hold the murderer in frame while frequently moving behind staircases and other objects in order to lose sight of his figure and hence prevent spectator identification. Gorris carefully prefigures this objectification in the opening sequence where the murderer is shot adjacent to an electricity pylon with similarly straggled legs. The metaphorical association marks the murderer's world as mechanical and nonhuman.

In opposition, the brothel *mise-en-scènes* are intimate spaces where women's friendships and communal support (and bitchiness) can flourish. Moving from the downstairs room (where the camera frequently frames six or seven figures at once both by tracking and by Gorris's carefully choreographed actress movements) the prostitutes work upstairs. The fluidity of movement between on-screen and off-screen space combined with a naturalistic use of sound, like street noises, makes the spatial interactions especially convincing. Similarly in the bedroom interiors the camera focus allows women to be powerful controllers of their spaces. Gorris avoids typical film objectifications of naked women by means of a very controlled camera focus. Undressed, the women are not framed voyeuristically for the viewer but are frequently in close up with the camera at their own eye level even when seated.

Similarly in *A Question of Silence* Gorris underlines Janine's growing involvement with the three women with specific authorial compositions. Importantly, it is the framing which connects Janine with each of the three women she visits in prison. As each interview builds on another the camera focus changes from static profiling to medium shot and to close up. The dyadic visual rhythm connects two women in turn with techniques such as profiling faces in close up. While there is no physical matching in each paired scene since Christine, Annie and Andrea are of very different heights and shapes, Gorris's compositions suggest overlap, similarities and intensity which matches Nancy Miller's concept of 'inflection'. Miller characterises 'inflection' as a deliberate display of the personal voice perhaps an accented emotion or a repeated image not unlike, for example, Alice Walker's repeated image of flowers which appear throughout her novels. In *Antonia's Line* the 'inflected', constant mutual gazing of mother and daughter is established from the tight opening close-up.

In addition Gorris's genre subversions match Gilbert and Gubar's 'anxiety of authorship'. Her first two films subvert a conventional thriller format which encourages viewers to identify with a strong, purposeful hero. Gorris refuses to have such heroic protagonists. Janine and Dora/Diane are not in charge of their emotions or their lives and clearly do not seek to affirm the continuity of social institutions whether legal or sexual, nor do they avoid psychic contradictions. In *Antonia's Line* the women's cyclical attention to birth subverts the village's harsh social values. The curate leaves the Church; Farmer Bas's sons cease tormenting Loony Lips and eventually murder the rapist, now fascist soldier, Pitte; and Crooked Finger's belief in Schopenheur's 'the world is hell' results in his suicide not that of women. In addition *A Question of Silence* is synchronic not diachronic. Gorris breaks with linear chronology by starting the film with the murderers already known to the audience and to the investigator. The generic convention where a detective progresses, singlemindedly to the solution of the crime is displaced in favour of Janine's consciousness raising.

Gorris further 'anxiously' problematises the thriller genre by introducing multigeneric elements like myth and fairytale. The narrative of

Broken Mirrors is shot through with references to Beauty and the Beast as when in deepest winter, André gives a blossoming rose to Dora who carries it through brambles to her boat. In Diane's revised story of the frog prince, the kissed frog remains a frog. In *Antonia's Line* fairytale subtext becomes fairytale surtext. The recluse, Crooked Finger, like André, is a source of wisdom but it is the women, Antonia and Sarah, who tell the story in epigrammatic quasi-Brechtian sayings. In addition the murder of Pitte is triggered by Antonia's witch-like curses. Gorris, as Nancy Miller suggests, resolutely and gloriously subverts the masculine signature.

Miller's motif of 'intensity' could be said to mark Gorris's films. In *A Question of Silence* Janine mirrors Gorris and a similar mirroring of Diane/Dora with Gorris shapes *Broken Mirrors*. Thus, in *A Question of Silence*, there is a sharp distinction between the way in which the camera focuses on Janine and its focus on other women (except when framing each in relation to Janine as I have argued). In both films subsidiary characters occupy only a centripetal function rather than the typical centrifugal, dynamic function of conventional cinema. That is to say, a viewer's interest in Gorris's characters, like spectators of stage actresses, is drawn away from the actor to others and to the background/set whereas in traditional cinema the actor sucks in the viewer's attention (Davis and Wells 1992). But Gorris's camera is centrifugal, more mobile in scenes with Janine at home. For example, Gorris permits herself a rare zoom to close up at Janine's first dinner party. Perhaps the most telling scene in this context is the scene where Janine discusses the three case histories with her husband and is caressingly tracked by the camera thereby mimicking Janine's eye level, now near to the floor as she squats, for the moment of a crucial direct address to camera 'I don't think these women are insane'.

There is a similar intensity in Gorris's 'lending of herself' to Dora/Diane. There are only two uses of a circling camera in *Broken Mirrors*. One is the scene in which Dora listens to André describing the stable in Bethlehem like a prototypical brothel and with the Virgin Mary presaging the later iconography of the Stabat Mater. The other is the restaurant scene of Linda's 'wake' where Diane tells her revised and comic version of the frog prince to the vast enjoyment of the other women. Rather than a highly mobile camera it is significant that only Dora and Diane circle in close up and medium shot tightly framed by

Gorris such as in the scene where Diane succours Linda after her overdose and later when Dora and Diane dance together. Similarly, in *Antonia's Line* a circling camera intensifies the symbolic quality of baby Therese's birth, as she is handed lovingly from villager to villager in a communal blessing. The saturation of authorship in these scenes is marked.

Nancy Miller's notion of 'inflection' explains Gorris's other authorial gestures. In *A Question of Silence* Gorris cuts from Christine's hand on head to Janine's identical hand held head in her study.

In her films Gorris relies heavily on specific colours. The carrying of a red boutique bag by each of the three women enables the viewer to read the displaced temporal sequences of *A Question of Silence*. In *Broken Mirrors*, Dora enters the film carrying a similar red bag as if symbolically to link both films. Bea wears a red coat and the murderer drives a red car. Red invades the whole diegesis of *Broken Mirrors* when Irma is savagely stabbed and bloodily soaks the brothel bed sheets. In *Antonia's Line* Gorris repeats particular images rather than colours, for example Breugal-like motifs (the mother's coffin). In addition there is a recurring inflection of references to the Virgin Mary: religious statues move to the thoughts of women. In *Broken Mirrors* André sings about the Virgin and fantasises about how she 'used to stay the night' with him while Ellen is forced to add to the brothel's sadomasochistic attractions the possibility of being whipped while chanting 'Hail Mary, full of Grace'. Diane's baby, clutching Diane's arm as the mother glances at drug stigmata on the body of her dead partner, is framed as a *pietà*, and the film concludes with an aria from Haydn's *Stabat Mater*. In her essay 'Stabat Mater' Julia Kristeva also carefully positions her own autobiographical, psychic 'voice' of mothering alongside social narratives of mothering on each graphically doubled page of separate columns – one academic, the other more reflexive (Kristeva 1986).

A musical inflection is crucial to Gorris's authorial enterprise. As she explains when interviewed about *Broken Mirrors* 'Stabat Mater lifts the whole film out of the confines of the sex club and into a larger world' (Dickenson 1985, p. 12). While there are many similar hymns to the Virgin Mary it is perhaps worth noting here Gorris's preference for Haydn's *Stabat Mater* which was composed at a time before the rise of composer historicism began to deny a certain freedom of composition (Citron 1993). In addition, traditionally the Stabat Mater cannot bear the sight of ritualised violence. Through the hymn's resolution the music expresses something of the unity Gorris wishes her viewers to experience at the close of *Broken Mirrors*. This musical coherence heavily contrasts with the discordant musical motifs signalling the scenes of male aggression scored by Lodewijk de Boer, the same composer for both of Gorris's first two films.

A more troubling authorial signature is Gorris's representation of racial difference. The Black woman in *A Question of Silence* simply joins the other boutique customers in a silent, supportive chorus. Even more problematic is the figure of Tessa, the Surinamese prostitute in *Broken Mirrors*. In some ways, it could be argued that Gorris's 'Othering' of Tessa reveals an 'anxiety of authorship' which is characterised by Gilbert and Gubar as the resulting literary effect of many women writers' confrontation with culture. According to them women writers often create their own doubles as monstrous or madwomen characters, as Charlotte Brontë did with Berthe, in their struggle with authorial identity and the male tradition. While clearly neither monstrous nor mad, Tessa's character seems to have sprung – stereotypically exaggerated as she is – from 'anxious' authorship: Tessa is customarily framed in medium shot sitting passively at the far end of the brothel bar, an isolated, silent figure.

Tessa's iconography corresponds closely to the painting, *Portrait of a Negress* (1800) by Marie-Guihelmine Benoist, an artist known for her neo-classical portraiture (see Figure 3). Of course the representational language of racial bodies differs historically just as the meanings of nakedness/clothed, femininity/masculinity equally shift discursively over time, yet the similarity is striking. Benoist's portrait can be read as a Black citoyen – therefore man's social and political equal – yet her naked breast and naked hands, nevertheless, display the Black female body as evidently available to a male gaze. Similarly, in *Broken Mirrors*, Tessa is framed in half-profile, giving the same guarded look away from camera that speaks of a subservient passivity. Both figures embody a female passivity and availability in which the Black body is modelled to reflect the desires and anxieties of the artist/viewer. Tessa's very brief verbal insertions are not independently self-generated but reactive, triggered by white abuse. The distinct Otherness of Tessa's figuration is reinforced when the only prostitute to choose Tessa's stool, in her absence, is the sexually abused and victimised Linda. Yet if the

Figure 3 *Portrait of a Negress* (1800) by Marie-Guihelmine Benoist
(1768–1826), Musée du Louvre, Paris

immobilising framing of Tessa is problematic there is one more potentially progressive moment. The scene in which Dora physically attacks
Francine in response to Francine's racist denigration of Tessa's apparent
fertility is a gesture of disavowal.

A final example of Miller's concept of intensity in the lending of self
are the lesbian inflections of Gorris's films. Gorris acknowledges the
influence of Chantal Akerman on her work – a film-maker who more
overtly engages with lesbian issues. There are several episodes which
numinously identify lesbian desire. In *Broken Mirrors* Diane visits Dora's
house boat to try on the part-made shirt which Dora is sewing for
Diane in friendship. As Diane undresses she notices and does not
reject Dora's involved gaze. Reaching for Dora, Diane kisses her companion. There is a strong homoerotic tension between the two women.
By ending on the moment of a further mutual gaze the scene can be
read as embodying lesbian desire and reflecting Dora's metaphoric
desire to 'garb' Diane in 'different' clothes. The shirt, like the women's
lesbian 'experience' is incomplete at that point in the film but, and very
significantly, Diane is wearing the finished shirt as she shatters the
brothel mirrors with gunshots in the liberating closure of the film.

A fusion of author with character similarly marks *A Question of
Silence*. The most magnetically radiant authorial scene in the film is the
scene of Janine's final interview with Andrea in prison. In her cell
Andrea very slowly and sensually outlines by hand Janine's face and
body, almost but not quite touching at any point (see Figure 4). It is a
particularly devastating portrait of mutual desire. What has not been
noted by other critics, but I think is significant, is first the structural
placing of the scene, following on as it does, from the scene where
Janine strokes Christine's head, and second, the deliberate camera
superimposition of Janine's mirrored head onto Andrea in a suggestively metaphoric doubling. The eroticised interview ends not because
either woman desires closure but because – in an image of male intru-
sion that shatters female activity – a male guard mistakenly enters the
cell. In *Antonia's Line* Daniëlle's comic vision of lesbian desire presents
her future lover Lara as a penis-wielding Botticelli *Birth of Venus*.

In *Broken Mirrors* the daily brothel routines which are balletically
choreographed for the camera into a sequence of intimate and shared
moments – sharing coffee, arranging the rooms, dressing and make-up
– are frozen by the arrival of a male customer. Perhaps the final horror

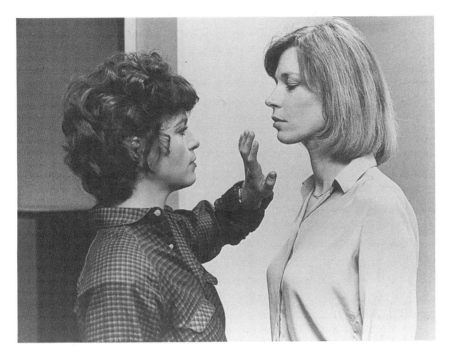

Figure 4   Andrea and Janine's 'lesbian continuum' in *A Question of Silence*
(1982)

for a male viewer of *A Question of Silence* is the textual prelude to the
murder: when all three women share a gaze they are empowered to
kill. Indeed the very escalating inventiveness of the murder tools: feet,
shopping trolleys, coat hangers, glass shelves and ashtrays, is deliberately orchestrated by the women's mutual gazing.

Gorris is very sure of her own emotional investment in her films and
of her deliberate mirroring of auteur and characters: 'For the actresses
Broken Mirror was very hard. On set they had to work through the
feelings I'd worked through privately when writing the script. I don't
want to see *Broken Mirrors* too often' (Dickenson 1985, p. 12).

Yet invoking the importance of authorship in the current postmodern crisis of representation might seem a curiously old fashioned
project. It is partly to interrupt the postmodern evacuation of subjectivity that I focus on the exciting possibilities of authorship in Gorris's
films. What I am suggesting is that feminist literary theory can offer

some strategically useful tools for feminist film study. Feminist literary critics have already made a firm decision that gender shapes signature and that there is an aesthetic difference in the way in which gendered signatures write. None of these critics argue that texts function only to give access to the author in some kind of essentialism. But neither do these critics, as postmodernists so frequently do, reduce the author to one of other textual functions or drop the author out of sight all together in favour of a focus on pure textuality. I have tried similarly to make visible Gorris's authorial identifications, to examine the force of the woman author as a textual presence. As Josephine Donovan optimistically claims this kind of gynocriticism can provide 'a validating social witness that will enable women today and in the future to see, to express, to name their own truths' (Donovan 1987, p. 107), because, as Antonia points out, if there is no heaven 'this is the only dance we dance'.

PART TWO

Chapter 5

BLACK FILM THEORY, BLACK FEMINISMS
Daughters of the Dust

————⊃⊂————

It is striking how Hollywood cinema confines Black women to comic roles, 'mammies', prostitutes and carers of whites at the very moment when Black women's writing is drawing vividly on Black culture. The reason why cinematic representations have not matched this progressive accomplishment is self evident. Black women are rarely the makers of movies; Julie Dash's *Daughters of the Dust* (1991) is the first full length mainstream film to be directed by an Afra-American. In addition, while Black women's creative writing and literary theory is now an established and popular body of work, Black women's film theory has lacked an institutional place (hooks 1992).

The late 1980s and 1990s witnessed a new phenomenon: a huge growth in Black film-making drawing on Black popular culture and Black anger at social and economic deprivations (the films of Spike Lee and John Singleton), and gay Black voices (Isaac Julien). Critical studies addressing issues of difference and Black representations are now growing in number and are having an impact on Black independent film-making if not, as yet, on Hollywood stereotypes (Gever 1993). The emergence of both Black mainstream and 'guerrilla' cinema (to use Spike Lee's term) together with a wide spectrum of Black feminist literature, both creative and critical, suggests a new threshold in Black aesthetics.

The films of Julie Dash join those of the British independent film makers Pratibha Parmar, Isaac Julien and others in consciously employing innovative techniques, particularly new forms of narrative. Such films require fresh critiques of difference more open to the strengths of hybridity and intertextuality such as critiques which draw on creative writing so long the *bête-blanche* of film theory. Kobena Mercer points out that white criticism rarely values Black cinema and generally focuses on issues of gendered spectatorship rather than on differences of history and Black subjectivities (Mercer 1994).

Recent film theory by Black women, including the work of bell hooks, Jacqueline Bobo and Michele Wallace, joins the literary criticism of Barbara Smith, Barbara Christian, Alice Walker and Audre Lorde, to share the task of redressing misrepresentations and omissions of Black women in white aesthetics (hooks 1992; Bobo 1993; Wallace 1993; Smith 1977; Christian 1989B; Walker 1984; Lorde 1984). Black feminist criticism is now wideranging while ironically, and paradoxically, a white critical omission of the body of Black women's creative work is accompanied by the centrality of stereotypical Black masculine bodies in mainstream cinema. Thus, American action cinema still depends heavily on stereotypical assumptions – exemplified in *Predator 2*'s jungle metaphor – about Black physical power, while denying its own sexualisation of the relations of power (Tasker 1993). While so-called Blaxploitation films of the 1970s such as *Shaft* and *Superfly*, introduced new urban Black narratives, these narratives constructed the Black hero as 'hyper- (hetero)sexual' in aggressive expressions of masculinity (Tasker 1993, p. 87). Mainstream cinema of the 1970s and 1980s offered no intellectual or emotional support to Black women.

Feminist theory in the 1990s is marked more than ever before by its addressing of Black issues and new configurations of difference triggered by the accurate attacks of Black feminists. The writing of Christian, Walker, hooks and others forces film theory into a dialogue with Black creative writing and history. What hooks and others create is a Black aesthetic which is neither monolithic nor transcendental but can mirror and affirm Black women film-makers' aim to tell Black women's stories in radically new ways. For example, by refusing to rely on star close ups, preferring to photograph community groups, there is no question that Julie Dash visibly matches Black feminist writers with their own attention to women's communal knowledge. Indeed, in 'revolutionary Black women', bell hooks specifically attacks writing which describes singular Black female identities as contributing to racism (hooks 1992). In other words, hooks prefers to describe differences within Black culture rather than describe Black as always the polar opposite of white. In addition to the Hollywood masculinisation of Black identity, there is a British tendency to assume that Black America is a uniform urban culture evident in, for example, the 1995 Channel 4 series *Baadasssss TV* in which the rapper and film star Ice-T stars as the signifier of Black culture. It seems hugely urgent then to return to the key feminist questions underpinning all my chapters: can there be, or is there, an alternative and feminist film language, in this case one which does justice to the literary power of Black feminist writers?

This chapter first considers how male Black film criticism and films neglect, or only selectively represent, Black women's experiences. I want to consider some of the ways in which Black feminist critics redress this absence through attention to the extra filmic discourses of literature and Afracentrism. Finally I turn to the work of Julie Dash, examining her specific debt to an informing Black feminist aesthetic and her 'rememory' of Black women's history. *Daughters of the Dust* is set in 1902 and portrays both the migration of the Peazants, a Gullah family clan, from the Sea Islands off the South Carolina coast to the mainland, along with the religious traditions and histories which shape Gullah culture. Produced for one million dollars in a mixture of public broadcasting and independent finance, the film reconstructs a moment of Gullah history through the conversations of Gullah women and the memories of the matriarchal figure Nana Peazant.

There are enormous and obvious dangers in any critique by a white British critic. First, there is a danger of celebrating Dash's *Daughters of the Dust* as a pioneering exemplary model of a Black feminist film in a way which would preclude attention to similarities and differences between aesthetic genres. My desire to redress the omission of Black women's films in most white-authored film theory risks another danger: an over emphasis on Dash's 'Otherness', for example, her invocation of Gullah culture. As Judith Williamson pertinently suggests in a British context 'it is particularly striking that the black British work that's been taken up most widely in the world of theory, been most written about and also picked up at festivals, on tours, and so on, is the work that fits most obviously into the category of avant-garde' (Williamson 1988, p. 35).

In addition, my focusing on a Black American director raises the question of whether I am distancing ethnicity as an American feature rather than my own? Clearly, though, what is at stake in any analysis of Black women's films is too important to be limited by an epistemological dispute about appropriation/distancing but should address the broader problematic of a Black feminist aesthetic. Hopefully through a careful reading of Black feminist writers, I can avoid the obvious pitfalls and focus Dash's daring work as a radical challenge to mainstream cinema and to film studies.

Before turning to Black feminist critiques, it is important to gain some sense of the recent film theories of Black male critics including the work of Clyde Taylor, Manthia Diawara and the gay British critic Kobena Mercer (Taylor 1993; Diawara 1993; Mercer 1994). Often what emerges in feminist work is not necessarily a new departure but a necessary critical return to issues repressed by male critics. Although differing politically and methodologically in approach, for example, Mercer is informed by British cultural studies, most male scholars write in response to what is sometimes called the new Black cinema wave (Black American cinema of the 1980s) focusing on the films of Spike Lee and John Singleton, and call for particular critical strategies such as Diawara's concept of 'resisting spectator' along with new practices of representation (Diawara 1993).

Kobena Mercer's edited collection *Black Film, British Cinema* contains papers from a key conference held at London's innovative Institute of Contemporary Arts, which includes Mercer's own essay 'Recoding Narratives of Race and Nation' (Mercer 1988). The collection is interesting to read in relation to the multigeneric work of Black feminist critics, because the text includes a mixture of reviews, letters and interviews alongside the more theoretical pieces by Mercer and Stuart Hall. In 'Recoding Narratives' and elsewhere, for example, in 'Diaspora Culture and the Dialogic Imagination' (reprinted in *Welcome to the Jungle*), Mercer argues that the future of Black film criticism lies in promoting a carnival creolisation of cultures and histories, that is, a destabilising of ethnic boundaries, rather than celebrating any ethnic uniqueness (Mercer 1988; 1994). This creolisation is crucial, Mercer claims, because however popular and commercial particular Hollywood or British Black and Asian films might be, *Boyz N The Hood* and *My Beautiful Launderette* among them, Black cinema has still not escaped being 'policed' into a 'minority' discourse. Mercer's essay follows Teshome Gabriel's in 'Thoughts on Nomadic Aesthetics and Black

Independent Cinema' (Gabriel 1982) in which, like the filmmakers he admires, Gabriel mixes narrative exegesis and travelogue, a combination he claims, which makes his aesthetic theory like a woman. While wholly progressive in intention, both critics fall into the trap of gendering the absences in existing film theory as female (Gabriel) or carnival (Mercer); that is to say equating absences with marginality. By contrast, Clyde Taylor's 'The Ironies of Palace-Subaltern Discourse', and other essays, do more radically attend to the extra diegic discourses of Black music and oral culture (Taylor 1993). In 'We Don't Need Another Hero' Taylor proposes what he calls a 'postesthetic' creative practice which can decolonise Western aesthetic categories (Taylor 1988). Yet his playful examples of 'postesthetic' are such disparate Black texts as Alice Walker's *The Color Purple* and Melvin van Peebles's notoriously misogynist *Sweet Sweetback's Baadasssss Song* which suggests that Taylor lacks critical fixity and certainly ignores historical and gender specificities.

The most substantial collection to date of Black American film criticism is *Black American Cinema* edited by Manthia Diawara (Diawara 1993). The text examines Black American cinema from two perspectives: an analysis of Black aesthetics in relation to Black politics and cinema institutions; and an analysis of Black spectatorship in relation to the spectator theories of white critics. The collection includes essays on the Black film industry of the 1920s; on Hollywood strategies of displacement, for example, the isolation of Whoopi Goldberg from Black culture, the biracial buddy movies of Richard Pryor and Eddie Murphy, as well as Diawara's own work on resisting spectatorship. The book is an important text in many ways. First, it tries to acknowledge the full extent and radicalism of the Black independent sector and second, it documents a long history of Black film-making starting with Oscar Micheaux's films in the 1920s. The outline of a Black film aesthetic which emerges is one drawing on W. E. B. DuBois's concept of 'twoness': that African Americans have two social identities, one which demands the assertion of a Black ethnic identity while the other encourages an acceptance of some artistic assimilation. One good example of such 'twoness' is Oscar Micheaux's visual mirroring of the poverty of his Black characters with dark interiors and grainy printing within a classic realist format.

In Diawara's own contribution he focuses on the ways in which Black spectators might circumvent stereotypical identifications and

resist the persuasive elements of Hollywood narratives. Diawara illustrates his argument with a sequence from D. W. Griffith *The Birth of a
Nation* (1915) often referred to as the 'Gus Chase' sequence in which
Little Sister, pursued by Gus, a caricatural Black aggressor, jumps from
a cliff and dies in the arms of her brother Little Colonel. As Diawara
points out, the film encourages the spectator to identify with the white
patriarchal order represented by Little Colonel. A 'resisting spectator',
Diawara suggests, can resist by invoking Afro-American history. There
are several issues caught up in Diawara's argument. First, what if a
spectator has little historical knowledge? Does this imply that only
literate Black professors are resisting spectators? Second, Diawara's
resisting spectator is a very masculine figure.

In a later more interesting and open response to the issue of resisting
viewing – 'Cultural Studies/Black Studies' – Diawara sees the future of
Black film studies as 'identification with the Black public sphere', a
quasi 'nationalistic' space but one which offers the positive pleasures of
hip-hop, funk, even 'Afrokitsch symbols' rather than victim images
(Diawara 1995, p. 209). However, while Diawara does justice to the
vibrancy of contemporary Black culture, by describing a Black aesthetic
as nationalistic this could reproduce some of the problems that Black
feminists encountered as members of the Black Arts Movement or the
Black Panthers. Specifically, gender issues are absent.

A very different approach to spectatorship is Jacqueline Bobo's
account of Black women viewing *The Color Purple* (Bobo 1993). Bobo
adopts a more contextual approach noting how Black women's cultural
consumption is hugely shaped by the contemporary renaissance of
Black women's writing. She also draws on cultural studies more than
on psychoanalysis and quotes verbatum from her own group interviews with Black women viewers rather than relying on an abstract
model like Diawara's hypothetical 'resister'. Utilising the concept of
'interpellation', or the way in which a subject is summoned into a text,
as well as the concept of 'interdiscourse', or the moment of encounter
between text/subject, Bobo identifies Black viewing pleasures in terms
of viewers' cultural competence (their intertextual cultural experience).

In many ways Bobo's essay matches work about other 'marginalised'
viewers such as lesbian spectatorship critiques which argue that
defining films' spectatorship pleasures in terms of male spectators
cancels the alternative viewing pleasures of lesbians. Jackie Stacey's

'Desperately Seeking Difference' similarly argues that films can offer more flexible spectator positions (her examples are *All About Eve* and *Desperately Seeking Susan*) when women bring very different subjectivities to the viewing experience (Stacey 1990). Bobo (and Stacey's) work, unlike Diawara's, foregrounds the significance of active and actual female looks. By discussing spectatorship as a cultural moment as part of real life subjectivities, Bobo makes a more politically informed reading than equivalent male-authored essays. As Gladstone Yearwood has pointedly argued, an iconic Black aesthetic is not particularly useful when the mere appearance of Blacks in no way defines the blackness of film (Yearwood 1982).

Black male film-makers illustrate this issue of gender absence in similar ways. Many contemporary Black films such as Spike Lee's *Do The Right Thing* and John Singleton's *Boyz N The Hood* are rightly celebrated for their unprecedented introduction of Black urban culture into mainstream cinema and their numinous identification of key Black social issues such as family problems, urban violence and the lack of economic opportunities and mobility. By inflecting narratives with hip-hop, rap music and jazz, Lee and Singleton give urban Black Americans a chance to see their lives reflected, for once, at the centre of representations. So, Singleton's transparent 'window on the world' of Los Angeles police surveillance, gang violence and the hip Black street language of gang resistance, gives his films an intense immediacy and 'realism'. Yet these films follow at least in part, the misogynist representation of Black women as 'bitches' and 'hos' which featured in Blaxploitation films of the 1970s. As Ed Guerrero points out, both critical and filmic discourses are effectively blind to the gender hierarchies which structure their looks (Guerrero 1993): of the 450 commercial films released in 1991, white women directed five per cent while Black women directed none at all. It is no coincidence that the Black masculinity which structures Blaxploitation, for example Sweetback's 'revolutionary' rape of a woman at knife point, emerges again in similar if metaphorical 'rapes' of Black women in Spike Lee's films.

Much of white feminist film criticism also fails to prioritise issues of race. Yet if we combine Black feminist film criticism to date together with Black women's literary critiques and creativity we witness a wide body of Black feminist critical work over the last two decades. Thus, Afra-American feminist criticism could be said to begin in 1974 with two events: the publication of a special issue of *Black World* containing essays by June Jordan and Mary Helen Washington which carried on its cover a photograph of Zora Neale Hurston, and the publication of Alice Walker's 'In Search of Our Mothers' Gardens' in *Ms* magazine (Humm 1994).

There is a wealth of ideas and conceptual handles in the literary and creative writing of Black women to support Black feminist film analysis. The interrelation of literary with visual perspectives is crucial to any analysis of Black women's culture because practices of representation are always caught up in processes of enunciation. In order to vacate stereotypical images Black women often turn to imaginative and hidden stories – to family histories and African culture including call and response (antiphony) and folklore. Black feminist literary critics have, for some time, been identifying and analysing key images and patterns which are clearly of use to visual theorists. These include: investigations into female centred culture and narrative, polyrhythmic structures (for example, Audre Lorde's multigeneric autobiography *Zami*) and personal or family languages. All of this produces what Hazel Carby calls a 'usable' past including the past produced through narrative (Carby 1987). Carby argues that the search for a usable past is an inevitable part of any diasporic experience but that, unlike archaeology, this search is always constructed by narrative or what we could call a film's diegesis. Writings such as Alice Walker's *In Search of Our Mothers' Gardens* (a collection named after that first germinal essay) and Audre Lorde's *Sister Outsider* eschew iconic or singular representations of black women in favour of more multiple histories. This work aims to highlight the mobility of black culture and to deconstruct the fixed binaries of white culture, a particularly important theme when diasporic cultures owe much to colonial pressures. Lorde's recognition in *Zami* is that black lesbian identities are heterogeneous: 'Being Black together was not enough. We were different. Being Black women together was not enough. We were different. Being Black dykes together was not enough. We were different' (Lorde 1982, p. 226). In Lorde's writing, identity is fluid, not singular or essentialist. The Black dykes of New York are a known social group sharing experiences and history, however identity is not predicated by social constructions but continually being remade in fresh relationships and experiences.

Julie Dash herself describes how Black feminist literature is a key and vital source of ideas and techniques for her films. The story of *Daughters of the Dust* she suggests:

> would come out and come in and go out and come in, very much the way in Toni Cade Bambara's work one character would be speaking to another and then it goes off on a tangent for several pages and then she brings it back and goes out and back again. (Dash 1992, p. 32)

To make vivid how Dash's intensely new visual appeal subverts mainstream representations Barbara Christian's descriptions of Black feminist strategies are exemplary. In 'The Race for Theory' Christian argues that Black women cannot simply be white women with colour (Christian 1989A). It is the white academic hegemony, or the 'race' of professional theory-creating critics, which has silenced women of colour, a silencing symbolised for Christian by the term 'minority discourse'. As Christian points out, Black women are central in much writing in the world, not minors (if not to the American academy). Black women have continually speculated theoretically about the world, she argues, although for the most part in stories, proverbs or what Christian calls 'hieroglyphs' – forms different from those of western logic.

Barbara Christian was the first Black feminist critic to write a book-length history of Black women's literature, *Black Women Novelists* (1980), which was followed by *Black Feminist Criticism* (1985) and many other essays, including 'The Race for Theory'. In these Christian clearly tracks and affirms the key features of an Afra-American feminist aesthetic. First, there are its positive images of Black womanhood, for example, mothers in Black slave narratives. Second, Christian draws attention to richer and more varied representations of Black women including the buried stories of Black lesbians. Christian's term 'rememory' refers to the force of reconstruction and family history. In 'But What Do We Think We're Doing Anyway?' (Christian 1986B), she summarises the aim of a Black feminist aesthetic as one of 'dialogue' both between foremothers and 'ordinary' Black women. Black hairdressers and typists are frequently more knowledgeable about contemporary Black writing, Christian claims, than the white academy, in W. E. B. DuBois's sense that Black thinking involves two processes: the practical and abstract ways of knowing.

Just as Christian enlarges the category 'literature' to include diaries, letters and songs, so she transforms literary criticism into an open process through her use of interrogatives. Christian's work is essentially an ideologically inspired criticism where what is meant by that is a critique which argues that literature uses historical ideas as part of the internal practices of each text. Christian highlights these historical and cultural specificities of Black women's writing as she points out that the strength of Alice Walker's novels lies in Walker's community politics of group survival.

Extrapolating Christian's ideas to *Daughters of the Dust* it is clear that Julie Dash subverts dominant cinematic codes by attention to Black Gullah history and culture. Women are at the centre of *Daughters of the Dust* and women emblematically refigure Black history; for example, Nana creates a Gullah history from her bottle tree with each bottle representing a family ancestor. Black literary critics similarly refigure literary history by mixing songs, autobiography and fiction. Mary Helen Washington's *Invented Lives* is a good example of such hybridity, juxtaposing critical essays with fictions and autobiography in a sustained attack on the neutrality of 'universal' criticism (Washington 1989). Similarly Alice Walker's *In Search of Our Mothers' Gardens* enlarged the field of Black literature to include crafts and autobiography (Walker 1984). Faced with the demands of traditional literary critics for a 'universal' model of Black writing, Audre Lorde describes alternative, more 'intuitive' forms of criticism incorporating the myths of Black community women (Lorde 1984). The controversy among Black Americans about the film *The Color Purple* shows how much the black community does think of literary and visual representations as a social battleground of sexual politics (Bobo 1989).

The key issue of audience, so pressing to Black film makers, is an issue already extensively explored by Black literary critics. As Barbara Smith said in her pathbreaking essay *Toward A Black Feminist Criticism* (Smith 1977) 'I do not know where to begin. Long before I tried to write this I realised that I was attempting something unprecedented' (Smith 1977, p. 1). What Smith was attempting to create, and with great success, was a new Black lesbian spectatorship by reading Toni Morrison's *Sula* as a lesbian novel. Smith specifically focuses on visual imagery in her account of the intersections of politics and text in Morrison's work. Smith went on to create the term 'simultaneity of discourse' to define Black feminist criticism. This is a way of reading which focuses on the interrelation of structures of discourse: race, gender and sexuality. Dash similarly opens up *Daughters of the Dust* to a lesbian reading by creating the character of Yellow Mary who 'would have a significant other person' – a phrase often used to point to a lesbian partner – and by creating 'many kinds of African-American women who appear in the film and in the world' – that is to say, a greater variety than stereotypical heterosexuals (Dash 1992, pp. 66–7).

For Black feminist critics, that world draws on an Afracentric feminist perspective; Patricia Hill Collins, suggests that Afracentrism constitutes itself in opposition to Western forms of thinking (Collins 1990). While Collins's argument does appear to deny Black writers Eurocentric tools and strategies, it is true that definitions of Black necessarily involve opposing definitions of white since, as James Snead points out, all signs can only be defined diacritically (Snead 1994). Afracentrism draws on African religions, on orality as a central tool of community culture and in particular, on the cultural significance, and veneration of, mothering. Alice Walker adopted the term 'womanist' rather than 'feminist' precisely to celebrate Afracentrism, the history of Black womenhood: 'Womanist is to feminist as purple is to lavender' (Walker 1984, p. xii). Similarly Audre Lorde steeps her work with mythical archetypes and particularly celebrates the Amazon women of Dan. Her autobiography *Zami* mixes narrative with Carriacou history, poetry and matriarchal myths. Lorde's sources of energy come from stories of mother/child symbiosis and from Black women's global networks such as identifying with Australian Aboriginals in *A Burst of Light* (Lorde 1988). In her much quoted essay 'The Master's Tools', Lorde explores issues of representation arguing that only non-patriarchal forms of thinking and writing can empower women, Black or white (Lorde 1984).

Literature is never outside, or distant from, history. Critics see Black literature as massively defined by an African woman's cultural diaspora while knowing that this vast cultural history is precisely marginalised by white culture. The whole force of *Daughters of the Dust* is Afracentric, with a narrative which centres on the Ibo landing in America and on Nana Peazant's memories of African myths. The language of the film is Gullah not American, while the film's entire visual imagery is African, so that even the hairstyles are 'based upon ancient hairstyles' from West Africa (Dash 1992, p. 53). As Filomina Steady's pathbreaking analysis of African feminism, *The Black Woman Cross-Culturally*, argues, any definition of African feminism must draw on linguistic subversions, the oral tradition and kinship relations (Steady 1981). I would suggest that Black feminist literature with its Afracentrism and its non-canonical texts displaying community culture and maternal iconography, can provide film study with major new tropes. That double voiced discourse of Black vernacular/Black literary rhetoric has implications for the 'double discourses' of film. Thus, Julie Dash radically favours innovative shared frames (wide-angle and deep focus rather than shot-reaction-shots) yet places these frames within a more conventional chronological narrative in order to create a spectacular cinematic equivalent of double voiced and community culture. In other words Dash can utilise while problematising realistic representations rather than, as some critics do, shortsightedly dismissing realism as somehow less radical.

The complex literary/visual transformations explored by Black literary critics and creative writers offer some crucial insights. For example, one important message to film-makers might be that in any reconstruction of Black women's history, forms of language are as foundational as the content of narrative. For this reason, perhaps, some of the most signif-icant Black feminist theories emerge in creative writing. Alice Walker's work is a particularly good example of the way in which writing can foreground differing political theories through the juxtaposition of different visual and literary forms. In this sense, Walker's *In The Temple of My Familiar* is a complex novel mixing the spiritual narratives of people speaking in tongues, with historical accounts, autobiography and dream tableaux in order to confront the knotty issues of body representation, sexual difference and racial and sexual violence (Walker 1989).

The Temple of My Familiar reveals Walker's commitment to spiritu-ality and her move 'away from sociology, away from the writing of explanations and statistics and further into mystery, into poetry and into prophecy' (Walker 1989, p. 8). The heroine Lissie with her past lives as a white man, and as a lion carries Walker's message of 'parent knowledge', of listening to ancestral voices. And Fanny resigns from her post as a Women's Studies teacher to become a masseuse believing that an holistic approach is more a source of healing than a narrow intellectual focus. By the end of the novel characters re-enter traditional thought. Since Walker's message is that prehistorical African spirituality survives in the culture of women, this work is a powerful feminist theology. Similarly, in *The Color Purple* it is Celie's friendship with a bisexual, economically independent Black woman which leads to profound spiritual experience (Walker 1983). Celie's transformed notion of God recognises the divinity as neither male nor female but as a spirit inviting her to create a liberation narrative. Alice Walker's knowledge claim in 'Saving the Life That is Your Life' is that Afra-American 'call and response', or testifying dialogue, is a very special interactive epistemology of connectedness with deep roots in African culture (Walker 1984). Many of Walker's pivotal images of women are drawn from African oral literature and myth. For example, 'womanist' has links with the Yorùbá deity Òsun – a strong fertile woman. Alice Walker argues that oral myths provide models of critical thinking. The crucial distinction between Afracentrism and white feminism is this attention to dialogue and to the cultural and spiritual history of Black women.

African feminist writers' attention to orality similarly undermines and subverts any notion of singular histories. For example in Zaire, Clémentine Faik-Nzuji has made a collection of Luba folklore; Bessie Head interweaves autobiography and historiography into her multi-generic novel *A Bewitched Crossroad: An African Saga* and Ellen Kuzwayo's autobiography *Call Me Woman* (1985) is replete with political speeches and the songs and letters of other South African women (see Busby 1993). Like Walker, these writers share a sense of the import of history, rejecting any static 'primitive' picture of Africa. Men and women are frequently figured, not as individuals, but as men and women in a cosmic scheme. For example, Bessie Head's *Maru* builds its framework on several African myths in which the characters Maru and Moleka represent the polarised opposition between the twin deities of the sun and the moon. African writers celebrate hybridity as a religious and cultural matrix dating from prehistory. In addition, African writing is dialogic, taking the view that Black writers are historical agents participating in a collective enterprise. Efua Sutherland's plays, for example, chart social issues within communal dramas (Humm 1994). Finally, African feminism argues that gender roles are shaped as much by matriarchy, kinships and Third World landscapes as by urban culture.

What is important in all of these sophisticated challenges to white western thinking is that Black representations, history and the arts go along with differing processes of representation with hybridity, spiritual schemas, and folklore. Hence, although Black women's film-making might be limited in quantity it can draw on, and interact with, a vast and rich spectrum of Afracentric literary and theoretical writing. Any individual film needs to be considered as much in relation to this background as to the history of American movie making. So Dash's *Daughters of the Dust* draws on subject areas explored in Black women's writing sharing literature's rhetorical power and larger versions of reality. African and Afra-American literature and film are intimately reflective and thus literary works are often major sources of material for film-makers. For example, Spike Lee's *She's Gotta Have It* is hugely informed by Zora Neale Hurston's *Their Eyes Were Watching God*, and contemporary Afracentric writing offers a new geography and new visual images – of spirituality and community culture. A novel such as Paule Marshall's *Praisesong for the Widow* (from which *Daughters of the Dust* draws its main story) explicitly dramatises Afracentric feminist themes through Marshall's depictions of place and displacement and the power of women's memory (Marshall 1983). In interview with Karen Alexander, Dash describes her debt to Black women's literature and to its celebration of the very special role women play in the work of retrieval:

> Discrepancies across space, across the Black Atlantic: in the new world it is the women who have become Griots (religious story tellers) of their culture. It was the literature of black women in the early 1970s that inspired me to become a film-maker of dramatic narratives. Before that I made documentaries, but after reading Toni Cade Bambara, Alice Walker, Toni Morrison, I wanted to tell those kinds of stories. I see myself as a disciple of Black women writers. They made me whole. (Alexander 1993, p. 22)

Dash aims to make cinematically palpable the great force of Black women's writing, and in the same interview, she describes her then current project: a remake of Michel Deville's *La Lectrice* substituting a Black heroine reading the classics of Black literature for Deville's Eurocentric lectrice (Alexander 1993).

Paule Marshall's *Praisesong for the Widow*, the immediate inspiration for *Daughters of the Dust*, takes its title from African ritual and describes the liberatory awakening of Avey Johnson from bourgeois suburban retirement (a suburb ironically named White Plains) as well as from the spirit of her dead husband. Cruising on the Caribbean like a dreadful inverted image of the Middle Passage, the name given to the movement of slaves across the Atlantic, Avey abandons ship to return to the culture and rituals of Carriacou. Avey's sense of her own identity is shaped by great-aunt Cuney's story of the Ibo landing in America and their decision to walk on water back to Africa away from American slavery. The novel abounds with ancestor figures, with an African sense of the duality of perception (the idea that we see with the soul as well as the eyes), with African dialect (adjectival intensification such as 'full-full') and with a suppression of linear chronology (symbolised by Avey leaving her watch on the cruise ship). Key scenes of the book match scenes in *Daughters of the Dust*. For example, Avey experiences an interdependence of past and present while close to water on the beach, and beach scenes are an important place of 'rememory' in *Daughters of the Dust*. Marshall's book is an enormously influential account of the importance of collective histories and of the ability of women in particular to remember ancient stories, rituals and praisesongs. Marshall's cultural rememory is visualised in *Daughters of the Dust* by Nana Peazant. What Marshall, Walker, Christian and Lorde offer film-makers is a way to connect, in Gayatri Spivak's terms, the verbal and the social text (Spivak 1987). As Barbara Christian suggests 'Audre Lorde so profoundly argues it is often in poetry that we imagine that which we have been afraid to imagine – that poetry is an important source of imagining new ideas for change' (Christian 1989B, p. 73).

Another and major source of ideas are the newer theoretical moves of Black feminist film critics. The first, crucial task for Black feminist film critics was to counter the racist images of mainstream cinema. Hence, the Black American film-maker and critic Alile Larkin's deconstructive attack on Hollywood stereotypes. In 'Black Women Film-makers Defining Ourselves' Larkin categorises these stereotypes into 'Contented Slaves', 'Brute Negro', 'Comic Negro', 'Exotic Primitive' and 'Tragic Mulatto' going on to describe the alternative practices of Black women's independent production including her own (Larkin 1988). Larkin offers new criteria for assessing Black artistic and cultural practices including the insistence that such practices should incorporate an interactive dialogue with the Black community. Jacquie Jones in 'The

Construction of Black Sexuality' looks more specifically at sexual stereotypes of Black women which she suggests are embodiments of mythical or archetypal images (Jones 1993). In mainstream cinema, Jones argues, Black female characters are not only paradigmatically morally inadequate, but metaphorically act as 'a link between the profane and the spiritual' (Jones 1993, p. 253).

The necessary move from deconstruction to reconstruction is made in the work of Karen Alexander's 'Fatal Beauties', an examination of positive images of Black Hollywood actresses (Alexander 1991). Alexander examines the career of the only 'genuine' Black female star Dorothy Dandridge seeing her as an inaugural and positive figure. Black feminist critics do register a note of caution about the limitations of any good/bad binary analysis, but, if only because racial stereotypes are so constantly remade by Hollywood, iconographic analysis does demand continuous critical attention.

That more complex question of the interaction of ideology and aesthetic form is answered by Valerie Smith in 'Telling Family Secrets' (Smith 1994). Examining *Suzanne, Suzanne* (1977) a film from the independent documentary sector directed by Camille Billops and James V. Hatch, what interests Smith is the visibility of the film's construction and processes. The director is both subject and observer of the film's family romance (her own niece's battle against drug addiction) placing herself at the juncture of different cinematic and extra cinematic discourses (home movies, snapshots, interviews). Smith's ideologically inspired analysis takes Black feminist film criticism a stage further from deconstruction and reclamation into a sophisticated account of how film form (in this case juxtapositions and multiple interrogations) can dismantle the white family romance.

This more ideologically inspired critique of looking, racial taboos and alternative frames is taken up by the major Black feminist cultural critic bell hooks. A further attack on white criticism informs hooks's *Yearning* and *Black Looks* (hooks 1991; 1992). As I have described in detail in Chapter One, hooks addresses the whole terrain of Black popular culture as well as the marked absence of that culture in the writings of white feminist critics. She asks us to acknowledge the agency of Black spectators pointing out that one of the effective strategies of white dehumanisation during slavery was to control the 'Black gaze' by brutally punishing slaves for looking at whites (hooks 1991).

hooks chooses Julie Dash's film *Illusions* as a key example of the development of a new feminist gaze as Dash problematises the issue of race and spectatorship in the film with a mirrored recognition between two Black women: Mignon Dupree, an executive passing for white, and Ester Jeeter a Black singer who Mignon employs to provide a voice for a white Hollywood star.

As the eponymous title suggests, the film examines illusions about racial identity and Black cinema history. Although not an exact historical facsimile, Dash's film does focus a key moment of Black cultural formation: the changing status of Black men and women during World War Two. Dash's inventive merging of newsreel, split screens, *film noir* and melodrama matches her characterisation of Mignon and Ester which draws on long standing extra-cinematic codes in Black women's culture. For example, Mignon's telephone conversations with her mother off screen are (clearly) a source of deep insight to her. Similarly the warm relationship which develops between Ester and Mignon gives Mignon the strength to admit to her racial identity. Dash's themes clearly correspond to those of Black women writers.

hooks is especially struck by the need of Black film-makers for a history that will both name and affirm Black identity but she proffers a more diverse portrait of that history than other critics to date. Thus, hooks suggests that Native Americans and Blacks share more than a common history of victimisation by whites; they also share a belief system in which ancestors contribute a formidable energy to community culture. hooks links the displacement of Native Americans into camps (reservations) with Black migrations across America (hooks 1991). The counter perspective of African and Native Americans is a vision of cross-cultural dialogue in which community and spirituality are central.

Daughters of the Dust shares many of these concerns, in particular an attention to multiethnicity (with Native American, Black and Arab characters), and to matriarchy and traditional culture. There is a significant continuity at the level of theme, language and representation between contemporary Black women's writing and Dash's film practice, particularly Dash's figuration of the matriarch Nana, the Unborn Child, spirituality (paths of *un*knowing) and Afracentrism.

Before engaging more fully with the film we need to gain a brief sense of what Dash specifically draws from Black history (and perhaps

what she ignores) in order to understand the full force of her achievement. In *'A Peculiar People': Slave Religion and Community Culture Among
the Gullahs* Margaret Washington Creel offers a complex account of the
dynamic, creative and cultural provenances of Africa among the Gullah
people (Creel 1988), and she was Dash's historical advisor during the
making of *Daughters of the Dust*. Creel groups the inherited and historically transmitted rituals, symbols and systems of communication in
Gullah culture – 'Gullah' is generally believed to be a shortened form
of Angola – into three main categories: community culture, religion and
resistance. In brief, Gullah beliefs include the concept of the perpetuity
of life typified in Bakongo cosmology in which spirituality is the major
element of culture integrating and co-ordinating other aspects of
communal behaviour. Creel's use of 'cultural focus' is clearly informed
by Melville Herskovits's pathbreaking study *The Myth of the Negro Past*
first published in 1941 (Herskovits 1990, p. xi). Herskovits attributes
the tenaciousness of African customs in America to the selling of
intransigent priests as slaves, as a result of African dynastic quarrels,
priests who would keep the constituent elements of African culture
vibrantly alive.

Gullah religion, Creel explains, is not set apart in a 'holy' building,
'sacred' day or set of dogmas but is part of a whole system of social
interaction and community values. For example, the decoration of slave
graves with sea shells and objects which hold water in *Daughters of
the Dust* is a Gullah practice expressing immortal existence and the
significance of a water underworld (Creel 1988, p. 319). When African
initiates left the bush to return to the village they underwent a wash-
ing ceremony. Africans regard their essential being as divided into
'little me' in the 'big me' and that 'little me', which exists before life, like
Dash's 'The Unborn Child', could continue to exist after death in the
spirit world (Creel 1988, p. 317). Creel's description of Gullah 'diviners'
as people 'who combined physical, religious and psychological
approaches in their healing treatments' matches both the character of
Nana Peazant and the work of Dash herself as a film-maker (Creel
1988, p. 57).

The appearance of water and journeys in Gullah culture metaphorically marks the history of the Black Atlantic, a dislocated peoples and
a plurality of Black identities drawn from several African nations. The
metaphor of the journey is the central theme of *Daughters of the Dust*,

as the Peazant family prepare to migrate to the mainland. Like the Gullahs, Dash proffers no simple reconstructed historical past. So, for example, she reproduces traditional forms – hair plaiting and bottle trees – as part of Nana Peazant's story telling preparation for the future journey. Dash's creation of an intertextual history, weaving Marshall's novel and other creative writings together with Creel's history, mediates the past metaphorically. By foregrounding new cinematic processes such as the dual narratives of the Unborn Child and Nana Peazant, Dash focuses this Black concern with the forms of telling as a property of Black history.

In *Daughters of the Dust: The Making of an African American Woman's Film,* Dash describes her extensive knowledge of Gullah culture which she gained from research in the Schomburg Center and the National Archives. 'One of the most fascinating discoveries I made was of the existence of over 60,000 West African words or phrases in use in the English language' (Dash 1992, p. 5). But Dash is very careful not to reproduce Gullah history as a static past event deliberately incorporating many contemporary images and drawing on the motor patterns of present day African Americans:

> For instance, the hand signals given by two of the men in *Daughters* is a reference to the non verbal styles of communication of ancient African secret societies which have been passed down across thousands of years and through hundreds of generations. Today these forms are expressed in the secrets of fraternities and in the hand signals of youth gangs. (Dash 1992, p. 6)

Herskovits confirms this American retention of African habits; for example, he connects an Afra-American erect bearing to the African habit of carrying burdens on the head (Herskovits 1990, p. 146). Similarly the West African ritual of pouring libations, a show of respect to the ancestors, survives, Dash argues, in the ritual of pouring drink onto basketball courts.

Rather than representing Gullah culture as a unified singular artifact, Dash is deliberately selective in her choice of symbols. For example, Creel suggested that indigo stains would not remain on the hands of those who processed the dye, but Dash loved the hyperbolic quality of the symbol'to create a new kind of icon around slavery rather than the traditional showing of the whip marks or the chains' (Dash 1992, p. 31). In other ways Dash directly incorporates Gullah cosmology as in the structuring of the film narrative like an anti-linear African griot (traditional oral poet) account of family history. Similarly, on learning about the multireligiosity quality of Gullah traditions which attracted adherents of Islam, Dash wished to include Muslim along with Baptist and West African religious beliefs. What she achieves in her remarkable intertextual work is to fill one key absence in many historical narratives: 'the psychic loss migrating Blacks experienced when we left the agrarian South' (Dash 1992, p. 42).

A major stumbling block in the early development of a wide ranging Black feminist aesthetic was film-makers' necessary financial reliance on short documentaries, although Val Smith argues that documentary can offer multiple interrogations (Smith 1994). Dash's creative jump from documentary through the threshold of Black literature encouraged her to more expansive aesthetic explorations drawing on European art films' often complex uses of space and time such as Jean-Luc Godard's montages. In many ways *Daughters of the Dust* incorporates features of avant-garde independent film-making: the belief that aesthetic difference is radical, the restructuring of time and spectator expectation and a disrupting of narrative chronology (Mellencamp 1990). But in other ways *Daughters of the Dust* is markedly anti avant-garde. Dash clearly does not privilege her own personal or unique viewpoint nor is she flexibly casual about technical quality but rather scripts a sophisticated cinematography. Dash's 'independence' lies in her portrait of more complex psychic and cultural images of Black women.

Dash is a very good example of the new Independent Black Cinema Movement whose film-makers trained with Charles Burnett at the University of California, Los Angeles. These 'Black insurgents' as Toni Cade Bambara argues, were informed by the Civil Rights struggles of 1954 to 1972 and made socially conscious films which interrogated many of the conventions of mainstream cinema (Bambara 1993). While narrative experimentation was a shared concern of other film-makers in the group, for instance, Barbara McCullough and Alile Sharon Larkin, Dash's attention to communal space in her cinematography, rather than a use of individual close up, marks a major departure from both Black independent film-makers as well as European avant garde feminist cinema.

Confounding conventional assumptions about the format and content of full length films, Dash creates fresh representations of Black culture by means of an intricate montage spiralling back in characters' memories while formally progressing chronologically through the Peazant family's day. *Daughters of the Dust* centres on a large family picnic to which Mr Snead the photographer has been invited in order to document a pivotal moment in any Black family history: the move to the North. The film's theme, a battle between the upwardly mobile, educated younger Peazants and the traditional Afracentric Nana who remains behind, is a familiar romantic theme. But rather than creating a simplistic binary division of old and new, Dash portrays several generations of the extended Peazant family all of whom hold differing beliefs: Nana and her African myths, Nana's Christian daughters-in-law, Haagar and Viola, who dismiss ancestor worship as 'voodoo', as well as the children and the Unborn Child, a possible returning ancestor figure who may 'revivify' Nana's beliefs. Dash's introduction of the Native American character St Julian Last Child matches bell hooks's call for the inclusion of Black and red histories. 'As red and Black people decolonize our minds we cease to place value solely on the written document. We give ourselves back memory. We acknowledge that the ancestors speak to us in a place beyond written history' (hooks 1992, p. 193).

Because *Daughters of the Dust* is about the retention of tradition and about the persistence of ancestor vision within the new, Dash deliberately incorporates Cherokee history: 'The Cherokees were some of the original inhabitants of the Sea Islands. So I thought it was important to have one remaining Native American there and that's why I named him Last Child' (Dash 1992, p. 46). As Herskovits points out, Native Americans and Black slaves shared many traditions including water cults: 'It is not generally recognized that the Cherokee Indians a tribe with whom Negroes were perhaps more in contact during the days of slavery than any other except Seminoles and Creeks, themselves had a well-developed river cult' (Herskovits 1990, p. 234).

Yellow Mary, by the end of the film, embraces a novel kind of Black spirituality by choosing to remain with Nana and her ancestral beliefs, while not renouncing her own more liberated experience of lesbianism even if she has to leave her partner. Dash subtly foregrounds the shaping pressure of Black writing cinematographically, through a dialectic of verbal and visual story telling. Hence, the hired photographer Mr Snead, extensively interviews as well as visually documents the Peazant family, juxtaposing oral memories with family photographs in a contiguous history. In interview with Zeinabu Irene Davis, Julie Dash describes *Daughters of the Dust* as one of a series of films in which she would examine the experience of Black women in the US from the turn of the century up to and beyond the year 2000 (Davis 1991). The film's title comes from Ezekiel 'O ye sons of the Dust' which Dash, with feminist intent, converts to daughters. Like Toni Morrison's analogous triptych fictional portrait of Black women in twentieth-century America, Dash focuses on intergenerational female relationships and women's memories precisely because it is women who carry cultural traditions into the future.

Dash chose actresses from the Black independent film sector: Nana Peazant is played by Cora Lee Day from Haile Gerima's *Bush Mama*, Haagar Peazant is Kaycee Moore from Charles Burnett's *Killer of Sheep*, and Alva Rogers was in Spike Lee's *School Daze* (Bambara 1993). And she deliberately employed fine artists rather than mainstream designers for production design to give a rich African visual quality to the film and to assist a more co-operative, rather than industrial, film practice.

The film is framed by two narratives: one in which Nana Peazant recalls Ibo and Peazant family histories and the other by the Unborn Child of Eula and Eli who takes Nana's narrative into the present, describing the events of the picnic day and the future. The two narratives are marked by a double visual syncopation in Dash's flexible exploration of aperture control. Utilising a computer operated speed control Dash has Nana speaking at twenty-four frames a second and clicks in and out of slow motion in the middle of scenes. The first use of slow motion occurs in the scene where Nana meets Eli while tending her husband's gravestone, as a visual analogue to Nana's call on family ancestors to help Eli come to terms with Eula's rape and pregnancy. As Nana says 'the ancestor and the womb are one'. Nana's understanding of the interconnectedness of women's bodies and morality is emblematically visible in the metaphor of the bottle tree when Nana explains that her 'griot' memory of births and deaths (each marked by a tree bottle) prevented incest in an illiterate slave existence. The image of the bottle tree draws on Black literature: Michelle Cliff's *Abeng* contains a similar image.

With exact precision Dash gives the sexually exploited Yellow Mary a parallel story in which Mary, too, carries an emblematic box matching Nana's tree and Kumbla containers. But because Mary is forcibly removed from Gullah culture while lactating to the mainland, Mary's 'pink satin case for jewellery' becomes a box of bad memories 'I don't want them inside of me', just as, in her role as wet nurse, Mary switches off 'her titties' when family memories become too painful. The careful articulation of Mary's lesbian figure with Nana's matriarchal tutelary figure is magnetic. The male Eli, on the other hand, has no faculty for such articulations and wails 'why don't memories protect us?' resentfully destroying Nana's ancestor bottle tree. Nana begins with knowing herself as 'both whore and virgin' and that 'old and new people are as in one body' which has its visual and historical apotheosis in the slave tradition of placing a lock of slave mother's hair in an infant's tiny quilt or charm before the baby is sold. I see Dash's representation of women's memory and history as an exemplary model of Barbara Christian's concepts of 'rememory' and of dialogue between 'foremothers' and 'ordinary' women (Christian 1989B).

Nana Peazant is a fully fleshed-out representation of what Mary Washington Creel calls griot culture and Alice Walker recreates as testifying figures. As Dash suggests 'myth, of course, plays a very important part in all our lives in everyone's culture. Without myth and tradition what is there? So there is the myth of the Ibo landing which helped sustain the slaves' (Dash 1992, p. 29). Afracentrism and multireligious complexity shape the film from the first opening prayer offered to Muhammed. African words are remembered 'Eena . . . Meena . . . Myna' but transmitted into a future new world of Sears Roebuck catalogues when the children use the mnemonic to choose catalogue items. Dash's richly expressive use of African and Gullah dialects highlights verbal differences. Like Paule Marshall's Avey, Nana frequently uses repetitive adjectival intensifications – 'done-done'. Women characters appear radiantly Afracentric with African make-up and hair-plaiting. Herskovits suggests that while hair straightening 'is decidedly not African, for nothing of the sort has been recorded from here' the multiplicity of West African hair braids does reappear in the New World (Herskovits 1990, p. 148). Dash even encouraged the use of West African gestures – Haagar frequently places her hand over her mouth while laughing which, Herskovits suggests, signifies a specific survival of African etiquette involving the turning of the head when laughing or covering the mouth when speaking to elders. Dash introduces other Afracentric elements such as when men, women and children engage in hand signals and secret signing to make the viewing experience as Dash, herself, points out 'like watching a foreign film' (Dash 1992, p. 116). In addition this 'foreign' quality is enhanced by the choice of Agfa-Geveart film stock, more flattering to Black women's skin than the conventional Kodak 5245 or 5297 of Spike Lee's movies. The entire theme of *Daughters of the Dust* can be summarised as 'scraps of memory' – a vital mechanism of bonding – following W. E. B. DuBois's recognition that African-Americans share scraps of memory, lacking as they do, a solid traceable lineage. Black women writers similarly depict women remembering and being empowered by African myths and motifs. In *Praisesong for the Widow*, with its evocative African title, Great-aunt Cuney lives simultaneously in the present and the past. 'Her body she always usta say might be in Tatum but her mind, her mind was long gone with the Ibo's (Marshall 1983, p. 39).

This Afracentric dialogic bringing together of young and old, future and memory both narratively and cinematically gives *Daughters of the Dust* a spectacular power. If any one thing defines Afracentrism, it is the centrality of spirituality. *Daughters of the Dust* responds to the overarching spirituality of West Africa most evidently in Dash's metaphoric use of water and sea shell imagery. As Mary Washington Creel suggests, significant African survivals include the placing of shells to mark the existence of ancestors. In *Daughters of the Dust* children have shells placed on their foreheads as a mnemonic device when the elemental African words 'water/fire' are spoken. The scenes of Nana's stories are immediately followed by scenes of a huge, floating wooden slave figurehead, sometimes appearing male and sometimes female, an icon of the Atlantic Crossing. The Unborn Child wears a water-coloured blue ribbon and the opening titles are in bold white over blue metaphorically anticipating the film's main theme of the Ibo walk over water and the Peazant journey to the mainland. Eula writes a letter to her own 'ancestor' mother who she invites to return by placing the letter under a glass of water by the bedside. Thus the film draws on similar African presences woven into Black women's writing. For example, Sula and Shadrack in Toni Morrison's *Sula* represents the same, traditional African spirit/water culture in which Shadrack is

Sula's 'ancestor' figure: a water spirit inhabiting Shadrack's formally shell-shocked body now earning his living as a fisherman (Morrison 1973).

One way of considering the remarkable echo between the narrative avowal of community values and Dash's cinematography is to note the astounding effect of Dash's choice of frame. Dash frames each scene of Yellow Mary, Eula and Trula (Yellow Mary's lover) to the left of screen following the beach photographs where men enter frame from the right. In addition the camera pans equally from right to left and left to right a technique which is rarely a feature of mainstream cinema. In conversation with bell hooks the British Asian film-maker Pratibha Parmar suggests how all uses of camera space are never ideologically 'free': 'The appropriation and use of space are political acts' (hooks 1991, p. 152). Equally, Dash draws attention to the spatial freedoms enjoyed by Native Americans before the white invasions both by a visual close up on St Julian Last Child's letter and by noting narratively that it was whites who took the old Seminole Creek land.

Disparate scenes are carefully overlapped with spoken dialogue from previous scenes to create a fluid sense of communal rapport, and Dash deftly, and with superb organisational skill, continually frames five or six Peazant family members simultaneously like a communal frescoe. Other overlaps include the Unborn Child's linkage of present and future with stereoscopic black and white film of an urban future which matches Snead's gift of the kaleidoscope with its 'beauty, simplicity and science, all rolled into one small tube'. Similarly the elder griots tell stories in silhouette watching the sky like a giant movie screen. In this way diegisic time is at one with a larger historical time. Although the film is episodic Dash's camera strategies and scenic montages ensure a strong metaphoric continuity.

Audre Lorde's *Zami* also meshes past and future by means of a narrative technique very like Dash's cinematography. *Zami* is an autobiography of Lorde's childhood in 1940s New York and her subsequent sexual, political and work experiences in America and Mexico. 'Zami' is a term from the Caribbean meaning 'women-identified-women' (Lorde 1982). To accommodate multiple experiences and stories, Lorde like Dash, creates two parallel voices: a poetic voice (usually in italics) describing myths and dreams, and a prose voice for the overall narrative. Like Dash's scenic overlays, Lorde, too, graphically interweaves her voices in a single 'frame', that is on pages where autobiography and myths flow in and out of each other.

Like Black women's writing *Daughters of the Dust* speaks most volubly and luxuriantly about Black women's culture. Dash's women figures are, like Walker's Celie and Morrison's *Tar Baby* independent, socially representative Black women, able to violate the spectacularised Black female representations of mainstream cinema. Chief among such women is Yellow Mary who is not a 'victim' of sexual exploitation but a complex and knowledgeable woman whose remitted independent earnings have enabled the Peazants to survive a racist, white judicial system. If, as Robert Townsend claims 'Hollywood is afraid that if you have more than one black person in a movie you have a black movie' than the lack of a single 'white face' gives *Daughters of the Dust* an immense Afracentric force (Gold 1987, p. 36). And, indeed, a woman-centric force for women are never shown in servile positions within the Black community. Dash avoids depicting the picnic preparations as women's quotidian and traditional lot by focusing in close up on a succession of hand gestures to deliberately match Nana's laying on of hands – her healing gesture to Mary and other characters – so giving women's food rituals a powerful potency. Similarly in *The Color Purple*, although much of what Nettie and Celie write about is male violence and the breakdown of male/female relationships, like *Daughters of the Dust* the novel elevates Black women's womanist skills and heritage over the world of men. The novel ends with Mr – learning to sew as a symbol of a transformed masculinity.

Daughters of the Dust flexibly represents multifaceted Black females with a visual iconography of hair (see Figure 5). The film has many moments depicting women's hair wrapping – a cinematic equivalent of Audre Lorde's erotic portraits of mother/daughter haircombing and plaiting in *Zami*. Women's hair 'work' operates as a kind of 'counter-discourse' by revealing how Black women can remember Black history as it were on their own bodies. As Dash suggests:

> the hairstyles we're wearing now are based upon ancient hair-styles and there is a tradition behind these hairstyles. They mean things. In any West African country, you know, if you are a pre-teen you have a certain hairstyle. If you are in puberty you have another. (Dash 1992, p. 53)

Figure 5   Nana, Yellow Mary and Eula in *Daughters of the Dust*
© Julie Dash (1991)

This tradition is totally at odds with Hollywood's star-system where a star's appearance often has little to do with a film's historical moment and hair in particular remains continuously similar in film after film. *Daughters of the Dust*, on the other hand, avoids star identifications by setting in play processes of collective work and storytelling which Dash parallels cinematographically in a multigeneric mixture of silent black and white film, still photographs and colour.

That the film is insistently Afracentric is helped by the John Barnes' background score. As Dash explains, Barnes assembled a variety of African instruments 'including the synclavier, the Middle Eastern santour, African bata drums and African talking drums' and drew on astrological beliefs for example, writing the Unborn Child's theme in 'the key of B, the key of Libra, representing balance and justice' (Dash 1992, p. 16). Dash matches this vibrant and varied music cinematically, by syncopating the Unborn Child's footsteps to harmonic patterns and using sound overlays instead of narrative, like the sound of steam trains, to suggest an urban future. Nana's stories are matched by a score which more strictly adheres to African instruments and folk tones. Musical notations model the rich interconnectedness of Peazant generations. The repetition of the Unborn Child's musical motifs for the final credits suggests Dash's hope for future communal harmony.

Daughters of the Dust paints an extraordinary canvas of Black feminist themes and representations. By avoiding mainstream cinema's addiction to contemporary urban Black landscapes, Dash can step away from its often sexist and essentialist Black female portraits. There are 'hos' and 'bitches' in *Daughters of the Dust* (Yellow Mary and Haagar) but Dash's recognition that 'Black woman' is a historic as well as cultural construction brings into play a much greater diversity of diasporic representations than urban images generally allow. Black women's feelings, knowledge and beliefs are at the centre of the film both visually in Dash's spatial organisation and narratively in the stories of Nana and the Unborn Child. *Daughters of the Dust* is aesthetically radical but it is not idiosyncratic. Unlike Western aesthetics in which idealised and individualised art objects, as well as the artists who make them, are divorced from the 'real' world, Dash's Black aesthetic is embedded in women's history and everyday worlds. But Dash's aesthetic is not mimetic, rather, it is one in which spirituality and matrilineality shape the truth and beauty of Black women's values and experiences. As Dash points out:

> I say, great, it is a foreign film because, as I've been saying, it's a film that privileges black women first, then the black community and white women. The feelings that evokes about African-Americans are foreign, because what audiences have seen over the years have been very simplistic. Things that appeal to basic instincts. And now we have a film that is both complicated and complete, with a lot of different meanings. (Dash 1992, p. 66)

Chapter 6

POSTMODERNISM AND *ORLANDO*

The postmodern signs yoking feminist with film theory figure in the work of several critics currently intrigued by futuristic cinema. Barbara Creed in 'Gynesis, postmodernism and the science fiction horror film' (Creed 1990A) argues that cinema's obsession with the theme of 'becoming woman' (the birthing metaphors of *Psycho*, *Alien*, *The Fly* and *Terminator*) represent the collapse of the symbolic and paternal function of individualism, authorship and other master 'truths' of the narratable world of pre-postmodern Anglo-American culture. In these films heroes cannot distinguish reality from fantasy (or in the 'case' of *Psycho*: phantasy) and this breakdown in the distinction between subject and object Creed, building on the work of Tania Modleski and E. Ann Kaplan, characterises as postmodern and potentially 'feminist'. Such optimism draws on the fact that heroes who cannot control the borders of their own material bodies cease to retain any masculine individuality (Creed 1990A; Modleski 1986; Kaplan 1988).

The key feature of postmodern cinema, then, is this new signification of gender. The degree to which postmodern signs differ from other cinematic effects also may mark the possibility of new figurations of individual and collective histories. For example, the too readily available plot of boyhood to manhood, and its metonymic brothers – the emerging nation and the last frontier – have little place in postmodern films. The power of a national history, or a *de*limited, gendered life story, is denied in favour of the pleasures of parody, pastiche and the spectacular. The discursive quotidian has little part in a postmodern world except in so far as its stories can be 'Othered' as in Julian Temple's witty pastiche of Californian Valley life seen through the eyes of friendly aliens in *Earth Girls Are Easy*. Leads in postmodern cinema are neither models of all-American manhood nor clues to men's desires.

At the same time part of feminism's interest in postmodern cinema, for example, Terry Gilliam's *Brazil* (1985), is in the compelling exposure of the impossibility of progressive history (Hutcheon 1988). In *Brazil's* future world discredited technology cannot offer any effective aid to progress. Instead, knowledge derives from cinematic and literary parodies. References abound to Orwell's *1984*, and to British movies of the 1940s, in conflicting discourses drawn from canonic texts and popular culture. There is no singular narrative functioning as a transparent window but an unreflecting anti-hero whose struggles encourage the spectator to doubt both character and film.

A similar concern shared by all feminist theorists is to challenge gender narratives in order to challenge dominant and stereotypical gender constructions. This concern involves feminists in the tangles of deconstruction, narrative transformations and transgressions between genres and between high and low art. An often cited example is Jenny Holzer's Times Square billboard. Holzer's active, feminist appropriation of the popular market place has some of the deauthorising, pluralising impulses of the postmodern. Angela McRobbie, in an interesting response to postmodernism's insistent reproduction of the popular, argues that its genuinely 'anti-foundationalist form of anti-social theory' offers a new way of understanding the popular (McRobbie 1994, p. 4). McRobbie's attention is to the visual; thus society is not 'one big picture' but a number of 'snapshots' (McRobbie 1994, p. 5). Only current postmodern thinking, according to McRobbie, can unfold the dense interwrappings of advertisements with classical and contemporary Hollywood films as well as the ongoing incorporation of street-style in *haute couture*.

These intersections will be at the heart of my project, in a discussion of Virginia Woolf's book and Sally Potter's film of *Orlando*, that is in two parts: the first, focusing on gender deconstructions in both film and book and the second, springing from that, focusing on their newer discursive reconstructions of history. Also, to make any postmodern sense of *Orlando* an interpretative lens needs to click from portrait to landscape to focus on surface and spectacle. It is the intersections between these themes which offer one model for reading both Woolf's and Potter's gender representations. Other feminists' reading of *Orlando*

(for example, Annette Kuhn in *Women's Pictures*), suggest that Woolf/
Potter's gender thinking is a perfect echo of social repressions and
transgressions. Kuhn argues that Potter's film shows:

> the pressure to be defined, in social terms, as either male or
> female remains; and that the gender identity assumed brings its
> own, often momentous, consequences. This is most evident when,
> in the nineteenth century, Orlando, as a woman, is constrained,
> deprived and dispossessed by laws that prevent her from owning
> or inheriting property in her own right. (Kuhn 1994, p. 235)

Kuhn's theme, that there is a mutuality between social identity and
gender identity, promises an anti-essentialist reading.

That 'man' and 'woman' cannot designate naturally distinct entities,
that gender representations will inevitably draw on/be drawn by their
effective social place, has been a constant theme in feminism of the
past decade. There is no question that *Orlando*, like Woolf's other
novels and essays and Potter's other films, answers spectacularly to any
linkage of the personal with the political, of socially constructed sexuality with private desires. Yet Kuhn's reading, though thoughtful, risks
collapse into a seductive model of social construction which renders
the superb spectacle of *Orlando* invisible. This understanding of *Orlando*
as primarily a commentary on the social and economic consequences
of tendentious gender fixities, does justice to the vibrant political energy
of the film, but nonetheless deprives both film and book of their sheer
delight in, what we now term, 'postmodern consumer spectacle'. While
Kuhn's political reading of *Orlando* is indispensably true it does seem
important to discuss what both book and film show not just what both
represent. What Kuhn neglects are the satisfactions of spectacle.

Because the invention of the cinema took place in tandem with
features of urbanisation and cultural change now labelled modernist,
the cinema was theorised for some time as the modern form. It is only
recently that critics have begun actively to celebrate as postmodern
those films which foreground the gap between cinematic illusion and
social reality. The stylistic agency of *Orlando* is visibly postmodern. That
is to say both book and film challenge, through the visible, the modernist assumptions that characters 'own' the text in some progressive
individual history. *Orlando* traverses the centuries from 1600 to Woolf

or Potter's present day. The eponymous hero favoured by Elizabeth I falls in love with Sasha a Russian princess visiting the court, is spurned first as a lover by Sasha, and then as a writer by Nick Greene. Appointed ambassador to Constantinople by King William, Orlando changes sex and, now a woman, returns to the literary salons of eighteenth-century London. In Potter's film, Orlando loses her estate by giving birth to a daughter in the twentieth century but in Woolf's biography Orlando retains her property with the birth of a son.

Both book and film parody the 'straight' forwardly representational with multiscenic elements (from Shakespeare to Botticelli) involving the spectator/reader as a self-conscious and active contributor to the narrative process. All of these features are commonly characterised as postmodern. I want to emphasise how little the ideas and technical processes of both book and film can really be valued unless we oscillate surface and meaning. Affirming the postmodern possibilities in Woolf's novel *avant la lettre* strongly validates Woolf's anti-realist project. So, for example, there is no question that the scenes of commerce in the Old Kent Road and Marshall and Snelgrove are exciting, and cinematic identifications of gender instability. It is the construction of the commercial as the vibrant source of *Orlando*'s deflation of diachronic or linear, history which exactly places *Orlando* within a feminist, postmodern frame.

Ironically, you could argue that the commodification of postmodernism itself, both by the high street and by the academy, has been the business success story of the decade. Hardly a week goes by without a casual and often imprecise synaesthesia of 'postmodern' with 'progress' and with 'pleasure' as in a typical description from *The Guardian* of the offices of MTV Europe as a 'postmodern palace resembling the set of Logan's Run' (Dutta 1994, p. 5). Terminological imprecision is even more vivid in the media critic Paul Morley's description of himself as a Sue-Ellen fan and a serious up-beat postmasturbator.

The other business success story preceding and continuing through the decade is, of course, the commodification of the sign 'Virginia Woolf'. First drawn as 'mad and asexual' by Leonard Woolf in his edition of *A Writer's Diary* (1953), differing and opposing Woolfian signs succeeded in a welter of popular cultural iconography including tee shirts, cushions, the *New York Review of Books* freebies, Channel Four's *J'Accuse*, Hanif Kureishi's 1987 film *Sammy and Rosie Get Laid*, and the hard rock group, Virginia Woolf, as well as the more feminist signs of sisterhood such as Shakespeare's Sister and feminist tee shirts produced by Historical Products Inc. (Silver 1992).

Radically disparate signs of contemporary culture then similarly encourage surface identifications rather than material change yet, perhaps perversely, I want to argue that attention to surface as history is precisely what makes postmodernism a distinctive and potentially radical cultural enterprise and that this is reflected both in Sally Potter's film of *Orlando* and in the original text. Both film and book suggest new ideas of subjectivity through the visual, by positioning the spectacular in new and interesting ways.

Now it is exactly this 'signature of the visible', the title of Fredric Jameson's collected essays about cinema, which so panics critics from the Left (Jameson 1992). Jameson's volume addresses the visibility of postmodern culture and specifically film. His uneasiness with postmodernism is by now well known (McRobbie 1994) and clearly revealed by the title of his book. It is a quotation from that text of high modernism, James Joyce's *Ulysses* 'signatures of all the things I am here to read' which stresses scriptibility – or the importance of texts – rather than visibility. And it is precisely the visibility of particular postmodern films which so distresses Jameson. In his analysis of *Diva* (1981) directed by Jean-Jacques Beineix (whose motorbike rider hero illicitly tapes the performance of a famous diva) Jameson praises the extraordinary luminosity of *Diva*'s images – breathtaking dawns – while deploring the very primacy of these images. It is because this, and other postmodern films such as de Palma's *Blow Out* (also 1981), insistently foreground the processes of reproduction, exhilarating in a surface aesthetic, that for Jameson such films lack effect. Anxiety is absent and new technologies are merely materials. While feminist critics might also deplore *Diva* it is for very different reasons than those chosen by Jameson. As Toni Cade Bambara points out, the film's young white male steals both voice and clothing from the African American opera star Wilhelmina Wiggins and this, Bambara rightly claims, is a 'theft-of-the-Third World shadow text' (Bambara 1993, p. 137).

A surrender to technological reproductions is one feature of postmodernism attacked by Jameson, others include the assimilation of neo-classic monumentality and its stylistic affinities with *art deco*. Postmodernism's effacement of 'some key boundaries or separations most notably the erosion of the older distinction between high culture and so-called mass or popular culture' Jameson famously dismisses as 'pastiche . . . blank parody, parody that has lost its sense of humour' (Jameson 1988, pp. 14–16). This pseudoculture has its apogee in *la mode retro* or nostalgia films which are 'mail-order houses of the spirit' (Jameson 1992, p. 85). In *Body Heat, The Conformist* and *American Graffiti* the use of quotation and pastiche, for Jameson, simply effaces 'real' history. Indeed, he sees this simulcrum of history as part of a more general waning of historical knowledge.

Jameson's speculations invite us to ask: Where is Woman? In Jameson's apocalyptic scenario 'woman' is the absent term. For both Woolf and Potter, it is precisely the waning of particular historical representations, for example, legal and militaristic pomp and circumstance which Woolf so wittily deflates in *Three Guineas*, which is a valuable loss of *history* – a loss of the paternal signifiers of history. Jameson's argument cannot take account of these moments of history (Woolf's famous 'on or about 1910', or second wave feminism) when pastiche/ parody, like the situationists equally famous motto 'the intelligentsia is power's hall of mirrors', might represent not a loss of historical knowledge but a radical break with existing historicised and misogynist constructions of knowledge (*Situationist International* ICA, 1989).

Jameson conceives of postmodernism as a 'litter of cultural artifacts' like a 'great junk pile of video cassettes' (Jameson 1992, p. 203). What Jameson particularly fears, of course, is postmodernism's representation of history as surface. The ransacking of preceding culture Jameson calls the 'cultural capital' of the postmodern and its 'new forms of cultural credit' (Jameson 1992, p. 157). The real distinction between postmodernism and classical modernism, for Jameson, is that modernism has truth value, an 'authentic vision', while postmodernism is text, sheer surface and superficial (Jameson 1992, p. 75). In short what Jameson most deplores in postmodern film is the obsession with a 'society of the spectacle' (Jameson 1992, p. 217).

From another direction, the American feminist critic Jane Marcus shares Jameson's anxiety about spectacle, and uses oddly similar terminology, in her savage attack on the film *Orlando* in *The Women's Review of Books*. Again titles are revealing. Marcus's 'Tale of Two Cultures' disparages *Orlando* in order to praise *Modern Fiction Studies'* academic essays about Woolf. *Orlando*, Marcus claims, is 'blancmange' and (curiously simultaneously) 'tapioca pudding' (perhaps Marcus is confused about British puddings) . . . 'a sweet white movie taken to the toothache level' . . . 'ridiculously bad' . . . 'the film-makers' didn't know of the novel's cult status in lesbian and gay culture' (this claim would surprise both Swinton and Potter). And finally the 'film slobbers' and 'I had to apologize', Marcus says, 'to my husband' in an interesting insertion of the circumscriptions of heterosexuality (Marcus 1994, p. 11). A more positive relation between spectacle, women and consumerism in the context of postmodernism is the much keener-eyed focus of those feminist critics of the postmodern, E. Ann Kaplan in America, and Meaghan Morris in Australia. In 'Feminism/Oedipus/Postmodernism' Ann Kaplan argues that transgressive strategies such as non-narrative devices and the surface repetitions of some rock videos might be potentially feminist and postmodern by undermining 'the usual oppositions between high and low culture; between masculine and feminine . . . between the private and the public sphere' (Kaplan 1988, pp. 35–6).

In 'Things to Do With Shopping Centres', Morris makes connections between spatial stories (here in debt to the anthropological writings of Michel de Certeau), the surface displays in Australian shopping centres and women's memories and local history whose admixture is a potential site of social conflict and therefore social change (Morris 1989B). Morris argues that, in the postmodern world, gender identity can be understood only in terms of the complex and contradictory ways in which consumerism, pleasure and power, and cultural languages are produced. She is intrigued by women's multifarious and active participation in the modernisation of social and cultural life in this century and in her collected essays *The Pirate's Fiancée*, follows Foucault in claiming that her discursive 'fields' such as shopping centres might construct women in stereotypical images but do provide mechanisms by which women transform their everyday lives (Morris 1988A). Women vibrantly enjoy shopping and hence frequently engage in a double coded postmodern world.

Because I want to display *Orlando* as an exemplary of some postmodern themes, let me quickly seize examples of similar insights from both book and film. Like Morris's postmodern women, Orlando actively participates in urban transformations. In the department store, Marshall and Snelgrove:

the lift gave a little jerk as it stopped at the first floor; and she had
a vision of innumerable coloured stuffs flaunting in a breeze from
which came distinct, strange smells; and each time the lift stopped
and flung its doors open, there was another slice of the world
displayed. (Woolf 1992, p. 286)

Marshall and Snelgrove is both a commodity spectacle of multiple,
uncontextualised and appropriated 'world' objects but also a source of
self-knowledge, of autobiographical memories: 'She was reminded of
the river off Wapping in the time of Elizabeth . . . how well she remembered the feel of rough rubies running through her fingers' (Woolf
1992, p. 287). Orlando turns from the plate glass mirrors of retail capitalism to her own(ed) reflective speculum 'a little looking-glass and a
powder puff' (see Figure 6) (Woolf 1992, 288).

In 'Modernity's Disavowal' Mica Nava makes a sophisticated reread-
ing of women and modernity to emphasise the transgressive gender
implications of 'discursive formations of shopping'. Nava suggests that
modernity placed a 'new stress on display and the visual – on looking'
(Nava 1994, p. 2). The fantasy palaces of department stores, Nava
points out, offered women in particular a spectacular environment 'a
context which legitimated the desire of women to look as well as to be
looked at' (Nava 1994, p. 14). In addition Nava powerfully stresses the
dynamic linkage of female consumerism and political change, for
example, the marketing of suffragette garments. Later in this chapter
I want to continue to trace intersections and differences between
modernism and postmodernism. Here I will simply state my view
that although the gendered features of modernity are at last being
recognised, for example, in Nava's exemplary essay, it is also true that
Woolf's kinship of 'women', 'subjectivity' and 'consumption' is precisely
postmodern. By the end of the biography the house has become 'like a
scraped new photograph' with a 'loudspeaker *condensing* [my italics]
on the terrace a dance tune' (Woolf 1992, p. 306). A world where technology reifies the human and 'condenses' and intensifies pleasure is
postmodern. As Lyotard suggests, the changed status of knowledge
brought about by information technology designates the state of
postmodern culture (Lyotard 1984). In *Orlando*, lifts and loudspeakers
condense and intensify Orlando's knowledge. All is surface, slices of
the world. Woolf's recasting of identities as mobile, multiple surfaces,

Figure 6 Tilda Swinton in *Orlando* (1992)

and I would add temporal and technological, is characteristically post-modern. By contrast, Jameson deplores the porousness of national borders which are allowing the Third World to be an economic, articulated area of American capitalism. In the corporate world of IBM or Levi-Strauss, demarcated economic boundaries make no sense.

Similarly the financing schema underpinning Potter's *Orlando* is characteristically post-Fordist: a homology of late capitalism and cultural postmodernism. In 1988 the producer Christopher Sheppard, known for his direction of documentaries (*Death of a Runaway*), as it were 'crossed genres' to produce *Orlando*. Sheppard's budget has the mixed pedigree of many post-Fordist films made up as it was from second-phase British funding, Italian money and post-*perestroika* Soviet production company finance. The tight budget necessitated a ten week schedule with one week of pickups and reshoots during editing. As Jameson points out 'the emergence of postmodernism is closely related to the emergence of this new moment of late, consumer or multinational capitalism. I believe also that its formal features in many ways express the deeper logic of that particular social system' (Jameson 1988, p. 28).

Yet it is important to realise that the aspect of postmodernism that now seems in many ways most immutably to characterise it – its attention to surface – is of recent gestation. As a descriptive label 'postmodern' came to be applied to film and television only in the 1980s. Postmodernism first gained currency in America in the 1950s and 1960s in literary criticism. The literary critics Irving Howe, Leslie Fiedler and Ihab Hassan made vigorous attempts to celebrate popular culture as much as the literary canon and projected a powerful sense of literary and cultural change as the title of Fiedler's book *Waiting for the End* suggests (see Humm 1994). Postmodern fiction is characterised by a knowing play with genres and a scepticism about realism and the values of high art. Indeed 'hyperreality' became a common theme in the postmodern architectural criticism of Charles Jencks. Attempts to specify the postmodern features of contemporary culture – buildings, novels, television, film – involved critics in one major recognition: that although culture was a multiple collection of many different forms, it could be read or understood as surface. This stress on surface, rather than on structure, by the leading postmodernists Baudrillard and

Lyotard, is the most obvious change from poststructuralism to post-modernism.

Cultural critics return repeatedly to the idea of postmodernity because its theories help us to explain changes in twentieth-century culture. Hence, the attempts to represent postmodernism as a coherent whole have inspired a plethora of writing including the now classic accounts by Jean-François Lyotard. Lyotard's *The Postmodern Condition* (1984) is regarded as the *ur*, or foundational, text of postmodernism giving, as it does, economic and cultural explanations for the new dissolution of boundaries between high and low culture and for the way in which contemporary culture is recklessly able to synthesise and reconstitute any artistic formation. Lyotard's central claim is that the grand narratives, or theories, of Marxism and Humanism have ceased to work as explanatory paradigms because these 'narratives' do not help us to understand constant and contradictory cultural change. Indeed Lyotard chooses these metanarratives or single, causal explana-tions of culture, as the key feature of postmodernism like Baudrillard, replacing metanarratives with an examination of cultural surface. That is to say, he argues that the meaning of culture derives both from its visual processes, like genre formation in film, and from the visible contexts in which these processes take place (Lyotard 1984).

The potential importance of that move, to theories of cinema and feminism, lies in its mobilisation of challenges. The first challenge, which Woolf struggled at great cost to herself to launch in her attack on fascism in *Three Guineas*, is to the concept of progressive social evolution – the idea that society inevitably mutates in some kind of progressive and linear development. The second challenge is to those irrepressible catachresis of 'universal manhood' and 'universal woman-hood': postmodernism's attack on gender abstractions and its assertion of more plural subjectivities is at the heart of *Orlando*.

The particular focus on the meaning-generating processes of cultural surfaces by those postmodern theorists working in the visual arts offers one creative way into *Orlando*'s representations. For example, the post-modern architect Charles Jencks flamboyantly designs with ad hoc, multigeneric and hugely eclectic historical 'thefts'. Jencks's The Elemental House (1980–2) abjures simple revivalism in favour of a suggestive stylised abstraction of representational themes. The Los Angeles site, Rustic Canyon, inspired him to construct the abstraction of a village in rustic pavilions whose classical 'temples' and high art pediments are matched but not diminished by 'a swimming pool in the shape of California with the pool lights marking the major cities' (Jencks 1977, p. 161). Jencks' games of 'hunt the symbol' could characterise the pleasures of both the book and the film *Orlando*. In *The Language of Postmodern Architecture* Jencks adopts the term 'double-coded' from communication studies to describe how postmodernism incorporates differing codes including the styles of many cultural groups. 'The style is hybrid, double-coded, based on fundamental dualities' (Jencks 1977, p. 5). He argues that postmodern architecture subverts, not evolves from, the aesthetic 'purity' of modernism—the international style of Le Corbusier and Mies Van der Rohe. Rather than a 'metanarrative' of classicism, postmodern architecture is fragmented: 'Through our repro-duction techniques . . . we can reproduce fragmented experiences of different cultures' (Jencks 1977, p. 5). Fragmentation is the representa-tional schema of Potter's *Orlando* whose filmic intertitles are neither summative nor introductory but offer the viewer scenic and Woolfian pauses for breath. Architecture is a 'verb', Jencks claims, 'an action where the image of a city becomes inchoate, the architecture evasive' (Jencks 1977, pp. 104 ; 91).

'Inchoate' street scenes are commonplace in Virginia Woolf's novels. An important contribution to *Orlando*'s characterisation comes from Orlando's reflections on the surface detail of urban scenes. Orlando pursues his locomotor pleasures as a man in Constantinople and, as Victorian woman, equally enjoys the restless detail of London's depart-ment stores and the Old Kent Road. Urban journeys allow Orlando a space for self-reflection. Rather than a panoptic eye, Orlando has a capacity for the optical point of view of a Hollywood camera: 'Nothing could be seen whole or read from start to finish. What was seen begun – like two friends starting to meet each other across the street – was never seen ended' (Woolf 1992, p. 293). Potter similarly stages the scene as an image of fractured experience by transferring Orlando from a motor vehicle to a motorbike with side car and placing the spectator in intimate close up with Orlando's perspective, on London's hybrid urban iconography as buildings are vectored in our direction.

In *Illuminations* Walter Benjamin flags 'fragmentation' as a key feature of cinematic form. The 'tactile quality' of Dadaist Art, Benjamin argues, 'promoted a demand for film' in which 'no sooner has' the spectator's 'eye grasped a scene then it is already changed' (Benjamin 1973, p. 240). James Donald lists a number of Woolf's contemporaries including Pound, Simmel, and Moholy-Nagy who described urban culture in cinematic terms (Donald 1995): the rhythms of the urban street match the rhythms of the cinema. *Orlando*'s hybrid mixture is matched in two now classic urban films from the 1920s: Walter Ruttmann's *Berlin: Symphony of a Great City* (1927) and Dziga Vertov's *The Man With the Movie Camera* (1928). Although as Peter Wollen points out; 'the history of film coincides almost exactly with the history of the skyscraper ... being consolidated during the early 30s', it is crucially significant that urban scenes in postmodern films such as *Blade Runner* exactly match Woolf's abandonment of 'stylistic realism' (Wollen 1992, p. 25). In a revealing footnote Benjamin remarks: 'the film corresponds to profound changes in the apperceptive apparatus – changes that are experienced on an individual scale by the man in the street in big city traffic' (Benjamin 1973, p. 252).

Orlando's active acquisition of knowledge through the spectacular in the Old Kent Road finds a ringing echo in Benjamin's essay and Wollen's later reflection. Similarly, Sally Potter's almost fetishistic dedication to mirroring Orlando's states of minds with external objects, for example, house facades and garden topiary, matches Woolf's: after 'twenty minutes the body and mind' (an interesting emphatic material reversal of the usual mind and body) 'were like scraps of torn paper tumbling from a sack' (Woolf 1992, p. 293). Woolf's anthropomorphising of the urban (its litter) is endorsed albeit in a more attractive metaphor, in postmodern theory. Jencks often describes buildings as actively human, 'dressed' with faces.

Orlando's scene of the Old Kent Road is the moment when spectacle and consumerism as knowledge creating are dramatically vivid and postmodern. At this point in the book what had been a continuous narrative by Orlando in the first person becomes fragmentary, split into cinematic points of view. Like contemporary American cinema the narrator favours medium shots and close ups rather than long shots. For example, and very uncharacteristically for Woolf, the passage explodes into extremely short sentences clicking from still to still: 'People spilt off the pavement. There were women with shopping bags. Children ran out' (Woolf 1992, p. 292). An irresistible testimonial to the power of shot-reaction-shot follows: 'When this happened, Orlando heaved a

sigh of relief, lit a cigarette, and puffed for a minute or two in silence'
(Woolf 1992, p. 293).

What Woolf achieves, through Orlando's survey of the surface terri-
tory of South London, is the illusion that surface movement can assist
self-knowledge. As Jeanette Winterson argues, Woolf shades and fades
as a painter does flying across the surface of time and space as if on a
magic carpet (Winterson 1995).'Cities and peoples pass beneath us in
a moment we are in England, in another moment in Persia, then the
carpet flies on (Winterson 1995, p. 73). Jencks's description of postmodernism as a'Chinese garden space'which'suspends the clear, final
ordering of events for a labyrinth, rambling"way" that never achieves
an absolute goal' (Jencks 1977, p. 134) is a perfect analogue both to
Orlando's enjoyment of the surface incoherence of the Old Kent Road
as well as Sally Potter's equally inventive scene of Orlando's race
through a century in a twisting garden maze.

This question of postmodernism – is what Woolf is writing, or Potter
depicting, parodic, anti*historical* (not ahistorical), slippery with gender
instabilities? – of course looks like the question of modernism *tout
court*. The crucial features of modernity, those explored by Marx,
Baudelaire and Benjamin, are that modernity is transitory, challenging
the concept of evolutionary progress and urban. Marx's *Das Kapital* is a
theory of commodities; Baudelaire's 'The Painter of Modern Life' is a
study of fashion; and in *One-Way Street*, Walter Benjamin chose the
shopping arcades of Berlin as his vanguard example of modernity. How
then are Woolf's continual venues – the street, the department
store – any different from modernist locations?

As Susan Buck-Mores has argued, Benjamin's massive work on the
significance of the Paris arcades is a seminal theorisation of modernity
and consumerism (Buck-Mores 1989). Benjamin prophetically anticipates the social possibilities of popular culture such as cinemas and
department stores. The cinema and shopping had a natural affinity in
the 1920s (the decade of *Orlando*) since 87.5 per cent of cinema goers
were women, young people and children (Nava 1994).Yet, as Nava so
insightfully points out, Benjamin is manifestly ambivalent about women,
when he considers them at all. In most of Benjamin's work it is 'the
prostitute who is presented as the key female figure in the iconography
of the city and at the same time, as *the* embodiment of commodification' (Nava 1994, p. 23). In addition women's urban spectatorship was

markedly distinct from that of men. Women made a functional use of shops and streets rather than voyeuristically looking at others (Jenks 1995).

It is gender which marks the 'difference' between modernism and postmodernism. Although modernism as a definitional term appears in art history in the 1830s, the practices of modernism are usually dated much later, from the post-Impressionism which so excited Bloomsbury and the arrival of Cubism in the early twentieth century. The anti-representational impulse in painting was matched by *vers libre* in poetry and narrative experimentation like stream-of-consciousness in the novel. Yet although particular examples of modernism, such as Marcel Duchamp's readymades, are revivified in postmodernism, modernism never lost faith in the belief that singular identity, and hence moral meaning-making, could transcend fragmentation. In other words, although modernist texts might share postmodernism's heterogeneous genres yet modernism still confidently clings to metaphors of masculine individualism, such as Bloom's Odyssean voyage through Dublin. Ironically in retrospect, it was the mediating function of myth in *To The Lighthouse* which encouraged Erich Auerbach to select Woolf as an apogee of modernism. Auerbach's point, well supported by close reading, is that the famous brown stocking knitted by Mrs Ramsay has no social metaphorical or metonymic meaning and can therefore take meaning only from myth (Auerbach 1971). Yet to a feminist eye it is the relationship between Mrs Ramsay's point of view and the domestic sign of the stocking, which is paramount. *Orlando*, both book and film, similarly adopts an Othered view point. In the biography Orlando sweeps past the Crystal Palace:

> Draped about a vast cross of fretted and floriated gold were widow's weeds and bridal veils; hooked on to other excrescences were crystal palaces, bassinettes, military helmets, memorial wreaths, trousers, whiskers, wedding cakes, cannon, Christmas trees, telescopes, extinct monsters, globes, maps, elephants, and mathematical instruments – the whole supported like a gigantic coat of arms on the right side by a female figure clothed in flowing white; on the left by a portly gentleman wearing a frock-coat and sponge-bag trousers. The incongruity of the objects, the

association of the fully clothed and the partly draped . . . afflicted
Orlando with the most profound dismay. (Woolf 1992, p. 222)

This is Woolf's description of Orlando's move from the strangling,
knotting together of bourgeois objects with gender values. In Potter's
film the equivalent scene pictures an even more active move to freedom, to a place outside.

'*A wild hand-held point of view video image – running through long
grass* ORLANDO: (voiceover) She's no longer trapped by destiny. And
ever since she let go of the past, she found her life was beginning' (Potter
1994, p. 61). Both scenes intensifying Orlando's detachment from imperial and bourgeois 'destiny', signify a breakdown in a master narrative
and hence are characteristically postmodern. And as Alice Jardine
suggests in *Gynesis* any such breakdown is 'gendered as female' (Jardine
1985, p. 60). One of Jardine's strengths is her compelling mapping of
the feminine as a sign of absence in male-authored texts, and her
observation that the breakdown has happened through postmodernism, or what Jardine calls denaturalisation. Derrida and Foucault
had offered proof that ideology is based on naturalised categories and
that modernism's 'ideology', as Andreas Huyssen argues, is based on
the naturalised categories of 'women' and mass culture as 'the Other'
(Huyssen 1986).

Modernists do not inevitably throw into crisis sexual difference.
Postmodern texts on the other hand often transcend gender binaries.
For example, Potter characterises the feminine as masquerade with
Quentin Crisp's homosexual, cross-dressed performance as Queen
Elizabeth I (see Figure 7). Woolf's *Orlando* pastiches gender categories
in the above passage by exposing the arbitrariness of bourgeois
associations 'whiskers/wedding cakes', 'cannons/Christmas trees',
fully-clothed males and 'partly draped' female. If one tries to read
Orlando as a picaresque modernist text, as the narrative of an alienated
intellectual, for example, one occludes its gender instabilities. There are
multiple Orlandos:

Then she called hesitatingly, as if the person she wanted might
not be there, 'Orlando?'. For if there are (at a venture) seventy-six
different times all ticking in the mind at once, how many different

Figure 7 Tilda Swinton and Quentin Crisp in *Orlando* (1992)

people are there not – Heaven help us – all having lodgement at one time or another in the human spirit? Some say two thousand and fifty-two. (Woolf 1992, pp. 293–4)

Woolf's character portrait typically and crucially involves interpellation, and instability.

If Woolf's work is so clearly marked by its grappling with a post-modern gender instability *avant la lettre*, from where does this forward-looking pressure emerge? *Orlando* is profoundly shaped by Woolf's immediate antecedent essays. She wrote *Orlando* between October and December 1927, completing the final third in March 1928, and in the same year explored ideas about biography, gender and modernism in 'The Narrow Bridge of Art' published in August 1927 – a discussion of Sterne's novel *Tristram Shandy*. Like Woolf, Sterne made a frequent use of parenthetical asides and mixed genres creating a cinematic spread of narrative. Woolf's essay describes more than this as she develops one of her central themes: the biographical (fictional or factual) should dispense with limited representations of gender which were 'merely the psychology of personal intercourse' (Woolf 1966–7, 225). As Woolf explains in 'The Art of Biography', 'biography will enlarge its scope by hanging up looking glasses at odd corners. And yet from all this diversity it will bring out, not a riot of confusion, but a richer unity' (Woolf 1961, 67). Woolf's intense interest in the relation between refractions of light and the representation of character is a continuing theme in *Orlando*. The year previously she had recognised that correspondence in an essay directly about film – 'The Cinema' – published in *Arts* in New York in 1926. Persistent attention to the surface appearance of characters in her novels is the theme of that essay (Woolf 1978). Leslie Hankins has argued that Woolf's essay draws on film theory of the twenties (Hankins 1993), but far more striking are her descriptions of cinema as an abstract space, making this perhaps the first British essay to describe cinema as avant-garde. Woolf has a unique and singular focus in her theme of spectacle, avidly responding to *Dr Caligari's* expressionist perspectives and new angles and shapes. She claims that these surface representations offer a new visual aesthetics:

The most fantastic contrasts could be flashed before us with a speed which the writer can only toil after in vain . . . we get intimations only in the chaos of the streets, perhaps, (a point later echoed by Benjamin) when some momentary assembly of colour, sound, movement suggests that here is a scene waiting a new art to be transfixed. (Woolf 1978, pp. 185–6)

That'new art'was *Orlando*. In an interview in 1993, Potter suggests that her attention to surface is a similar and integral part of the script writing process since she 'reaches out viscerally through the senses, through a feeling of seeing things for the first time. There's a sense of the abstract, almost the metaphysical' (Dargis 1993, p. 42). *Orlando*, as Woolf suggests in her *Diary*, 'taught me . . . how to keep the realities at bay' (Woolf 1953, p. 136). In the course of writing, Woolf realised how much was involved in creating new gender representations in a productive, performative way:

One can see anything (for this is all fantasy). Everything is to be tumbled in pell mell . . . Sapphism is to be suggested. Satire is to be the main note – satire and wildness . . . my own lyric vein is to be satirised. Everything mocked. And it is to end with three dots. . . . (Woolf 1953, p. 105)

Woolf's fragmented punctuation, for example, the use of ellipses, frequent question marks and parentheses, are signifiers of a breakdown in the master narrative of biography. *Orlando* took on a life of its own: 'After two days entirely gave up my time chart and abandoned myself to the pure delight of this farce' (Woolf 1953, p. 117). 'How extraordinarily unwilled by me but potent in its own right, by the way, *Orlando* was! as if it shoved everything aside to come into existence' (Woolf 1953, p. 120).

If what defines gender identity in canonic literature are familiar discursive formations focusing a core subjectivity, then Woolf's aesthetic attention to restlessness, to 'abandonment', rejects this closure. As Jeanette Winterson wittily suggests'Woolf wanted to say dangerous things in *Orlando* but she did not want to say them in the missionary position' (Winterson 1995, p. 68). Love works in mysterious ways but not 'in the confines of heterosexual desire . . . the Orlando who holds Sasha in his arms is still the Orlando who holds Shelmerdine in hers' (Winterson 1995, p. 67). Woolf's investment (and Potter's active endorsement of that investment), in gender transitivity presages post-modernism. An acutely critical view of heterosexuality forms a crucial part of some postmodern theory, for example, the work of Judith Butler. *Orlando* was also being written and published at a time of crisis in the legitimising categories of sexuality. The first decades of the twen-tieth century witnessed a feminisation of the urban scene and a specif-ic masculine fear of sexuality, of a loss of identity, in the face of women's advancement (Huyssen 1986; Nava 1994). Following the First World War's decimation of the male population, suffrage challenges combined with the demographic crisis were perceived to delegitimate Victorian sexual mores. Havelock Ellis and Radclyffe Hall had added a third sex, or Uranians, to existing binaries based on Ellis's research into sexual identities. The *grands récits* of contemporary masculinity and femininity were in crisis and Vita Sackville-West and Virginia Woolf organised support for *The Well of Loneliness* while Woolf agreed to appear at Radclyffe Hall's obscenity trial.

We need to note the historical moment in which the film *Orlando* enters the social discourse of sexuality. Following second wave femi-nism, new mappings of sexual identifications matched the progressive economic liberation of contemporary women. As Susan Faludi notes the annual sales of women's business suits rose by six million units between 1980 and 1990 and in a less trivial gesture a historic House of Lords ruling the year before the completion of *Orlando* enabled the British judiciary for the first time to sentence a man to imprisonment for raping his wife (Faludi 1992). The film reflects that newer terrain outside of motherhood, the family and heterosexuality, a terrain endorsed by Tilda Swinton, an actress known for her cross-dressing roles.

One of the implications of cross-dressing is that personal identity is independent of gender. So, in scene 45 Orlando in close-up looks directly at the audience: 'Orlando: same person. No difference at all. Just a different sex' (Potter 1994, p. 40). Here is Woolf:

'The change of sex, though it altered their future, did nothing whatever to alter their identity' (Woolf 1992, p. 133).

Woolf attacks both enforced gender binaries and, at the end of *Orlando*, the heterosexist prohibition that inheritance is gained through the continuity of a male line. 'The chief charges against her were (1) that she was dead, and therefore could not hold any property whatsoever; (2) that she was a woman, which amounts to much the same thing' (Woolf 1992, p. 161).

The speculations of recent feminist theory about the importance of masquerade to newly imagined forms of gender is relevant here. A critique of visual constructions of gender is the theme of Mary Ann Doane's analysis of film and cinema 'Film and the Masquerade'. Where for Lacan masquerade is inherently nostalgic, gesturing towards the lack of phallus, according to Doane masquerade both destabilises the female image and confounds the masculine structure of the look because masquerade defamiliarises female iconography (Doane 1990).

If in Hollywood cinema the female spectator, following Mulvey, gains pleasure only in masochism 'the effectivity of masquerade lies precisely in its potential to manufacture a distance from the image, to generate a problematic within which the image is manipulable, producible and readable by the woman' (Doane 1990, p. 54). Hollywood's increasing preoccupation with themes of cross-dressing and transsexualism (*Tootsie, Mrs Doubtfire*) marks a commercial interest in a postmodern collapse of confidence in fixed gender roles. As Judith Butler suggests: 'the loss of gender norms would have the effect of proliferating gender configuration, destabilizing substantive identity and depriving the naturalizing narrative of compulsory heterosexuality of the central protagonists: "man" and "woman"' (Butler 1990, p. 146).

An account of masquerade as agency was the pioneering work of Joan Riviere's 'Womanliness as a Masquerade'. Riviere's claim is that masquerade is implied in any construction of 'womanliness' because cultural constructions already involve impersonation (Riviere 1986). Similarly Sandra Gilbert and Susan Gubar turn to representations of cross-dressing in the work of Djuna Barnes and Gertrude Stein because cross-dressing is such a wonderfully visible sign of the social transgression of gender (Gilbert and Gubar 1988). Marjorie Garber argues more radically that cross-dressing offers 'a challenge to easy notions of binarity' because it is a continuous mode of articulation 'a space of possibility' (Garber 1992, p. 11). In saying this, Garber may be drawing on the formulations of Adrienne Rich. In 'Compulsory Heterosexuality and Lesbian Existence', Rich, too, rejects historicised gender representations following de Beauvoir's thesis that women are originally homosexual (Rich 1980):

Lesbian existence suggests both the fact of the historical presence of lesbians and our continuing creation of the meaning of that existence. I mean the term 'lesbian continuum' to include a range – through each woman's life and throughout history – of women-identified existence, not simply the fact that a woman has had or consciously desired genital sexual experience with another woman (Rich 1980, p. 56).

Rich makes a radical lesbian critique of the arbitrariness of sexual dichotomies (lesbian or heterosexual), meaning, when she talks about the construction of sexuality, a psychic and representational construction as well as a social construction. Although Rich's essay provoked feminist hostility with its 'over evaluation' of female bonding, yet in many ways the essay is marked by pacifist maternal anarchism and invites us to ask, as Riviere and others don't quite do, not only about the politics of sexuality but also about the importance of destabilising the master narrative: excising the narrative not simply punning or playing with its costume.

More than any other moment in the film, the moment of Orlando's sex change, or rather the motivation for his sex change, speaks eloquently of Rich's argument. Potter deliberately 're-visions' Woolf's originating narrative in which Orlando's sex change is not overtly transgressive of social constructions of gender. Through the sex change, Potter attempts a concrete realisation of Woolf's pacifist politics which figure more explicitly in *Three Guineas, A Room of One's Own* and in Orlando's own constant refrain that he never ran his sword through anyone. In Potter's film, Orlando becomes female in a shocked reaction to the masculine demands of war. In scene 42 Orlando tends a wounded man, disregarding Archduke Harry's cry 'Leave him! Leave him'. Orlando responds with 'This is a dying man!', only to be told: 'He's not a man, he is the enemy' (Potter 1994, p. 38).

Orlando rejects the master narrative of militarism. In interview with Manohla Dargis, Potter explains

what Orlando is doing as a man at that point is facing the ultimate test every boy grows up holding somewhere in his psyche, that he may have to go to war, fight, kill or be killed. That is the moment

Orlando realizes he cannot, will not be a man in the sense he is being asked to. (Dargis 1993, p. 42)

The potential importance of this move does not depend, as it might seem to do, on an Irigarayan model of the death drive. According to Irigaray a masculine gender identity depends on the death drive which is unavailable to women who unable to symbolise their drives, merely act as representations of men's death drives in the symbolic (Irigaray 1985B). Irigaray's model would deny the constructed difference of Orlando's pacifism, since the linkage of social violence with masculinity presupposes that anti-militarism inevitably results in gender transitivity: Orlando would have to become a woman. But Potter does not stabilise a dyadic gender inversion: 'We talked all the time about Orlando as a person rather than as a man or woman' (Donohue 1993, p. 10).

Where Lyotard envisaged the social-psychological androgyne as a goal of postmodernism, Potter is more critical, aware that the androgyne does not address repressive gender roles (Lyotard 1984). Potter claims to have retained Woolf's 'notion of the androgynous mind and dissolving gender boundaries' but characterises this as 'polymorphous sexuality rather than specific sexual identities' (Florence 1993, p. 283). The arbitrariness of gender is a specific focus of the film. For example, the library scene juxtaposes a gay, falsetto singing voice with an unusually deep voiced woman. Potter parodies the artificial catachresis 'truly feminine' with Orlando's absurd and exaggerated eighteenth-century blue dress hindering her unwieldy passage through the picture gallery. Again the sound track provides dissonance and irony as an exotic peacock's cry parallels Orlando's walk. Gender is always performance – most transparently in the brief scene where Orlando watches *Othello* whose actors are necessarily male but model women's 'treachery' and the horrific consequences of 'compulsory heterosexuality'.

Potter subverts filmic gender fixities primarily by usurping the masculine gaze. The artificiality of gender construction has a metonymic counterpart in the open artificiality of *Orlando*'s cinematic process. Tilda Swinton encouraged Potter to allow Orlando direct speech to camera. In rehearsal, Swinton first spoke her lines to Potter and the intimacy of that address is reflected in her performance. Conventional spectatorship is deconstructed as Orlando with her daughter turns to camera: 'this really is a good film'. Potter describes her aim which is 'to weave a golden thread between Orlando and the audience through the lens of the camera' (Donohue 1993, p. 10). Significantly, Shelmerdine, Orlando's lover, cannot hold his gaze.

The issue of gender identity opens the film. Swinton's extraordinarily luminous and unmarked complexion and studied performance of a non-masculine yet non-feminised male draws attention to the instability of traditional gender motifs (see cover). Swinton's physical beauty connotes femininity (slight, fine-featured) throwing into relief that her masculinity is a performance. The association of whiteness with female desirability has a long cinematic history. Marilyn Monroe, Richard Dyer suggests, similarly acted as a 'visual analogue for a basic conception of female sexuality as itself formless' (Dyer 1987, p. 58). Monroe, Dyer claims, anticipates the vaginal imagery of feminist art of the 1970s because her 'image is reaching out to embody an experience [the Irigarayan two lips] that does not in fact exist' (Dyer 1987, p. 66). As Dyer suggests, stardom is an unstable phenomenon which is never constant and hence can never be successfully mapped onto a particular sexuality. Significantly, Swinton looks into camera when invited by Queen Elizabeth into the royal chamber, allowing the Queen to 'kiss his forehead sensually' and concludes '(*To Camera*) very interesting person' (Potter 1994, p. 9).

The scene highlights the possibility of forging and reforging sexual preferences since Quentin Crisp's 'Queen' would undoubtedly admire a young beautiful boy but the historic Queen may have favoured both sexes. The direct address of the gaze is of course, in the pornographic tradition an expressive, specularised relation to the spectator *qua* spectator. Potter dialectically contrasts Swinton's masculine control of the gaze with the feminine quality of her 'to-be-looked-at-ness' fragile female beauty. Swinton is both the fetishistic object of our gaze and actively governs the camera frame. The doubling of vision is a metonymy of the doubling of gender. Swinton's use of direct address and epigrammatic, often touchingly conversational asides to camera, momentarily freezes the narrative *and* sensitises us as spectators to the activity of gazing.

Potter's postmodern attack on 'the innocence of representation' has been an underlying theme of her work for some time. In an essay about her performance art published in 1980, Potter pinpointed her key strategy as 'reversing the gaze' and 'understanding the role of the audience in producing the meaning of a performance' (Potter 1987, p. 292). In *Gender Trouble* Judith Butler similarly asserts that all gendered selves can be read as a series of performances:'The performance suggests a dissonance not only between sex and performance but sex and gender, and gender and performance' (Butler 1990, p. 137). This is because to Butler,'the very notions of masculinity and femininity stem from unresolved homosexual cathexes'(Butler 1990, p. 54). Gender can only be understood inside discourse and therefore gender identity is made up of different signifying practices.

Potter wittily captures this theme in the opening lines of the film:

(*Voiceover*) 'There can be no doubt about his sex – despite the feminine appearance that every young man of the time aspires to' [note Potter's more positive endorsement of feminine gender performance than Woolf's original] . . . But when he –' (ORLANDO *Turns and looks into the camera*) – that is, I –'. (Potter 1994, p. 3)

As Butler argues there is no 'I' before discourse. As here, the 'I' can only be spoken when the codes of masculinity and femininity are established.

Costume and masquerade are key elements in *Orlando*'s postmodernity. Potter's production design team of Ben Van Os and Jan Roelfs regularly collaborate with Peter Greenaway, while the costume designer Sandy Powell worked with Derek Jarman, Mick Jaggar and on the homoerotic *Interview With A Vampire* – all parodies of gender representations. Orlando is engendered in performance: in recitation of *The Faerie Queen* to Britain's leading'Queen', Quentin Crisp, in formal dances, and in elaborate toasts to the desert and so forth. Orlando exposes contemporary notions of gender to be culturally determined givens of a chauvinistic Elizabethan court, for example, the discussion with the Earl of Moray about Russian women'growing beards as they grow older.

EARL OF MORAY: It was told to me on good authority by Lord Francis Vere
ORLANDO: Has he travelled to Muscovy?
EARL OF MORAY: He knows someone who did
ORLANDO: Ah. (Potter 1994, p. 12)

The eighteenth century is similarly misogynist evidenced by Jonathan Swift's:'Women have no desires, only affectations' and Alexander Pope's 'indeed women are but children of a larger growth' (Potter 1994, p. 45).

The film, like the book, shows how gender meanings are produced in the heterogeneous discourses of travellers, historians and writers and how none of these meanings singularly can capture 'Orlando'. As Potter suggested in interview with Patricia Dobson

> there is no naturalism in the film, but there is a 'natural' feel running through it. Orlando is the golden thread through the story and through her, the clothes and the shifting environments we have this feeling of an exaggerated essence of each period of history . . . there are about fourteen different styles in the film. It's as though every week we are making a new film. (Dobson 1992, p. 23)

Like Maya Deren, Yvonne Rainer and Shirley Clarke, Potter's training in contemporary dance, particularly in improvisation and interpretation, encouraged her self-conscious play with mimicry and pastiche. For example, Potter makes a constant use of doubles: Elizabethan double portraits, two child pickpockets in Constantinople. Finally the act of sex can only be performed after Orlando and Shelmerdine mutually agree a 'doubled' gender:

> SHELMERDINE (*Struggling*) 'you might choose not to be a real man at all. . . say if I was a woman'.
> ORLANDO: 'You?' (Potter 1994, p. 54)

As Luce Irigaray argues, social constructions of gender appear only in these kinds of catachresis ('real man'). Potter exposes the dysfunction of such figures as phrases which are used to describe something that does not properly exist (Irigaray 1985). Potter's performance training specifically taught her to attack fixities: 'The thing about working as a performer . . . it makes you realise that there isn't a fixed audience and therefore you can't have a fixed product that is going to be universally appealing, you need different points of access' (Swanson and Moy-Thomas 1981, p. 42). By the moment of *Orlando* Potter was arguing that 'for me *Orlando* is not so much about femininity and difference as

aboutVirginia Woolf's notion of an essential self that lies beyond gender'
(Glaessner 1992, p. 14).

In some senses Potter quite radically and with originality shows
same-sex desire between Sasha and Orlando (in that the audience
knows Orlando is the female actress Tilda Swinton) without Orlando
being fixed to a stable gender identity. The effect is not a naturalistic
portrayal of a positive androgynous model, or at least not only this.
Orlando's gender, in biography and film is free – Swinton negotiates
gender and lacking any consistent and core gender identity, Swinton's
cross-dressing becomes, not a trendy fashion choice, but a conspicuous
visible site of play and spectacle. As Sally Potter suggested when asked
about the lesbian politics of an earlier film, *The Gold Diggers* 'those
ideas were there, but stated at an angle like everything else in the film'
(Ehrenstein 1993, p. 3).

Potter's projects are charged with gender transitivity as well as left
wing politics and irony. If Virginia Woolf wrote *Orlando* in one year at
white heat, the gestation of the film had a much longer pregnancy.
Both Sally Potter and Tilda Swinton read the novel in the late 1960s.
Interviewed by Mansell Stimpson, Potter claims that in adolescence –
a generative and gendering moment – 'it was very inspiring to first
read *Orlando* as a teenage girl, to have a central character who lived
first as a man and then as a woman' (Stimpson 1993, p. 23).

In 1984, following the release of *The Gold Diggers*, Potter was invited
by the National Film Theatre to choose a season of sympathetic and
ambient films for its premiere. Many, like *Lola Montes*, dealt with the
theme of performance as well as with the iconic power of the female
face – *Orlando*'s key motifs. Some had Russian landscape as backdrop,
for example, *Alexander Nevsky*, and many reflected on the nature of
cinema in a number of ways: a use of film-within-film or play-within-
film scenes, or 'the use of backstage scenes to illuminate the devices of
illusion making', as in *Hellzapoppin* (Potter 1984, p. 3). All twenty films
dealt directly or indirectly with the instability of gender. Similar interests
surface in Tilda Swinton's career such as a short membership of the
Communist Party of Great Britain while studying for a Social and
Political Science degree at Cambridge (Sawtell 1993, p. 4). Sally Potter
went on to make a documentary history of Russian women in film: *I
Am An Ox, I Am A Horse, I Am A Man, I Am A Woman* (1987/8). The
choice of St Petersburg as a location venue for her film of *Orlando* was

determined, not only by financing arrangements and by the suitability of the locale for *Orlando*'s winter sequences, but also by Potter's admiration for Alexei Rodionov's impressive cineliteracy (cinematographer on Elem Klimov's film *Come and See*) (Glaessner 1992, p. 15).

It matters then that Potter's film gives gender instability specific political and historical inflections. In *Orlando* the seriousness of gender transitivity is indistinguishable from, and underpinned by, a deliberate and sustained pastiche of history. Any theory of postmodernity relies on subverting the traditional stories of history. In postmodernism, history ceases to be a totalising singular discourse but an ever-moving constellation. The American feminist historian Joan Kelly-Gadol, similarly and powerfully repudiating conventional historical categorisations of women, offers a fresh conceptualisation of history from the perspective of women in her pioneering essay 'The Social Relation of the Sexes: Methodological Implications of Women's History' (Kelly-Gadol 1976). By ignoring women's experience, traditional ways of representing history, Kelly-Gadol suggests, also falsify it. In her reassessment of periodisation and historical change, Kelly-Gadol argues that there was no 'renaissance' for women at least not during the Renaissance when women lost economic power and status.

The major success of postmodernism, among its other achievements, is this radical break from *history*. Postmodernists violently disagree about historical dating since they reject the notion that history is packaged in neat, delimited periods. So Cook and Kroker in *The Postmodern Scene* date postmodernism from the fourth century with the Augustinian subversion of embodied power, while Roy Boyne and Ali Rattansi, in *Postmodernism and Society*, more conservatively ascribe its genesis to the Spanish writer Frederico de Onis who in the 1930s first used the term in *Antologia de la poesie espaniola e hispanoamerican* (1934) (Cook and Kroker 1985; Boyne and Rattansi 1990). Woolf mimics traditional versions of history in *The Journal of Mistress Joan Martyn* and creates in *Orlando* a bespoke history which becomes less verifiable as the book progresses. The 'great' and 'representative' male literary figures are not more 'real' than the figure of the fictional writer Nick Greene:

'There, Ma'am, a little to the right of the lamp-post, one of 'em humped, t'other the same as you or me – were Mr. Dryden and Mr Pope. The Captain must have been mistaken, as a reference to

any textbook of literature will show, but the mistake was a kindly
one, and so we let it stand'. (Woolf 1992, p. 160)

Similarly in the film, history is circular not progressive. 'Death' and
'Birth' structure the film as Orlando is miraculously recalled to life.
Scenic closures occur in smaller units than the totality of historical
periods. Near the close of the film in *The Observer's* Marco Polo building, Orlando's 500 year old manuscript is disdainfully dismissed by
corporate publishing:'I think it will sell (*There is a pause as* ORLANDO *listens impassively*) providing you re-write a little. You know, develop the
love interest and give it a happy ending. (*He fingered the stained manuscript rather gingerly*)' (Potter 1994, p. 59). In characteristic postmodern
fashion, Potter parodies this conventional narrative closure with Jimmy
Sommerville's hovering golden angel harking back to his falsetto song
for Queen Elizabeth at the beginning of the film. The reference is to
Walter Benjamin's *Theses on the Philosophy of History,* also taken up by
another postmodern performance artist Laurie Anderson in her album
Strange Angel, in the shared image of history as an angel being blown
backwards into the future (Benjamin 1973; Anderson 1989). The
feminist historian Sheila Rowbotham has drawn attention to this
postmodern perception most significantly in the title of her book *The
Past is Before Us* (Rowbotham 1989). As Rowbotham explains 'the past
has gone by and is already evident for scrutiny. It is after all the future
which is behind us. For with all our gazing and peering we cannot see
what is not yet' (Rowbotham 1989, p. xi).

The song is a perfect anti-closure device. What the film's ending
does is to problematise the fiction of a traditional 'happy ending' while
simultaneously foregrounding that possibility through the video camera
of Orlando's little girl. As Potter explained in conversation with Penny
Florence, the ending of the film, together with the choice of female
rather than male gender for Orlando's child, was:

> one part that I must have rewritten hundreds of times ... The
> whole of the rest of the film up to that point, is determined by,
> if you like, the male line of inheritance ... At the end there is
> another kind of inheritance that becomes possible. I'm certainly
> well aware of how I'm standing on my mother's shoulders and
> grandmother's shoulders. (Florence 1993, p. 282).

Virginia Woolf's own and major parodic gesture is, of course, her writing of Orlando's history. The subtitle of the novel 'a Biography' indicates Woolf's intent. Orlando's biographer is historically malleable rather than having the certainty of masculinity. Historical certainty is thus austerely withheld: 'It is these pauses that are our undoing. It is then that sedition enters the fortress and our troops rise in insurrection' (Woolf 1992, p. 78).

Woolf exposes not just the arbitrariness of historical periods but also linearity. Orlando asks 'what's an "age", indeed? What are "we"? and their progress through Berkeley Square seemed the grouping of two blind ants' (Woolf 1992, p. 196). The notion of Zeitgeist is undermined. Woolf continually contrasts the brief time of exterior events with extended interior musings and undercuts conventional representations of historical periods as separate and legitimate entities: 'This method of writing biography, though it has its merits' [where month follows month] 'is a little bare, perhaps, and the reader, if we go on with it, may complain that he could recite the calendar for himself' (Woolf 1992, p. 254).

Woolf deflates linear history by creating an intrusive biographer who openly questions the historical biographical model: 'The true length of a person's life, whatever *The Dictionary of National Biography* may say, is always a matter of dispute' (Woolf 1992, p. 291). *Orlando* continually revises literary history, including revisions of Woolf's own writings as well as the literary canon: Ariosto's *Orlando Furioso*, Shakespeare's *As You Like It* while the 'Time Passes' sequence from *To The Lighthouse* becomes in *Orlando* 'Time Passed'(and here the exact amount could be indicated in brackets) and nothing whatever happened' (Woolf 1992, p. 94). Parodies abound of Jacobean masques (the Ladies Purity, Chastity and Modesty), sentimental letters, and Victorian romantic verse. One particularly clear example is of orientalism's Othering. As Orlando, now female, leaves behind masculinity for a gypsy life she also has to leave behind the correlate of masculinity: romantic individualism. At first Orlando attempts a Wordsworthian sublime:

The purple iris wrought her to cry out in ecstasy at the goodness, the beauty of nature ... raising her eyes again, she beheld the eagle soaring and imagined its raptures and made them her own ... all the young gipsies laughed. But Rustum el Sadi ... had the deepest suspicion that her God was Nature . . . He showed her his right foot, crushed where a rock had fallen. (Woolf 1992, pp. 138–9)

Woolf deflates Orlando's 'masculine' appropriation of Nature and romantic abstraction with Rustum el Sadi's life history of rural hardship.

Book and film share in deflating *Wuthering Heights*. In Potter's *Orlando* the maze opens onto a heath and Orlando runs in Cathy Earnshaw fashion through the hugely exaggerated dry ice of Gothic and melodrama costume films. Similarly Woolf continues to parody Orlando's absurd belief in a union with nature: 'Then, some strange ecstasy came over her. Some wild notion she had of following the birds to the rim of the world and flinging herself on the spongy turf . . . her ankle was broken' (Woolf 1992, pp. 236–7).

But, as Sally Potter suggests in interview with Walter Donahue, postmodern literary strategies do not necessarily work in cinema:

> Because the book is almost a running commentary on the history of literature as the vehicle for consciousness there had to be a cinematic equivalent to what happened to that kind of consciousness post war. In other words the fracturing of her consciousness and the arrival of the electronic age. (Donahue 1993, p. 12)

Potter's most sustained cinematic equivalent to literary parody is her use of motifs and scenes from the films of Michael Powell to whom *Orlando* is dedicated. As she herself admits 'my favourite film by Michael Powell and Emeric Pressburger is *A Matter of Life and Death* and when interviewing Powell for a television film Potter sketches him with a Powell-like palette of colours 'shiny apple-red cheeks' (Potter 1992, p. 25). Potter chose Powell's *The Red Shoes* for her National Film Theatre programme and she points out that Powell's hovering 'between realism and nonrealism' puts him in 'a magic zone' (Dargis 1993, p. 42). Just before his death it was Powell's active support which enabled Potter to complete *Orlando* and a more direct pastiche of Powell's *Gone to Earth* appears in the scene of Orlando running in the garden.

As befits the thick complexity of postmodernism, *Orlando* mimics singular histories and a singular aesthetic with multiple visual references. Shelmerdine mimics Rochester's entrance in *Jane Eyre*, galloping 'towards her out of the mist' on a similar large black phallic horse and, like Rochester, *'is flung to the ground and lies spreadeagled in front of* ORLANDO'. Not insignificantly the postmodern gesture receives the imprimatur of the intimate gaze. *'ORLANDO looks questioningly into the camera'* (Potter 1994, p. 51). *Alice in Wonderland* is recalled in Potter's giant topiary teacups fronting the house. *Dr Zhivago* has a diagonal relation to Orlando's snow-sleigh ride with Sasha. The doors of John Ford's *The Searchers* frame the scene of Orlando's sex change recalling and deflating that famously misogynist Ford gesture of framing women characters in smaller versions of the larger doorways open to male characters.

Other visual references which Potter parodies are from high art. Tilda Swinton's red hair and pale skin (much like Potter's own) matches both the Lely miniature referred to in the novel as well as the Hatfield House portrait of Elizabeth I. The scene where Orlando surveys her naked female form (*Orlando* was the first film to show pubic hair in Japan) echoes Botticelli's *Birth of Venus*. There are postmodern inflections in Potter's other films. In the shooting and editing process of *The Gold Diggers* Potter 'attempted to create "layers" in each scene of genre references and internal cross references in order to create a spectator tension with filmic expectations' (Cook 1984, p. 15). *Thriller* parodies the sexual politics of Puccini's *La Bohème* from Mimi's point of view. Similarly *Orlando* puns on the jumpy quality of lantern slides with Brechtian chapter headings 'Politics', 'History'.

In interview with Valentina Agostinis in 1981, Potter suggested that *Thriller* worked through 'engagement rather than necessarily with identification. There is a pleasure in analysis, in unravelling, in thinking' (Agostinis 1981, p. 47). I would argue that *Orlando's* postmodernism similarly resists easy identifications: 'It is time for women to take up our inheritance, an inheritance of a different kind. That's why the daughter is at the end playing with a little movie camera' (Dowell 1993, p. 16). Potter creates an active-looking subject woman rather than the object of traditional historians or film directors; Orlando's constant looks to camera reject any object status (see Figure 8). In addition *Orlando's* narrative deconstructs history into a series of fragmented scenes. As Potter puts it: 'I have tried to subvert what is being set up . . . that seemed to me a useful way of looking at British history. In each scene, in each frame even there is an element of contradiction' (Francke 1993,

p. 5). Potter captures and then deflates historical periods in several ways. For example, Orlando receives the Order of the Bath, the imprimatur of imperial history, ironically framed by an Islamic arch and watched by an audience merely of a few servants. Again Orlando's eighteenth-century femininity is parodied by juxtaposition with excessively 'feminised' and absurdly shaped and draped furniture: 'The premise of *Orlando* is that all history is imagined history and leaves out all the most important bits anyway. There are traces of historical information that can be reinterpreted in various ways, so we are in a situation of artifice' (Florence 1993, p. 278). *Orlando* decentres conventional narrative with its rapid sequencing of scenes, and sharp and contrasting juxtapositions of sound with image. Orlando's 'we'll fly away as free as birds' to Sasha is parodied with usual excess in the script '*Fireworks shoot up into the night sky* . . . Orlando can be heard declaiming' (Potter 1994, p. 19). In postmodern fashion, objects/surface/music (which Potter composed) are crucial signifiers, not linear narrative.

Texture and colour coding replace the cause and effect of narrative continuity. Each period has a precise palette from Elizabethan

Figure 8   Tilda Swinton and her niece Jessica Swinton in *Orlando* (1992)

black/white to Constantinople blue which floods both costume and background objects (the Khan's blue cuffs and Khiva's blue tiles). Potter's cinematic choreography is extremely precise. For example, in the scene where Orlando loses her house the door opens into an apparently endless hole (see Figure 9). Odd objects in each scene underscore and symbolise a perceptual and metaphorical mapping of character, as much as a cognitive mapping. And as she, herself, suggests:'framing is the magic key to other scenes. (Donahue 1993, p. 12): Orlando and Sasha erupt into love through an arch; gauzes and veils frame Orlando in Constantinople and so forth. Potter replaces character motive and narrative expectations (which to some extent are already foreclosed by the'mothering' text) with sensual pleasures.

In a letter to R. C. Trevelyan about *Orlando,* Virginia Woolf felt herself to be similarly decentering historical and gender perspectives.

> Of course the effort to break with strict representation is very unsettling, and many things were not controlled as they should have been ... but the method was not so much at fault as my ignorance of how to do it psychologically ... I'm sorry about the obscurity. (Woolf 1976, p. 588)

Jane Flax has presciently argued that the common ground of feminism and postmodernism is precisely this new theory of subjectivity which can draw on memories, on the unconscious to construct new social subjectivities (Flax 1987). Part of the interest of *Orlando* for any exploration of postmodernism is that the book dates from a time before such ways of rethinking gender identity and historical pressures were termed postmodern. Yet as Orlando's biographer herself suggests, Orlando is a spectacular example of the contradictions of the post-modern:

> This extraordinary discrepancy between time on the clock and time in the mind is less known than it should be and deserves fuller investigation ... What is love? What friendship? What truth? but directly he came to think about them, his whole past, which seemed to him of extreme length and variety, rushed into the falling second, swelled it a dozen times its natural size, coloured it a thousand tints, and filled it with all the odds and ends in the universe. (Woolf 1992, p. 95).

Figure 9   Orlando loses her house

Virginia Woolf questions the gender meaning-making processes of history. This question is at the heart of postmodernism. Woolf pluralises historical knowledge and asks important questions about gender dimorphism. In *A Poetics of Postmodernism*, Linda Hutcheon suggests that 'historiographic metafiction' 'use parody not only to restore history and memory' but also at the same time 'to put into question the authority of any act of writing'. One of the effects of this 'discursive pluralising' is to give value to the 'ex-centric' 'that which is "different" is valorized in opposition to, élitist alienated Otherness' (Hutcheon 1988, pp. 129–30). *Orlando* the film mixes intertexts of dance, a child's video, 'great' literature and *Orlando* the novel is similarly multigeneric with a wealth of poetry, letters, masque and biography. This explicit decentering of historical/narrative authority is postmodern.

There are, however, problems in identifying postmodernism too closely with feminism. To date, postmodernism has been a very masculine enterprise often answering to post-Fordism by marketing past architecture and dead artists. And I think it highly significant that the architect Charles Jencks should date postmodernism from the destruction of a domestic environment – the dynamiting of St Louis Pruitt-Igoe Housing. Postmodernism often ignores the crucial instabilities of ethnicity and homosexuality both as historically constituted and in living speakers. The radical lesbian theorist, Sheila Jeffreys, is suspicious of attacks on the concept 'woman' at a time when lesbian, Black and other oppressed groups making use of these categories, are only just beginning to make space for themselves historically, culturally and in the academy' (Jeffreys 1994, p. 112). While the certainties of regulatory sex/gender regimes remain in place, she suggests that we have to have some certainty about who we are in order to organise politically. Woman's body is absent in some postmodern writing which makes no serious consideration of women's subjective and social experiences of mothering, of the emancipatory needs of different ethnic groups, nor of the inequalities of difference, and the need of women, Black and white, for agency and historical truth. As Nancy Hartsock argues 'postmodern theories ... deny marginalised people the right to participate in defining the terms of interaction with people in the mainstream' (Hartsock 1987, p. 191).

However there is little doubt that *feminist* postmodernism has radical and forward-looking ideas about gender and history. Potter, resolutely postmodern, refuses the fixed term 'feminist' – 'I can't use the word any more because it's become debased' – while she embraces a feminist trajectory: 'I now try to find more subtle ways, more indirect or appropriate ways to be individual or the circumstances to express some of these ideas' (Florence 1993, p. 279). Tilda Swinton's erotic looks to camera, like Woolf's gentle interrogations, bond with viewer/reader in a shared process of historical meaning-making. The move to new meanings of history, the whole impulsive charge against those metanarratives of patriarchal, naturalised sexual divisions makes *Orlando* – film and book – perfectly postmodern.

Chapter 7

PRACTISING FEMINIST THEORY

———⟨≻⟨≻———

INTRODUCTION

Understanding the personal as political – how identity is constructed and represented – is the task of feminist theory. Questions about the place of sexual difference in our conscious and unconscious under-standings of identity, and the relation between difference, identity and social and economic inequalities are the specific questions which invite feminist theory into the political arena. As Chapter 1 above argues, the processes by which individual women recognise themselves as female are often caught up in compulsions of the visual. Indeed, the social face of femininity is constructed by mechanisms of visual representation, such as advertising and film, which gain women's collaboration and consent via specific forms of identification. The power of politics resides in the production and dissemination of ideology which in turn can rest on an ability to *re*-present the personal within a specific visu-al realm. The theme of *Feminism and Film* is that the power of feminism comes from its ability to show how individual women are collectively constructed politically in that realm and usually oppressed.

BRITISH FEMINIST FILM-MAKING FROM 1970 TO TODAY

During the 1970s, feminist independent film-makers and media groups joined other activists and academics in a counter-culture existing out-side mainstream cinema, theatre and television. The expansion of higher education including the founding of four new universities in the mid-1960s with their annual arts festivals, the ending of theatre censorship in 1968 and the growth of feminist and gay theatre (for example, the Almost Free Theatre's Women's and Gay Theatre Festivals of 1973–4), combined with feminist film production (the London Women's Film Group was founded in 1972), to create a progressive cultural force (Wandor 1981).

The initial aim was to produce alternative media narratives often with a specific political purpose or expressive of family or personal histories, supported by an independent exhibition circuit, including student film societies, arts laboratories and other fringe venues. Film and video contributed creative energy to the Women's Art Movement: the germinal 'Women's Images of Men' ICA exhibition (see Chapter 1) drew such an overwhelming response to its advertisement for submissions from video and performance artists that a second exhibition, 'About Time', purely devoted to film/video and performance was organised by Catherine Elwes and Rose Garrard, with a major catalogue contribution from Sally Potter. (Parker and Pollock 1987).

These fresh and distinctive media practices were often made possible by supportive left wing local authority funding such as the Greater London Council (GLC) and by Women's Aid and health groups' need for educational videos. In turn feminist radical aspirations were both political and personal; so, for example, video groups worked with miners wives documenting individual and collective struggles during the Miners Strike of 1984–5 (Jordan and Weedon 1995). Similarly, Catherine Elwes's film *With Child* (1984) was about her first pregnancy. Elwes suggests 'in opposition to the traditional masculinity of the camera eye, my work emphasises the presence of the female author' (Elwes 1986, p. 6). Often these new and marginal films deliberately subverted the narrative conventions of commercial cinema. Along with the privileging of the personal went a critique of temporality in a re-editing of television and film images for ironic critical effects. So, Sandra Goldbacher and Kim Flitcroft's *Polka Dots and Moonbeams* and *Night of a Thousand Eyes* are montages of Hollywood features, and television advertisements with live action. Alternatively, feminists humorously deconstructed the ways in which women are stereotyped in such advertisements, for example, Marty St James and Anne Wilson's *An American Romance* (O'Pray 1986).

What united feminist independent film makers, and distinguished them from their male counterparts, was an oppositional stance to purely avant-garde experiments. In 'A Bid For Radical Naturalism',

Catherine Elwes attacks Scratch Video and the New Narrative work of the early 1980s because, she argues, this work perpetuates the English avant-garde preoccupation with form to the exclusion of content. Feminist artists, Elwes claims, are more concerned about the reality of the nuclear age 'today's ultimate narrative' and for 'many feminist and gay activists narrative had always been an essential part' of practice (Elwes 1986B, p. 20).

By the mid 1980s feminist film and art practice along with media pressure groups were part of a broad-based move to de-centre conventional representations of women – the theme of the first National Feminist Film and Video Conference held in Cardiff in 1983. The 'personal is political' theme informed distribution and exhibition circuits with the founding of the feminist distribution companies, Cinema of Women and Circles, who promoted current work as well as revivifying the films of little known historic women film-makers. The typology of distribution is a microcosm of the political trajectory of feminism from the 1980s to the 1990s. For example, Circles' 1987 catalogue with its two hundred titles catered to newly-burgeoning women's studies with educational packages such as *All Work and No Pay* on domestic labour. With the launch of Cinenova in 1991 (which brought together Cinema of Women with Circles) the 1991 catalogue lists over 350 titles now organised into fresh themes for the 1990s: 'lesbian', 'race' and 'world view'. In addition, the curator Bev Zalcock points to the new and lively radical work of lesbian camp, for example, *Goblin Market* (1993) directed by Jo Smith (Zalcock 1994).

Feminist films coincided with a flurry of feminist media monitoring and institutional analysis. The Women's Monitoring Network held its first nationwide monitoring campaign in 1981 detailing with exact precision media representations on one day of women as sex objects (excluding pornography) and were inundated with over one thousand cuttings (Davies *et al.* 1987). The subsequent and rapid growth of feminist critiques drew on this work of activist groups such as the Women's Media Action Group, founded to oppose sexism in the media and the Women's Media Resource Project and Women's Film, TV and Video Network which provided media skills for women wishing to work in the media or who were already part of the industry (Brown *et al.* 1993). The parallels between feminist film work and feminist theory and women's studies are, as *Feminism and Film* has been arguing, quite uncanny and the current recognition of feminist and radical media activism – major British cities have feminist media visual enterprise centres such as VERA productions in Leeds – contradicts pessimistic claims about the death of British feminism.

As crucial as the system of film distribution and activist networks was, and continues to be, feminist independent film and video was funded and given visibility more dramatically, and paradoxically, by an institution. The launch of television's Channel Four in 1982 has, as Annette Kuhn argues 'changed the face of British independent film-making' and thus, Britain's cultural landscape (Kuhn 1994, p. 220). It was no coincidence, as the gay film-maker Stuart Marshall points out, that Channel Four chose to fund the first gay series *Out on Tuesday* 'at the same time that Section 28 was proposed and passed' in the House of Commons banning public funding for gay rights promotion (Chamberlain *et al.* 1993, p. 54). Building on the co-operative film-making of groups such as Cinema Action and the Berwick Street Collective, Channel Four specifically funded, and indeed made possible, a series of nationwide independent film workshops. From the first Festival of Independent British Cinema held in Bristol in February 1975, the rapid expansion of such workshops in Britain is attested to by the Labour Party's planned support for a structure of twenty-five small production units with permanent staff (Stoneham 1992). At its height, Channel Four's budget of £2 million considerably strengthened the production capacity of the independent sector and, importantly, it had a special remit to encourage Asian, Black and women's groups (Stoneham 1992).

Franchise workshops were franchised under the Workshops Declaration established in 1982 by the ACTT (Association of Cinemato-graph, Television and Allied Technicians) in consultation with funding organisations, including the BFI (British Film Institute) and regional arts associations. This enabled workshops to have one hour's worth of programmes transmitted by Channel Four each year. The Workshop Declaration encouraged staff to be multi-skilled rather than operating normal union agreements (Muir 1987). But by the 1990s the danger of monopoly institutional funding was clearer. With the decline of alter-native sources of finance, for example, local authority support, due to the abolition of the GLC by the Conservative government and the closure of women's committees nationally, Channel Four, *de facto*,

created a 'dependency culture' by funding a 'closed cartel' of self-per-
petuating workshops and commodifying projects into easier-to-screen
magazine formats such as the feminist programme *First Sex*.

Workshops, like Amber Films in Newcastle, set up with a specific
social or political emphasis to reflect the lives and values of a particular sector of society, not surprisingly moved away from small scale,
politically passionate work on social issues of the North East to more
'mainstream' films. Perhaps for these reasons Annette Kuhn now
pessimistically claims that 'the conditions of existence for a feminist
countercinema do not exist in the 1990s' (Kuhn 1994, p. 247). In addition, as Rod Stoneham points out, there are still 'a disproportionately
low number of women, non-white, or working class people in positions
of power in British TV (Stoneham 1992, p. 128). More significantly for
the future visibility of feminist film-making 'there were four women
among the original 13 commissioning editors' for Channel Four in 1983
and 'almost a decade later it is two out of 14' (Stoneham 1992, p. 128).

However, while it might be true that gender issues are less structurally central, issues of difference are directly addressed by Channel
Four. Black and lesbian film-makers did gain unprecedented access to
mainstream media in an institutional process of inclusion. Black film
workshops, such as Sankofa, where Black women are prominent
received production finance. Indeed James Snead describes how a
showing of Afro-British films in America at UCLA in 1987 made British
Black and women's film-making seem 'a vibrant and growing film
culture' (Snead 1988, p. 47).

The 1980s generation of film-makers like Pratibha Parmar and Joy
Chamberlain who emerged from the different Asian, Black and lesbian
communities of Britain, created a powerful new discursive opposition to
notions of 'mainstream' and 'Otherness' (Parmar 1993). Joy Chamberlain
points out that the larger budgets of the 1980s enabled her to move on
from making campaign documentaries for Women Against Rape to
more cathartic narratives (Chamberlain *et al.* 1993). Similarly Black
feminist artists were deeply involved in multigeneric art work creating
a plural and heterogeneous art incorporating video and photography,
supported by feminist journals such as *FAN* (*Feminist Art News*) (Sulter
1990).

What is at stake in this varied but potent history is that media work
is crucial to feminist cultural politics and theory. Firstly, the media are

a major influence on women's perceptions of themselves and constructions of identity since it is in the media that visual fantasies of, and
for, particular subjectivities are created. Second, although there is
currently a large body of feminist film theory beginning with Laura
Mulvey's pathbreaking essay, 'Visual Pleasure and Narrative Cinema'
practices of transformation have been under theorised (see Chapter 1
above). I want to elaborate on this strange situation of the dropping
out of sight in feminist film theory of community feminist practice,
through an illustrative case study of collaborative projects in tape slide.
I will analyse some small-scale, artisanal work in order to address the
congruence of the experiential, the political and the theoretical. Each
tape slide is described in detail because publishing costs restricted the
number of illustrations. Tape slide is a treasure trove for feminist praxis
and feminist theory since it questions reception, simulation, history
and media stereotypes. Tape slide has a special purchase on both the
political and the personal because when we watch tape slide we can see
the processes of manufacture in the narrative sequences community
activists and students choose in order to represent gendered, raced and
classed identities. Both collective labour and an affirmation of a
social/political message are often figured in the process.

FEMINIST PRAXIS: A CASE STUDY

From 1989 Women's Studies at the University of East London (UEL) has
collaborated with local community photographers in tape slide projects.
Tape slide is a cheap but potentially very powerful medium. Two or more
carousel slide projectors, pulsed by a Gemini machine from a four to
eight track audio tape, overlay still photographic images following a
sequence of both spoken and musical sound. The sense of narrative
combined with overlays or jarring juxtapositions is enhanced by music,
poetry and personal stories.

   The aim of this work is to teach media skills, utilising a high component of political, issue-based material. This means that academic
feminist theory can both respond to women's political concerns as well
as to their future employment success as 'owners' of multi-technical
skills (shooting, copying, editing, storyboard and soundtrack mixing).
Collaborative work routines play a fundamental part, as do anti-racist
working practices and disability awareness. Selecting images from

magazines, newspapers and elsewhere and setting up joint photographic shoots in groups provides students with the opportunity to work collaboratively by pooling ideas and skills.

Perhaps not surprisingly, students choose to deploy the personal as their main subject matter. Tapes creatively examine icons of mothering, reproductive technology, weight and beauty issues among others. Yet crucially, each time students locate personal representations in a political context by making a public performative act of experimental self-perception, the latter does not absorb the former but sets up interesting tensions and dualisms.

In the production of student tape slides the notion that 'the personal is political' is an intrinsic part of the medium. Students often enjoy reproducing personal material with a raw, rough, 'visible' editing style, delighting in the anti-élite, cheap, community conditions in which they work. They control the means of production. Unlike mainstream film, tape slide carries an inherent hostility to commercial representations, by, for example, often disrupting cause and effect narratives and privileging everyday experience. Tape slide forces the viewer to think about the sequencing of chosen events and the viewer's place in similar events. The disparity between sound and image highlights the message that the personal is not being smoothly re-presented to us but is part of a process we create, since sound can dominate more than vision. Revealing disjunctions in address, tape slide's anti-seamless process can be a visual political theory.

THEORY

In constructing a triad, film/feminism/femininity, we witness the same problem of the personal and the political which frequently plays itself out inside feminist thinking elsewhere. Two feminist theorists, Jacqueline Rose and Avtar Brah, have confronted these issues from different directions. Together both critics offer helpful ways of understanding the likely tensions between representations, politics and the personal.

Jacqueline Rose's *Sexuality in the Field of Vision* makes a feminist examination of the interface between the personal, sexual fantasy, the visual, and psychoanalysis (Rose 1986). In her work Rose draws attention to the visual processes by which we learn and come to understand the meanings of sexual difference. Her critique of visual forms involves a questioning of sexual differences and the ways in which normative representations 'reassuringly' stabilise these differences.

Avtar Brah is a Ugandan-Asian critic who has written extensively about the relation between race as a visual signifier and gender. In 'Questions of Difference and International Feminism' she argues that questions about cultural politics (in which we could include the media) should involve a 'politics of identification' rather than a 'politics of identity' (Brah 1991). That is, Brah argues that identity or the personal is always part of heterogeneous discursive processes. It is never a given intact essence.

For both critics, however, despite the very different disciplinary, ethnic and political positions they occupy, the scene of the personal is one in which processes of representation are fundamentally at issue. Artistic products (for example, tape slide) argues Brah, should not be read as static symbols of cultural essentialism but as expressions of the processes of psychological and personal diversity. Rose agrees that we should pay careful attention to the processes of film as much as to the film product in order to challenge constructed concepts of psychic identity.

Students, like anyone else, are drawn in by the fantasy formats of film and literature, but, students in women's studies are drawn to another question: how are representations of the personal (their mothers, children, bodies) tied to fantasies constructed by the media in order to limit women's political unconscious as well as our political actions. The issue of the representational process of the personal therefore leads outside the limits of the academy to an understanding of how sexual difference is politically in play. The dialogue between media representations and feminism is a space where the larger political complexity of the personal is 'visible'.

Rose's *Sexuality in the Field of Vision* engages in this dialogue and is a sophisticated thinking through of the tension between representations of the title's two terms 'sexuality' and 'vision'. The book's overall aim is twofold: firstly to assess the important relation of psychoanalysis and feminism in contemporary cultural debates, and second to assess how images of sexual difference at the heart of cultural institutions are tied to effects of the unconscious (or we could claim more generally to the personal). The book points out that Freud himself indissolubly links images and sexual difference in his essay 'Leonardo da Vinci and a Memory of His Childhood'. Freud often entangles the visual in constructions of sexual difference, for example, in scenarios where perception founders as boys refuse to believe anatomical differences or when the pleasure of looking becomes the excess of scopophilia (the drive to look). For Freud, Rose argues, the relation of viewer and scene is one of fracture. The representation of sexual difference has therefore less to do with the content of the scene and more to do with the subjectivity, and the processes of perception, of the viewer.

What Rose perceptively teases out is that the relation between sexuality/identity and the image (the visual) are caught up in 'artistic' processes because, following Lacan, we understand that sexual identities and their representations involve constructed fantasies. The problem for Rose is that in psychoanalysis, the staging of sexual difference has already taken place. But processes of the visual are crucial because they can demonstrate oscillations in the domain of difference. Where Freud takes the visual to be a simulacrum of the unconscious, post-Freudian thinking takes a more complex view. Representation is understood to be more arbitrary. To postmodernists such as Meaghan Morris representation is always a problem, never a reality (Morris 1988A).

The strength of Rose's work and its pertinence for feminist theory, film practice and women's studies, is that she points to the potential dangers this cultural move into postmodernism might entail. Firstly, psychoanalytic concepts of the unconscious (the personal) have less prominence. Second, the political value of cultural artifacts is diminished. Third, the concept of textuality (or process) is often detached from sexual difference. Rose subtly suggests that how we see – the personal engagement with the image – belongs to 'a political intention'. More than this the 'intention is historical'. I am particularly intrigued by Rose's interest in process and 'mutual relation' because this relates to a debate about issues of difference currently occupying feminist philosophers and sociologists. For example, discussions of epistemological processes particularly in science draw attention to the ways in which experience and analysis are not dichotomous but interactive in that all analysis is shaped by the political context and conjectures of the viewer (Bleier 1986; Collins 1990; Harding 1991; Hirsch and Fox Keller 1990; Pateman and Gross 1986; Smith 1987; Stanley 1990).

Avtar Brah's 'Questions of Difference and International Feminism' is a good example of these concerns. Brah's extensive research into British labour markets, Asian women's representation and identity formation is too complex to summarise here. But in brief, she argues that respect for cultural differences is more likely if cultures are conceived less in terms of collections of reified artifacts and more as processes. An important issue in feminism is recognising the processes of women's diversity with regard to class, race and sexuality. The degree to which we can work across our differences may depend on conceptual representations drawing on aspects of the visual with which we understand those differences. As suggested above, rather than a politics of identity, Brah persuasively suggests that we will better achieve coalitions through a politics of identification. That is, we often learn to see ourselves as part of 'imagined communities' and we can identify with the politics of these groups without ever having been part of a specific history. Brah concludes that if cultural forms are conceived collectively, then cultural products are much less likely to be reified or essentialist. Cultural diversity, particularly in the media, encompasses an immense range of psychological and emotional expressions to remind us, amongst other things, that our personal experiences are not constituted solely within oppressions.

While Brah's focus is largely on the social, her suggestive concepts of 'imagined communities' and a 'politics of identification' are highly relevant to Rose's visual concerns. Placing both accounts side by side we could argue that collective media practice within a feminist 'vision' might very well set up a 'mutual relation' between the unconscious and the social, between the personal and the political. The aim is to pull media work in the direction of recognising the political construction of the personal and back again to personal fantasies. The issue is to reconcile the personal with forms of representation which in their process recognise women's need for political change. Media study necessarily throws into question any division between an assumed 'real' world of politics and a fantasy/imagined existence of the personal because it helps us think through how the political is always imagined 'fantastically'.

Yet in feminist activism in the late 1960s and early 1970s the personal was often narrowly defined – largely in terms of personal oppressions and experiences of victimisation. The purpose of women's groups, both outside and inside the academy then, as today, was empowerment. But 'empowerment' was often taken to mean simply the provision of a safe place for women – a space where women could share different experiences and personal realities in a safe environment (Kramarae and Spender 1992).

In addition, the concept of a 'women-centred perspective' was frequently proposed but its precise methodology remained unfocussed. Following Bowles and Duelli-Klein (1983) feminist thinking has fractured into a poststructuralist rejection of the essentialism inherent in such a perspective (Riley 1984), attacks on the ethnocentrism implied by its exclusions (Spelman 1988; Spivak 1987), psychoanalytic (Lacanian) attacks on a unified perspective (Mitchell and Rose 1982) and anxieties about the heterosexism of a singular perspective (Fuss 1991). Yet a desire to retain the category for feminist analysis is felt very strongly, not least by students entering women's studies. Attempts to define a feminist standpoint epistemology have been more thorough-going in sociology, particularly in Liz Stanley's work (Stanley 1990). Of all the elements that are condensed in the notion of feminist standpoint, the visual, to date, has been occluded. The strategy of this chapter is to engage the visual through feminist praxis, as an element of feminist identity.

In visual productions students can make connections between private and public personae, can question the authenticity of public selves and can generate ideas about the nature of knowledge and authority. But I have written elsewhere of the possible dangers involved in encouraging students to deny their social subjectivities by allowing the work of academic deconstruction to become their new 'identity' (see Humm 1991B). An oscillation between the poles of the personal and political and the exploration of tensions between these poles can sometimes harness the personal as a means to educational change as long as this is not buried in the therapeutic so that means become ends.

Women's studies is not unique in this regard. Personal growth movements characterised many educational worlds of the 1970s in a post-60s belief that giving personal experience more representational weight in intellectual life and work would magically transform education and result in a transformation of society. Movements for educational reform, such as humanistic psychology, argued that the acquisition of positivistic scientific knowledge inhibits the personal changes needed to bring about social change (Halmos 1978; Rowan 1976). But, as Chandra Mohanty suggests, because issues of gender are contested differentially in different historical conjunctures, our theoretical constructs must come from 'the context being analysed', not simply from personal analysis (Mohanty 1984, p. 345). In other words the empowerment of women is indissolubly linked to discursive contexts which include the visual.

TAPE SLIDE

The feminist subject for feminist theory and visual practice and women's studies must be more a collective subject representing heterogeneous differences. Media work, by involving the multiple variables of viewer, subject and collective makers sometimes simultaneously represents both dominant (white), and potentially dominated, experience (sexual orientation). It is this sense of continuous and creative counterpoint between identifications (personal) and process (collective) which underpins media work. Engaged with the practical issues of costing and skills deployment, such study can never be accused of neglecting power forces because inevitably a media product is a historically specific result of particular production relations. Tape slide addresses its own conditions of production and reception within the context of the personal, matching what Liz Stanley defines as the aim of feminist praxis which is 'to draw the *process* of knowledge production in research and theorising, into its *product* (Stanley 1990, p. 4).

A constant theme in contemporary feminism is its resistance to dominant representations of women in advertising, photography and film. Tape-slide images often address the dominant but can establish unexpected juxtapositions between the bounded areas of high and popular culture, most obviously, for example, by mixing family photos with slides of oil paintings. These reconnoitres defamiliarise the familiar as well as the family. It is the process of meaning-making which is crucial. Tape slide offers a mediating 'neutrality' between life-world and social-world as the 'I' moves to 'we' and collective dialogue produces the possibility of new subjectivities.

One good example of this at UEL was *Beauty From Within* a tape slide dealing with issues of weight. Large and slim students photographed themselves and deconstructed dominant images from magazines, re-staging moments of food obsession and the powerful forbiddens of femininity by deliberately emphasising the grotesqueries of size. The students speculated visually on how to be heavy women in a society which aims to make powerful heavy women unrepresentable. The tape slide made a double move – of collective critique and playful/painful reconstruction – aiming to destabilise the power of social representations. Thus, statistical body measurements were overlaid onto fantasy images combined with a strong voiceover reading of a diary of bulimea. This combination impressively disarticulated the power of advertising. The tape slide took up the critical challenges of both Rose and Brah: to *re*-present the process of 'mutual relation' between the personal and representations, and to create a 'politics of identification' with heavy women which any viewer could share. Self imagery was not the starting point but rather the collective work of identity creation.

Tape slide can never be 'arty' because its multi-media 'crudity' inevitably challenges the concept of an immaculate art work. Its shaky generic status challenges originality and essence. The personal as political often emerges more strongly through tape slide than it does through other photographic genres. Tape slide is sometimes eccentric in technical execution, if precise in intention, but the preoccupation with juxtaposition allows tape slide's role as a political process to be registered. The aberrant use of advertisements and readings against the grain are often compelling. The construction of deconstruction sets loose a range of unintended associations, by their nature invalidating transparent reality. There is no 'painterly' gesture.

Tape slide offers a great flexibility and potential for dislocating existing representations and for constructing new knowledges. If one of the stylistic norms of magazines and advertising is a constant deployment of a fleeting, arrested 'woman' then tape slide offers continuous flowing superimpositions and multiplicity. Its fluid 'photomontage' can display recognisable people and objects, while inviting political thinking through visual effects. The juxtapositions of original photographs and advertisements create fractured images of femininity and graphically portray the motley ways in which women experience the personal.

TROPISMS

Other tape slides at UEL addressed the question of high culture in itself, for example, traditional art's representation of mothering. *Reproducing Ourselves* displayed figurative, representational art from the Renaissance to the present in order to show how the personal experience of mothering is never satisfactorily represented (Rich 1976). Yet the work deconstructed itself by revealing an interplay between the students' unconscious desire for motherhood with the conscious political activity of destabilising representations of motherhood. The powerful visual juxtapositions of, say, Bellini's paintings with *Prima* magazine stereotypes contrasted oddly with strangely mood-enhancing music of strong triads. The tape slide seemed outside the rules of intelligibility since its meaning was not located on screen but as a process of disruption. The writer Nathalie Sarraute devised a term 'tropisms' for her similar 'attempt to record experience as it is felt before it passes through the filter of language' (Kramarae and Treichler 1985, p. 459). It was no surprise to learn several months later that one of these graduating students had given birth, since tape slides often bring up unspoken and repressed experiences (tropisms), here for example a desire to mother, making a kind of public visual knowledge invoking unconscious personal quests.

Studying Women: Five Student Autobiographies gained political strength from representing both the attractions of domesticity as well as its dreariness, and from a politicisation of domestic issues including sexual abuse. On the one level the chosen images were personal – domestic objects – appropriate to a very personal event. On the other hand, the tape slide made the 'personal' 'political' by accompanying these images with a strong plea for a more public means of telling. The tape slide was organised around the need to tell. Words printed on gels were superimposed on images at regular points. The message varied in graphic style, size and duration and broke with narrative continuity. The graphic information carried its own resonances and associations, matching and mismatching the gentle voiceover. The direct personal moments placed the viewer in contact with a positional politics. Words and images clarified, or sometimes undercut, each other and, enhanced by the compulsions of soundtrack and darkened viewing space, the personal gained a public credibility. The re-presentation of the personal allowed new political questions to emerge about family histories, sexual practices and identity.

As a result of identifying the issues involved in cinema's determinisms, Rose points to what a feminist politics of representation must address: the collision between a feminism drawn to images from the personal with a technological apparatus involving an optics of realism

and perfect reproducability designed to gain the consent of the unconscious. She argues that 'putting the concept of sexual difference back
into the discussion of the cinematic apparatus', is the problem of
cinema, but the question of the processes which this activity inevitably
entails could be part of the solution (Rose 1986, p. 213).

I find it fruitful here in *Feminism and Film* to have briefly explored
tape slide as a film form since the principle of sound/image juxtaposition at the heart of tape slide is similar to the principle of montage in
the cinema. For feminist praxis the possibility of working with an
interpellation of the unconscious (through processes of camera projection) and subverting these processes by contrasting the visual with a
distanced scripto-audio offers the possibility of political art. As the
viewer moves from subject to subject position 'historical specificity and
universalism need not be counterposed against each other' (Brah 1991,
p. 174). As women work collectively, swapping skills and blurring
authorship, the film techniques and political content criss-cross into a
new identity – constituting visual form.

CONCLUSION

What I have been trying to convey, both with these historical examples
of British feminist film praxis and the student work, is to show how
filmic processes can be exploited to create representations operating on
several interconnected levels of the personal, the political and visual
pleasure. The core of feminist theory is a struggle with representations
and with established forms of knowledge which align the personal
with specific representative (or usually unrepresentative) social identities. To deconstruct these false selves involves applying a constant
pressure of something repressed – the personal – that can come
sharply into focus through alternative practices. For example, Asian,
Black and white students often open up a visual space for images
normally marginalised or made invisible in traditional curricula. This is
because they control both the means of production – slide projectors,
tape recorders, cameras – and the forms of representation – the images
and languages of, for instance, anti-racism. With tape slide students
can undertake the political task of addressing social issues in a public
way while making visible and legitimate their personal views and lives
in a visually pleasurable way.

The affinity between film/feminism/female cannot, of course, in itself create political change but equally, recognition of this affinity through collective practices could reveal the fallibility of traditional knowledges. All this is well covered ground. What remains important is that a recontextualisation of personal experience and the move from the personal as private to the personal as publicly visible raises issues about the relation of the two. Of course, as Lucy Lippard realistically argues 'feminist art has had to exist for the most part outside the boundaries imposed by the male-nominated art world' (Lippard 1987, p. 233). But if the function of the feminist visual is to open up political possibilities then who knows what new images of our persons and of our politics we may see?

AFTERWORD

—◁▷—

There is no tidy conclusion to be reached from evaluating and valuing the ways in which gender and film mesh together. This is particularly so because one of the aims of *Feminism and Film* is to braid and unbraid many and various elements of gender representation involving differing ethnicities, sexual preferences, and aesthetic issues: the chapters of *Feminism and Film* criss-cross disciplines to engage psychoanalysis, postmodernism as well as literary and other theories. But if there is no conclusion, as such, one assumption which pervades this book has certainly been confirmed. That assumption is that the relationship between gender and film is primarily cultural – a web of constituent social, psychological, political and aesthetic presences and absences which catch all women (and men) in complicated negotiations too dissonant to be netted in a singular, racially undifferentiated psycho-analytic sweep. For this reason the experimental, disciplinary diversity of feminist theory can be a crucial comfort to film analysts eager to see a wider range of filmic desires and representations than those sighted by a singular white 'spectator'.

Many critics now fast forward and rewind films in search of evidence of family histories, political obsessions and sociological concerns (Kuhn 1995; Medhurst 1995; Plummer 1990). I hope that others might be intrigued to find how many telling representational effects of gender surface in feminist theories which range from a broad analysis of same-sex experience to specific questions about scientific stereotypes. Feminists are using the tools of theories to deconstruct representations of gender discrimination in exciting and radical ways. I hope that the force of feminist theory will stimulate a consideration of broader issues than those currently centred in film theory. For example, Barbara

Christian and Evelyn Fox Keller are not names customarily indexed in film studies but I think that their particular perceptions dramatise visual issues very well (see Chapters 6 and 3). In any case, from its inception, film study has been overtly, if not accessibly theoretical and incorporating new angles of vision enriches our visual lives.

Why feminist theory matters and why it matters to film, is because of its adventurous legacy in global feminist studies. One of the key aims of feminist theory is to resist monolithic and nationalist reproductions. When Betty Friedan's *The Feminine Mystique* appeared in 1963 feminism, like the American women's angst which she uncovered, was invisible in the media (Friedan 1963). Second wave feminism gained its impetus in America from the assertiveness of the New Left, the Civil Rights and the anti-psychiatry movements, and in Britain from socialist and Marxist anti-Vietnam campaigns and from CND. Pre-dating the growth of feminism, came a growth in women's employment, in women's entry into higher education and an increase in rates of divorce.

The recognition that public policies could be crafted from private experience is unique to feminism. By connecting issues of reproduction with issues of production, the personal with the political, second wave feminism has changed contemporary thinking. The narrative of second wave feminism weaves its way from the widely read and popular books of Betty Friedan and Germaine Greer – whose *The Female Eunuch* (1970) explored the destructive misrepresentation of women by patriarchy – through the reassessments of socialism and psychoanalysis undertaken by Sheila Rowbotham and Juliet Mitchell; and through the radical feminism of Kate Millett, Adrienne Rich and others (Greer 1970; Rowbotham 1973, Mitchell 1974; Millett 1977; Rich 1980). Feminist theory underpinned the activism of groups like the New York Radicalesbians and the British Wages for Housework Campaign. Such theory and activism has been followed by the major categories of response, some of which are described in this book. The dissemination of feminist ideas through the media and women's publishing presses worldwide, for example Manushi, Kitchen Table Press and Virago, gave women's issues public visibility. But it was the development of radical women-centred activism, exemplified by the women's refuges, which highlighted the connections between representation, sexuality and violence and other forms of women's oppression such as the patriarchal family and the sexual division of labour (Humm 1992).

Second-wave feminism takes as its starting point the politics of representation while sharing first-wave feminism's politics of legal, educational and economic equal rights for women. As contemporary feminist theory evolves, the word 'representation' shifts its meaning. Among feminists who came from a socialist/Marxist background in the late 1960s 'representation' means 'political and ideological work' (Barrett 1979, p. 14). In the essays of Audre Lorde, 'representation' means reproducing the erotic power of each others' differences (Lorde 1984). Feminist theory has changed from the 1970s when it minimised differences between women to, in the 1990s, celebrating the electric charge of racial and sexual 'difference' and women-centred perspectives. That change liberates women from the conviction of a single, universal experience into a world of multiple and mobile racial, class and sexual preferences.

Feminist theory rarely resembles the 'propagandist', 'lesbian plot', 'narrow', 'ideological' labels stored in the filofaxes of politically correct conservatives. Rather, feminist theorists of the visual take advantage of the coupled term by making critiques about gender representations while remaining within a shared vocabulary of knowledge. Feminism is not prescriptive or essentialist, but inhabits visual practices in stimulating shapes. There is no single feminism but many different interpretative methods, including those in this book: Black feminisms, postmodernism, the psychoanalytic and so forth. Feminist theory has no party line but brings together many ways of looking, which in turn draw on different disciplines and debates. What brings feminist theorists together is a common belief that gender is constructed through the visual and that representations must thus articulate, consciously or unconsciously, gender constructions. By giving a systematic account of the interaction between gender and visual forms, feminist theorists hope to open up visual culture to issues of power and sexual divisions.

In the 1970s and 1980s feminism was preoccupied with new visual issues in cultural and intellectual thought. Like Catherine Elwes' expression of discomfort with the masculine avant-garde (Elwes 1986B), feminists prominent in the independent film and television sector in Britain highlighted issues of institutionalisation, racial and

sexual stereotyping in newly complex ways. Nadine Marsh-Edwards of
the Black film collective Sankofa, describes the historical and political
reasons for new Black British representations in her account of meeting
Black activists of the 1960s and 70s.

> It was sad the way they turned round and viewed us. Instead of
> looking at us as the next generation who could maybe carry on
> some of their work, they were trying to keep the history that they
> had created for themselves. It felt to me quite static and didn't
> envisage how the future could be changed. (Attille *et al.* 1988, p. 55)

In addition feminism's productive permeability of the boundaries of
film and fine art, of private and public in performance work and of
collaborative film work, is more than one country's historical event,
even if it has been to date inadequately historicised.

There is now a span of work exhibited across the globe in which we
can see the outlines of more open, diverse feminisms. Feminist media
work is everywhere to be seen. In the Southern hemisphere Australia's
Women in Film and Television is a powerful networking and lobbying
group: Europe, meanwhile, boasts many training and practical workshops, for example, Belgium's VDAB Vilvoorde and France's Asprocep.
South and Central American creativity embraces Santiago's Women's
Alternative Media Unit and Santa Domingo's Women Technicians in
Communication, promoting research and publications on women in the
media (Brown *et al.* 1993). Africa's internationally powerful federation
of African Media Women is based in Zimbabwe and the Tanzania
Media Women's Association was formed in 1987 to provide a forum for
the exchange of ideas and resources in action days as well as in video
and radio programmes (Tanzania Media Women's Association 1991).

The recent, exciting visibility of queer cinema, for example, *Go Fish's*
erotic diversity, is exactly mirrored by feminist theory. Judith Butler's
concepts of performance and abjection give leverage to queer cinema's
new representational effects (Butler 1993): Pratibha Parmar's *Khush* uses
'a diverse range of visual modes' including the reworking of classical
Asian dance sequences (Parmar 1993, p. 10).

There is also a creative explosion of visual imagery in Black queer
culture in order to disavow social invisibility. The films of Cheryl Dunye
(shown in Channel Four's 1995 Dyke TV season), Dawn Suggs and

Yvonne Welbon among others,'challenge the boundaries of experimental, autobiographical, and documentary genres' (Parkerson 1993, p. 235).
Nor is this work closeted in the gay community but now forms part of
the alternative mainstream which is just what the screening of Dunye's
films on British television suggests. As Michele Wallace points out, the
status of women of colour in the mainstream is a crucial issue:'Oprah
Winfrey will really be the first powerful black female TV and film
producer . . . for the first stage of feminism or black feminism, it will be
a momentous advance for black women' (Wallace 1992, p. 671).

Feminist theory/women's studies is itself pioneering in the field of
international new technologies; for example, the American National
Council for Research on Women has created a huge databank and *The
International Encyclopedia of Women's Studies*, which I help to edit, will
make its 1.5 million words and over 600 contributions available in
electronic form (CDROM) as well as in print.

In other words, as a result of sexual, cultural and ethnic complexities
veining the adventurous feminist media work and theories of the 1990s,
films cannot any longer be remote from feminism. The inevitable and
common sense corollary of our times suggests we recognise the creative diversity and new identifications which feminist theory offers,
while not losing sight of cultural and political pressures.

As Trinh Minh-ha the feminist film director argues feminism/film is
a new'border traffic' (Humm 1991):

> The personal politicised and the political personalised is the in-
> between ground where the questioning work materialises itself
> and resists its status as mere object of consumption. It is this
> critical stance maintained toward the self-other, personal-political
> relationship that informs feminist consciousness of the oppressive
> workings of both patriarchal and hegemonic ideology. (Trinh, T
> 1984, p. 8)

BIBLIOGRAPHY

Adlam, D. *et al.* (1977) 'Psychology, ideology and the human subject', *Ideology and Consciousness*, 1 (May), 5–57.

Agostinis, V. (1981) 'An Interview with Sally Potter', *Framework*, 14 (Spring), 47.

Alexander, K. (1991) 'Fatal Beauties: Black Women in Hollywood', in Gledhill (ed.), *Stardom: Industry of Desire*, London: Routledge.

Alexander, K. (1993) 'Daughters of the Dust', *Sight and Sound*, 3:9 (September), 20–2.

Althusser, L. (1971) *Lenin and Philosophy and Other Essays*, London: New Left.

Anderson, L. (1989) *Strange Angel*, London: Warner Bros.

Andrew, D. (1992) 'Concepts in Film Theory', in Mast, Cohen and Braudy (eds), *Film Theory and Criticism*, New York: Oxford University Press.

Astruc, A. (1948) 'The birth of a new avant-garde: la caméra-stylo', *Ecran Francais*, 144 trans. in Graham (ed.), *The New Wave*, London: Secker and Warburg/BFI.

Astruc, A. (1959) 'What is *mise-en-scène?*' '*Qu'est-ce que la mise-en-scène*', *Cahiers du Cinema*, 100 (October), 266–8 trans. L. Heron in Hiller (ed.), *Cahiers du Cinema The 1950s Vol. 1*, London: Routledge and Kegan Paul.

Attille, M. et al. (1988) 'Interview with Sankofa Film Collective', in Mercer (ed.), *Black Film, British Cinema*, London: Institute of Contemporary Arts.

Atwood, M. (1982) *Second Words*, Toronto: Anansi.

Auerbach, E. (1971) 'The Brown Stocking', in Sprague (ed.), *Virginia Woolf: A Collection of Critical Essays*, Englewood Cliffs, NJ: Prentice Hall.

Bambara, T. C. (1993) 'Reading the Signs, Empowering the Eye: *Daughters of the Dust* and the Black Independent Cinema Movement', in Diawara (ed.), *Black American Cinema*, London: Routledge.

Baron, S. (1985) 'Splinters', *City Limits*, 184 (12 April), 16.

Barrett *et al.* (1979) *Ideology and Cultural Production*, London: Croom Helm.

Barrett, M. and Phillips, A. (eds) (1992) *Destabilizing Theory*, Cambridge: Polity.

Barry, J. and Flitterman, S. (1987) 'Textual Strategies', in Parker and Pollock (eds), *Framing Feminism*, London: Routledge and Kegan Paul.

Bart, P. (1985) 'The Different Worlds of Women and Men: Attitudes Toward

Pornography and Responses to *Not A Love Story* – a film about Pornography', *Women's Studies International Forum*, 8:4, 307–22.

Barthes, R. (1977) *Roland Barthes by Roland Barthes*, trans. R. Howard, New York: Hill and Wang.

de Beauvoir, S. ((1949) 1972) *The Second Sex*, Harmondsworth: Penguin.

Benjamin, W. (1973) *Illuminations*, London: Fontana.

Berger, J. (1972) *Ways of Seeing*, Harmondsworth: Penguin.

Bergstrom, J. (1988) 'Enunciation and Sexual Difference', in Penley (ed.), *Feminism and Film Theory*, London: Routledge.

Bhabha, H. (1983) 'The Other Question', *Screen*, 26:6, 18–37.

Billen, A. (1995) 'The Billen Interview: Stripping Yarns', *The Observer*, May 28, p. 8.

Billson, A. (1989) 'Cronenberg on Cronenberg', *Monthly Film Bulletin*, 56:660 (January), 4–6.

Bleier, R. (ed.) (1986) *Feminist Approaches to Science*, New York: Pergamon.

Bloom, H. (1973) *The Anxiety of Influence*, New York: Oxford University Press.

Bluestone, G. (1966) *Novels Into Film*, Berkeley: University of California Press.

Bobo, J. (1989) 'Sifting Through the Controversy: Reading *The Color Purple*', *Callaloo: A Journal of Afro-American and African Arts and Letters*, 12:2 (Spring), 332–42.

Bobo, J. (1993) 'Reading Through the Text: The Black Woman as Audience', in Diawara (ed.), *Black American Cinema*, London: Routledge.

Boss, P. (1986) 'Vile Bodies and Bad Medicine', *Screen*, 27:1 (Jan/Feb), 14–26.

Boston Women's Health Book Collective (1973) *Our Bodies, Ourselves: A Book by and For Women*, New York: Simon and Schuster.

Boyne, R. and Rattansi, A. (1990) *Postmodernism and Society*, London: Macmillan.

Brah, A. (1991) 'Questions of Difference and International Feminism', in Aaron and Walby (eds), *Out of the Margins: Women's Studies in the Nineties*, London: Falmer Press.

Brown, L. *et al.* (1993) *The International Handbook of Women's Studies*, Hemel Hempstead: Harvester Wheatsheaf.

Brownmiller, S. (1975) *Against Our Will: Men, Women and Rape*, New York: Simon and Schuster.

Buck-Mores, S. (1989) *The Dialectics of Seeing: Walter Benjamin and the Arcades Project*, Cambridge MA.: MIT Press.

Burlingham, D. (1952) *Twins: A Study of Three Pairs of Identical Twins*, London: Imago.

Burroughs, W. (1969) *The Naked Lunch*, London: Corgi Books.

Busby, M. (ed.) (1993) *Daughters of Africa*, London: Vintage.

Buscombe, E. (1973) 'Ideas of Authorship', *Screen*, 14:3 (Autumn), 75–86.

Butler, J. (1990) *Gender Trouble*, London: Routledge.

Butler, J. (1993) *Bodies that Matter*, London: Routledge.

Camera Obscura (1989) The Spectatrix, 20/21.

Carby, H. (1987) *Reconstructing Womanhood*, New York: Oxford University Press.

Carter, A. (1979) *The Sadeian Woman*, London: Virago.

Caws, M. A. (1990) *Women of Bloomsbury: Virginia, Vanessa and Carrington*, London: Routledge.

Centre for Contemporary Cultural Studies (1977) *On Ideology*, London: Hutchinson.

Chamberlain, J. *et al.* (1993) 'Filling the lack in everybody is quite hard work, really . . .', in Gever, Greyson, Parmar (eds), *Queer Looks*, London: Routledge.

Chambers, I. *et al.* (1974) 'Introduction', *Cultural Studies*, 6 (Autumn), 1–6.

Chatman, S. (1992) 'What Novels Can Do That Films Can't (and Vice Versa)' in Mast, Cohen and Braudy (eds), *Film Theory and Criticism*, New York: Oxford University Press.

Chicago, J. (1979) *The Dinner Party: A Symbol of Our Heritage*, Garden City, NY: Anchor/Doubleday.

Chicago, J. (1985) *The Birth Project*, Garden City, NY: Doubleday and Co.

Chodorow, N. (1978) *The Reproduction of Mothering*, Berkeley: University of California Press.

Christian, B. (1980) *Black Women Novelists: The Development of a Tradition 1892–1976*, Westport, Conn: Greenwood Press.

Christian, B. (1985) *Black Feminist Criticism*, Oxford: Pergamon.

Christian, B. (1989a) 'The Race for Theory', in Kaufmann (ed.), *Gender and Theory*, Oxford: Blackwell.

Christian, B. (1989b) 'But What Do We Think We're Doing Anyway? The State of Black Feminist Criticism(s) or my version of a little bit of history', in Wall (ed.), *Changing Our Own Words: Essays on Criticism, Theory and Writing by Black Women*, New Brunswick: Rutgers University Press.

Christian, B. (1990) 'The highs and lows of Black feminist criticism', in Gates (ed.), *Reading Black: Reading Feminist*, London: Penguin.

Ciment, M. (1972) 'Entretien avec Alan J. Pakula', *Positif*, 136 (Mars), 32–9.

Citron, M. J. (1993) *Gender and the Musical Canon*, Cambridge: Cambridge University Press.

Cixous, H. (1976) 'The Laugh of the Medusa', *Signs*, 1:4 (Summer), 875–93.

Cixous, H. and Clément, C. (1987) *The Newly Born Woman*, Manchester: Manchester University Press.

Collins, P. H. (1990) *Black Feminist Thought*, London: Unwin Hyman.

Collins, P. H. (1995) 'Pornography and Black Women's Bodies' in Dines and Humez (eds), *Gender, Race and Class in Media*, London: Sage.

Cook, D. and Kroker, A. (1988) *The Postmodern Scene*, London: Macmillan.

Cook, P. (1981) 'The Point of Self-expression in Avant-garde Film', Caughie (ed.), *Theories of Authorship*, London: Routledge.

Cook, P. (1984) '*The Gold Diggers*: Interview with Sally Potter', *Framework*, 24 (Spring), 12–30.

Cook, P. (1985) '*Gebroken Spiegels (Broken Mirrors)*' *Monthly Film Bulletin*,

52:615 (April), 113–14.

Cook, P. (1993) (ed.) *The Cinema Book*, London: British Film Institute.

Cook, P. and Johnston, C. (1990) 'The Place of Woman in The Cinema of Raoul Walsh', in Erens (ed.), *Issues in Feminist Film Criticism*, Bloomington: Indiana University Press.

Copjec, J. (1988) '*India Song/Son Nom de Venise dans Calcutta désert*: The Compulsion to Retreat', in Penley (ed.), *Feminism and Film Theory*, London: Routledge.

Coward, R. (1992) '"This Novel Changes Lives": Are Women's Novels Feminist Novels?', in Humm (ed.), *Feminisms: A Reader*, Hemel Hempstead: Harvester Wheatsheaf.

Cowie, E. (1984) 'Fantasia', *m/f*, 9, 71–104.

Cowie, E. (1992) 'Pornography and Fantasy: Psychoanalytic Perspectives', in Segal and McIntosh (eds), *Sex Exposed: Sexuality and the Pornography Debate*, London: Virago.

Cowie, E. (1993) 'Women, Representation and The Image', in Alvarado *et al.* (eds), *The Screen Education Reader*, London: Macmillan.

Creed, B. (1990a) 'Gynesis, Postmodernism and the Science Fiction Horror Film', in Kuhn (ed.), *Alien Zone: Cultural Theory and Contemporary Science Fiction Cinema*, London: Verso.

Creed, B. (1990b) 'Phallic Panic: Male Hysteria and *Dead Ringers*', *Screen*, 31:2 (Summer), 125–47.

Creel, M. W. (1988) '*A Peculiar People*': *Slave Religion and Community Culture Among the Gullahs*, New York: New York University Press.

Cronenberg, D. (1992) in Rodley (ed.), *Cronenberg on Cronenberg*, London: Faber and Faber.

Daly, M. (1987) *Webster's First New Intergalactic Wickedary of the English Language*, Boston, MA: Beacon Press.

Dargis, M. (1993) 'Sally Potter: a director not afraid of Virginia Woolf', *Interview*, 23:6 (June), 42–3.

Dash, J. (1992) *Daughters of the Dust*, New York: The New Press Ltd.

Davies, K. *et al.* (1987) *Out of Focus: Writings on Women and the Media*, London: The Women's Press.

Davis, A. and Wells, S. (1992) (eds) *Shakespeare and the Moving Image*, Cambridge: Cambridge University Press.

Davis, Z. I. (1991) 'An Interview with Julie Dash', *Wide Angle*, 13:3/4 (July/ October), 110–18.

Deleuze, G. and Guattari, F. (1978) 'The Interpretation of Utterances, Politics and Psychoanalysis', in Foss and Morris (eds), *Language, Sexuality and Subversion*, Darlington, AUS: Feral Publications.

Diawara, M. (ed.) (1993) *Black American Cinema*, London: Routledge.

Diawara, M. (1995) 'Cultural Studies/Black Studies', in Henderson (ed.), *Borders, Boundaries and Frames: Cultural Criticism and Cultural Studies*, London: Routledge.

Dickenson, F. (1985) 'Dutch Courage', *Time Out*, 765 (18 April), 12.

Dines, G. (1995) '"I Buy It for the Articles": *Playboy* Magazine and the sexualization of consumerism', in Dines and Humez (eds), *Gender, Race and Class in Media*, London: Sage.

Dittmar, L. (1988) 'Beyond Gender and Within It: The Social Construction of Female Desire', *Wide Angle*, 8:3, 79–88.

Doane, M. A. (1990) 'Film and the Masquerade: Theorizing the Female Spectator' in Erens (ed.), *Issues in Feminist Film Criticism*, Bloomington: Indiana University Press.

Dobson, P. (1992) 'Orlando', *Screen International*, 853 (17 April) 23.

Donald, J. (1995) 'The City, The Cinema: Modern Spaces', in Jenks (ed.), *Visual Culture*, London: Routledge.

Donohue, W. (1993) 'Immortal Longing', *Sight and Sound*, 3:3 (March), 10–14.

Donovan, J. (1987) 'Toward a Women's Poetics', Benstock (ed.), *Feminist Issues in Literary Scholarship*, Bloomington: Indiana University Press.

Douglas, M. (1966) *Purity and Danger: an analysis of concepts of pollution and taboo*, London: Routledge and Kegan Paul.

Douglas, M. (1975) *Implicit Meanings*, London: Routledge and Kegan Paul.

Dowell, P. (1993) 'Demystifying Traditional Notions of Gender: An Interview with Sally Potter', *Cineaste*, xx:1, 16–18.

Dutta, R. (1994) 'Low-key Master of the Whole Vibe', *The Guardian*, October 18, p. 5.

Dworkin, A. (1981) *Pornography*, New York: Perigree.

Dyer, R. (1987) *Heavenly Bodies: Film Stars and Society*, London: Macmillan.

Dyer, R. (1990) *Now You See It: Studies on Lesbian and Gay Film*, London: Routledge.

Ecker, G. (ed.) (1985) *Feminist Aesthetics*, London: The Women's Press.

Ehrenreich, B. and English, D. (1978) *For Her Own Good: 150 Years of the Experts' Advice to Women*, New York: Anchor Press.

Ehrenstein, D. (1993) 'Out of the Wilderness: An Interview with Sally Potter', *Film Quarterly*, 47:1 (Fall), 2–8.

Eisenstein, S. (1992) 'Dickens, Griffith and the Film Today' in Mast, Cohen and Braudy (eds), *Film Theory and Criticism*, New York: Oxford University Press.

Ellis, J. (1982) *Visible Fictions*, London: Methuen.

Elwes, C. (1986) 'With Child: Programme Note', in Finch (ed.), *ICA Video and Library Guide*, London: Institute of Contemporary Art.

Elwes, C. (1986b) 'A Bid for Radical Naturalism', in Finch (ed.), *ICA Video and Library Guide*, London: Institute of Contemporary Art.

Evans, M. (1985) *Simone de Beauvoir*, London: Tavistock.

Faludi, S. (1992) *Backlash: The Undeclared War Against Women*, London: Chatto and Windus.

Ferguson, A. (1981) 'Patriarchy, Sexual Identity and the Sexual Revolution', *Signs*, 7:1 (Fall), 158–72.

Firestone, S. (1979) *The Dialectic of Sex*, London: The Women's Press.

Fischer, L. (1989) *Shot/Countershot: Film Tradition and Women's Cinema*, Princeton: Princeton University Press.

Flax, J. (1987) 'Postmodernism and Gender Relations in Feminist Theory', *Signs*, 12:4, 621–43.

Flitterman, S. (1981) 'Women, desire and the look: feminism and the enunciative apparatus in cinema', in Caughie (ed.), *Theories of Authorship*, London: Routledge.

Flitterman-Lewis, S. (1990) *To Desire Differently: Feminism and the French Cinema*, Urbana: University of Illinois.

Florence, B. (1991) 'The Making of "TOTAL RECALL"' *Cinefantastique*, 21:5 (April), 34–48.

Florence, P. (1993) 'A Conversation with Sally Potter', *Screen*, 34:3 (Autumn), 275–85.

Floyd, N. (1988) 'Double Trouble', *Time Out*, 952 (16 Nov), 18–19.

Floyd, N. (1990) 'Barker and Cronenberg', *Time Out*, 1049 (26 Sept), 23.

Forster, H. (1985) *Recodings: Art, Spectacle, Cultural Politics*, Port Townsend, Washington: Bay Press.

Foucault, M. (1972) *The Archaeology of Knowledge*, trans. A. M. Sheridan-Smith, London: Tavistock.

Foucault, M. (1977) *Discipline and Punish*, Harmondsworth, Penguin.

Fox Keller, E. (1990) 'From Secrets of Life to Secrets of Death', in Jacobus, Fox Keller and Shuttleworth (eds), *Body/Politics: Women and the Discourses of Science*, London: Routledge.

Francke, L. (1993) 'A Director Comes in From the Cold', *The Guardian*, 11 March, p. 5.

French, M. (1978) *The Women's Room*, London: Sphere.

Friedan, B. (1963) *The Feminine Mystique*, New York: W. W. Norton.

Fuss, D. (ed.) (1991) *Inside/Out: Lesbian Theories, Gay Theories*, London: Routledge.

Gabriel, T. (1982) *Third Cinema in the Third World*, Ann Arbor: University of Michigan Research Press.

Gaitskill, M. (1992) 'David Cronenberg', *Interview*, 22:1 (January), 80–2.

Garber, M. (1992) *Vested Interests: Cross-Dressing and Cultural Anxiety*, Harmondsworth, Penguin.

Gedda, L. (1961) *Twins in History and Science*, London: Charles C. Thomas.

Gentile, M. (1985) *Film Feminisms: Theory and Practice*, Westport, Connecticut: Greenwood Press.

Gentile, M. (1990) 'Feminist or Tendentious?: Marleen Gorris's *A Question of Silence*', in Erens (ed.), *Issues in Feminist Film Criticism*, Bloomington: Indiana University Press.

Gever, M., Grayson, J. and Parmar, P. (eds) (1993) *Queer Looks: Perspectives on Lesbian and Gay Film and Video*, London: Routledge.

Gilbert, S. and Gubar, S. (1979) *The Madwoman in the Attic*, New Haven, CT: Yale University Press.

Gilbert, S. and Gubar, S. (1988) *No Man's Land* vol. 2, *Sex Changes*, New Haven: Yale University Press.

Gilligan, C. (1982) *In A Different Voice: Essays on Psychological Theory and Women's Development*, Cambridge, MA: Harvard University Press.

Glaessner, V. (1992) 'Fire and Ice', *Sight and Sound*, 2:4 (August), 12–15.

Gledhill, C. (1980) '*Klute* I: a contemporary *film noir* and feminist criticism' and '*Klute* 2: feminism and *Klute*' in Kaplan (ed.), *Women in Film Noir*, London: British Film Institute.

Gleiberman, O. (1988) 'Double Meanings', *American Film*, 14:1 (October) 38–43.

Gold, R. (1987) 'Hiring of Black Talent a Grey Area', *Variety* (25 March), p. 36.

Goodman, L. (1992) 'Pornography and Representation', in Bonner *et al.* (eds), *Imagining Women: Cultural Representations and Gender*, Cambridge: Polity Press.

Gordon, B. (1990) '*Variety*: The Pleasure in Looking', in Erens (ed.), *Issues in Feminist Film Criticism*, Bloomington: Indiana University Press.

Gordon, B. and Kay, K. (1993) 'Look Back/Talk Back', in Gibson and Gibson (eds), *Dirty Looks: Women, Pornography, Power*, London: British Film Institute.

Greer, G. (1970) *The Female Eunuch*, London: McGibbon and Kee.

Grosz, E. (1994) *Volatile Bodies*, Bloomington: Indiana University Press.

Guerrero, E. (1993) 'Framing Blackness', *Cineaste*, 20:2, 24–31.

Halmos, P. (1978) *The Faith of the Counsellors*, London: Constable.

Hankins, L. (1993) 'Woolf's "The Cinema" and Film Forums of the Twenties', in Gillespie (ed.), *The Multiple Muses of Virginia Woolf*, Columbia: University of Missouri Press.

Haraway, D. (1989) 'A Manifesto for Cyborgs: Science, Technology and Socialist Feminism in the 1980s', in Wood (ed.), *Coming to Terms*, London: Routledge.

Harding, S. (1991) *Whose Science? Whose Knowledge?*, Milton Keynes: Open University.

Hartsock, N. (1987) 'Rethinking Modernisms: Minority vs Majority Theories', *Cultural Critique*, 7, 187–206.

Haskell, M. (1973) *From Reverence to Rape: The Treatment of Women in the Movies*, New York: Holt, Rinehart and Winston.

Heath, S. (1973) 'Comment on "The Idea of Authorship"', *Screen*, 14:3 (Autumn), 86–92.

Heath, S. (1977/8) 'Notes on Suture', *Screen*, 18:4 (Winter), 48–77.

Hein, H. (1993) 'Refining Feminist Theory: Lessons from Aesthetics', in Hein and Korsmeyer (eds), *Aesthetics in Feminist Perspective*, Bloomington, Ind.: Indiana University Press.

Herskovits, M. J. (1990) *The Myth of the Negro Past*, Boston: Beacon Press.

Hibbin, S. (1983) 'Justifiable Homicide', *Stills*, 6 (May/June), 92.

Hickenlooper, G. (1989) 'The Primal Energies of the Horror Film', *Cineaste*, 17:2, 4–7.

Hiller, S. (ed.) (1991) *The Myth of Primitivism: Perspectives on Art*, London: Routledge.

Hirsch, M. and Fox Keller, E. (eds) (1990) *Conflicts in Feminism*, London: Routledge.

hooks, b. (1984) *Feminist Theory: From Margin to Center*, Boston MA: Turnaround Press.

hooks, b. (1991) *Yearning: Race, Gender and Cultural Politics*, London: Turnaround.

hooks, b. (1992) *Black Looks: Race and Representation*, London: Turnaround.

hooks, b. (1993) 'The Oppositional Gaze: Black Female Spectators', in Diawara (ed.), *Black American Cinema*, London: Routledge.

hooks, b. (1994) *Outlaw Culture: Resisting Representations*, London: Routledge.

Humm, M. (1991) *Border Traffic: Strategies of Contemporary Women Writers*, Manchester: Manchester University Press.

Humm, M. (1991b) 'Thinking of Things in Themselves: Theory, Experience, Women's Studies', in Aaron and Walby (eds), *Out of the Margins*, London: Falmer Press.

Humm, M. (1992) *Feminisms: A Reader*, Hemel Hempstead: Harvester Wheatsheaf.

Humm, M. (1994) *A Reader's Guide to Contemporary Feminist Literary Criticism*, Hemel Hempstead: Harvester Wheatsheaf.

Hutcheon, L. (1988) *A Poetics of Postmodernism: History, Theory, Fiction*, London: Routledge.

Huyssen, A. (1986) *After the Great Divide: Modernism, Mass Culture, Postmodernism*, Bloomington: Indiana University Press.

Irigaray, L. (1977) 'Women's Exile', *Ideology and Consciousness* 1 (May) 62–77.

Irigaray, L. (1985) *This Sex Which Is Not One*, trans. C. Potter, Ithaca, NY: Cornell University Press.

Irigaray, L. (1985b) *Speculum of the Other Woman*, trans. G. C. Gill, Ithaca: Cornell University Press.

Jacobowitz, F. and Lippe, R. 'Dead Ringers: The Joke's On Us', *Cineaction!*, 16 (Spring), 64–8.

Jacobus, M., Fox Keller, E. and Shuttleworth, S. (eds) (1990) *Body/Politics: Women and the Discourses of Science*, London: Routledge.

Jaehne, K. (1988) 'Double Trouble', *Film Comment*, 24:5 (Sept/Oct), 20–7.

Jameson, F. (1988) 'Postmodernism and Consumer Society', in Kaplan (ed.), *Postmodernism and its Discontents: Theories, Practices*, London: Verso.

Jameson, F. (1992) *Signatures of the Visible*, London: Routledge.

Jardine, A. A. (1985) *Gynesis: Configuration of Woman and Modernity*, Ithaca, NY: Cornell University Press.

Jay, M. (1993) *Downcast Eyes: The Denigration of Vision in Twentieth Century French Thought*, Berkeley, CA: University of California.

Jeffreys, S. (1994) *The Lesbian Heresy*, London: The Women's Press.

Jencks, C. (1977) *The Language of Postmodern Architecture*, London: Academy Editions.

Jenks, C. (ed.) (1995) *Visual Culture*, London: Routledge.

Jensen, R. (1995) 'Pornography and the Limits of Experimental Research', in Dines and Humez (eds), *Gender, Race and Class in Media*, London: Sage.

Johnson, W. (1985) 'Broken Mirrors', *Film Quarterly*, 39:1 (Fall), 43–4.

Johnston, C. (ed.) (1975) *The Work of Dorothy Arzner: Towards a Feminist Cinema*, London: British Film Institute.

Johnston, S. (1983) *'De Stilte Rond Christine M. (A Question of Silence)'*, *Monthly Film Bulletin*, 50:589 (February), 48.

Jones, J. (1993) 'The Construction of Black Sexuality: Towards Normalizing the Black Cinematic Experience', in Diawara (ed.), *Black American Cinema*, London: Routledge.

Jordon, G. and Weedon, C. (1995) *Cultural Politics: Class, Gender, Race and the Postmodern World*, Oxford: Blackwell.

Juhasz, A. (1994) '"They said we were trying to show reality – all I want to show is my video": The politics of the realist feminist documentary', *Screen*, 35:2 (Summer), 171–91.

Kallmann, F. J. (1953) *Heredity in Health and Mental Disorder*, London: Chapman and Hall.

— Kaplan, E. A. (1976) 'Aspects of British feminist film theory: a critical evaluation of texts by Claire Johnston and Pam Cook', *Jump Cut*, 12/13, 52–5.

Kaplan, E. A. (1980) *Women in Film Noir*, London: British Film Institute.

— Kaplan, E. A. (1983) *Women and Film: Both Sides of the Camera*, London: Methuen.

Kaplan, E. A. (1987) 'Feminist Criticism and Television', in Allen (ed.), *Channels of Discourse: Television and Contemporary Criticism*, London: Methuen.

Kaplan, E. A. (ed.) (1988) *Postmodernism and its Discontents: Theories, Practices*, London: Verso.

Kaplan, E. A. (ed.) (1990) *Psychoanalysis and Cinema*, London: Routledge.

Kaplan, E. A. (1992) *Motherhood and Representation: The Mother in Popular Culture and Melodrama*, London: Routledge.

Kaufman, E. (1985) 'Broken Mirrors', *Hollywood Reporter*, 287:19 (June 10), 3.

Kaupen-Haas, H. (1988) 'Experimental obstetrics and national socialism: the conceptual basis of reproductive technology today', *Reproductive and Genetic Engineering*, 1:2, 127–33.

Kay, K. and Peary, G. (eds) (1977) *Women and the Cinema: A Critical Anthology*, New York: Dutton.

Kay, S. (1989) 'Double or Nothing', *Cinema Papers*, 74 (July), 23–35.

Kelly-Gadol, J. (1976) 'The Social Relations of the Sexes: Methodological Implications of Women's History', *Signs* (Summer), 809–24.

King, K. (1994) *Theory in Its Feminist Travels*, Bloomington: Indiana University Press.

Klein, M. ((1945) 1991) *Love, Guilt and Reparation and Other Works 1921–1945*, London: Virago.

Klein, M. (1991b) *The Selected Writings of Melanie Klein* (ed.) J. Mitchell, Harmondsworth, Penguin.

Klein, M. (1993) *Envy and Gratitude and Other Works 1946–1963*, London: Virago.

Kofman, S. (1985) *The Enigma of Woman*, Ithaca: Cornell University Press.

Kotz, L. (1993) 'An Unrequited Desire for the Sublime: Looking at Lesbian Representations Across Works of Abigail Child, Cecilia Dougherty, and Su Friedrich', in Gever, Gregson and Parmar (eds), *Queer Looks*, London: Routledge.

Kramarae, C. and Treichler, P. A. (1985) *A Feminist Dictionary*, London: Pandora.

Kramarae, C. and Spender, D. (eds) (1992) *The Knowledge Explosion: Generations of Feminist Scholarship*, New York: Teachers College Press.

Kristeva, J. (1980), 'Motherhood According to Bellini' in *Desire in Language*, Columbia: Columbia University Press.

Kristeva, J. (1983) *Powers of Horror*, New York: Columbia University Press.

Kristeva, J. (1986) 'Stabat Mater' in Moi (ed.), *The Kristeva Reader*, Oxford: Blackwell.

Kuhn, A. (1975) 'Women's Cinema and Feminist Film Criticism', *Screen*, 16:3, 107–12.

Kuhn, A. (1978) 'Introduction to *Riddles of the Sphinx*', *Culture Handbook*, London: British Sociological Association, p. 12.

Kuhn, A. (1981) trans. H. Cixous 'Castration or Decapitation', *Signs*, 7:1, 41–55.

Kuhn, A. (1984) 'Dear Linda', *Feminist Review*, 18 (Winter), 112–21.

Kuhn, A. (1984b) 'Women's Genres', *Screen*, 25:1, 18–28.

Kuhn, A. (1985) *The Power of the Image: Essays on Representation and Sexuality*, London: Routledge and Kegan Paul.

Kuhn, A. (ed.) (1990) *Alien Zone: Cultural Theory and Contemporary Science Fiction Cinema*, London: Verso.

Kuhn, A. (1994) *Women's Pictures: Feminism and Cinema*, 2nd ed., 1st Edition 1982, London, Verso.

Kuhn, A. (1995) *Family Secrets: Acts of Memory and Imagination*, London: Verso.

Kuhn, A. (ed.) (1995b) *Queen of the 'B's: Ida Lupino Behind the Camera*, Trowbridge, Wilts: Flick Books.

Kuhn, A. and Wolpe, A. (1978) *Feminism and Materialism: Women and Modes of Production*, London: Routledge and Kegan Paul.

Lacan, J. (1977) *Écrits: A Selection*, London: Tavistock.

Lakoff, R. (1975) *Language and Woman's Place*, New York: Harper and Row.

Larkin, A. S. (1988) 'Black Women Film-makers Defining Ourselves: Feminism in Our Own Voice', in Pribram (ed.), *Female Spectators: Looking at Film and Television*, London: Verso.

Lauretis, T. de (1984) *Alice Doesn't: Feminism, Semiotics Cinema*, London: Macmillan.

Lauretis, T. de (1987) *Technologies of Gender: Essays on Theory, Film and Fiction*, London: Macmillan.

Lauretis, T. de (1990) 'Guerrilla in the Midst: Women's Cinema in the 80s', *Screen*, 31:1 (Spring), 6–25.

Lee, N. (1988) 'Visuals for *Dead Ringers* Inspire Belief', *American Cinematographer*, 69:12 (December), 38–42.

Lefanu, S. (1983) 'A Matter of Murder', *Time Out*, 652 (18 February), 26.

Lichtenberg-Ettinger, B. (1995) *The Matrixial Gaze*, Leeds: Feminist Arts and Histories Network.

Lippard, L. (1976) *From the Center*, New York: Dutton.

Lippard, L. (1987) 'Issue: An Exhibition of Social Strategies by Women Artists', in Parker and Pollock (eds), *Framing Feminism*, London: Pandora.

Lorde, A. (1982) *Zami*, London: Sheba Press.

Lorde, A. (1984) *Sister Outsider*, Trumansburg, NY: Crossing Press.

Lorde, A. (1988) *A Burst of Light*, London: Sheba.

Lovell, T. (1980) *Pictures of Reality: Aesthetics, Politics and Pleasure*, London: British Film Institute.

Lukács, G. (1971) *Theory of the Novel*, London: Merlin Press.

Lyotard, J.-F. (1984) *The Postmodern Condition: A Report on Knowledge* trans. G. Bennington and B. Massumi, Minneapolis: University of Minnesota Press.

MacKinnon, C. (1989) *Toward a Feminist Theory of the State*, Cambridge MA: Harvard University Press.

MacKinnon, C. (1995) 'Sexuality, Pornography, and Method: "Pleasure Under Patriarchy"' in Juana and Tong (eds), *Feminism and Philosophy: Essential Readings in Theory, Representation, and Application*, Boulder: Westview Press.

MacKintosh, H. (1983) 'Asking Why', *City Limits*, 72 (18 February), 13–14.

McRobbie, A. (1994) *Postmodernism and Popular Culture*, London: Routledge.

Mainardi, P. (1982) 'Quilts: the Great American Art', in Broude and Garrard (eds), *Feminism and Art History*, New York: Harper and Row.

Marcus, J. (1994) 'A Tale of Two Cultures', *The Women's Review of Books*, xi:4 (January), 11–12.

Marshall, P. (1983) *Praisesong for the Widow*, London: Virago.

Mayne, J. (1994) *Directed by Dorothy Arzner*, Bloomington: Indiana University Press.

McGregor, G. (1992) 'Grounding the Countertext: David Cronenberg and the Ethnospecificity of Horror', *Canadian Journal of Film Studies*, 2:1 (Spring), 43–62.

Medhurst, A. (1995) 'Myths of Consensus and Fables of Escape: British Cinema 1945–51', in Fyrth (ed.), *Labour's Promised Land? Culture and Society in Labour Britain 1945–51*, London: Lawrence & Wishart.

Mellen, J. (1974) *Women and Their Sexuality in the New Film*, New York: Dell.

Mellencamp, P. (1990) *Indiscretions: Avant-Garde Film, Video and Feminism*, Bloomington: Indiana University Press.

Mellencamp, P. (1995) 'Five Ages of Film Feminism', in Jayamann (ed.), *Kiss*

Me Deadly, Sydney: Power.

Mercer, K. (1988) 'Recoding Narratives of Race and Nation', in Mercer *et al.* (eds) *Black Film British Cinema*, London: Institute of Contemporary Arts.

Mercer, K. (1994) *Welcome to the Jungle: New Positions in Black Cultural Studies*, London: Routledge.

Merck, M. (1992) 'From Minneapolis to Westminster', in Segal and McIntosh (eds), *Sex Exposed: Sexuality and the Pornography Debate*, London: Virago.

Metz, C. (1974) *Language and Cinema*, The Hague: Mouton.

Miller, N. (1986) 'Changing the Subject', in *Feminist Studies/Critical Studies*, (ed.) T. de Lauretis, London: Macmillan.

Miller, N. (1991) *Getting Personal*, London: Routledge.

Millett, K. (1977) *Sexual Politics* (1970 1st edn), London: Virago.

Mills, S. *et al.* (1989) *Feminist Readings, Feminists Reading*, Hemel Hempstead: Harvester Wheatsheaf.

Mitchell, J. (1966) 'Women: The Longest Revolution', *New Left Review*, 40 (November/December), 11–37.

Mitchell, J. (1974) *Psychoanalysis and Feminism*, Harmondsworth: Penguin.

Mitchell, J. and Rose, J. (1982) *Feminine Sexuality: Jacques Lacan and the École Freudienne*, London: Macmillan.

Mittler, P. (1971) *The Study of Twins*, Harmondsworth: Penguin.

Modleski, Tania (1986) 'The Terror of Pleasure: The Contemporary Horror Film' in Modleski (ed.), *Studies in Entertainment: Critical Approaches to Mass Culture*, Bloomington: Indiana University Press.

Modleski, T. (1988) *The Women Who Knew Too Much: Hitchcock and Feminist Theory*, London: Methuen.

Modleski, T. (1991) *Feminism Without Women: Culture and Criticism in a 'Post-feminist' Age*, London: Routledge.

Moers, E. (1977) *Literary Women*, New York: Anchor Doubleday.

Mohanty, C. (1984) 'Under Western Eyes: Feminist Scholarship and Colonial Discourses', *Boundary*, 2, 12–13 (3), 333–58.

Morley, D. (1995) 'Television: Not So Much a Visual Medium, More a Visible Object', in Jenks (ed.), *Visual Culture*, London: Routledge.

Morris, M. (1988a) *The Pirate's Fiancée*, London: Verso.

Morris, M. (1988b) 'Things To Do With Shopping Centres', in Sheridan (ed.), *Grafts*, London: Verso.

Morrison, T. (1973) *Sula*, New York: Alfred A. Knopf.

Muir, A. R. (1987) *A Woman's Guide to Jobs in Films and Television*, London: Pandora.

Mulvey, L. (1975) 'Visual Pleasure and Narrative Cinema', *Screen*, 16:3 (Autumn), 6–19.

Mulvey, L. (1987) 'You don't know what is happening, do you, Mr Jones?' in Parker and Pollock (eds), *Framing Feminism*, London: Pandora.

Mulvey, L. (1989a) 'Individual Responses: Laura Mulvey', *Camera Obscura*, 20/21, 248–52.

Mulvey, L. (1989b) 'British Feminist Film Theory's Female Spectators: Presence and Absence', *Camera Obscura*, 20/21, 68–81.

Mulvey, L. (1989c) 'Afterthoughts on "Visual Pleasure and Narrative Cinema"', in Mulvey (ed.), *Visual and Other Pleasures*, London: Macmillan.

Nava, M. (1994) 'Modernity's Disavowal: Women, the City and the Department Store', unpublished paper forthcoming in Nava and O'Shea (eds), *Modern Times: Reflections on a Century of English Modernity*, London: Routledge.

Neale, S. (1983) 'Masculinity as Spectacle', *Screen*, 24:6, 2–16.

Nguyen, D. T. (1990) 'The "Projectile" Movie Revisited: The Female Body in *Track 29* and *Dead Ringers*', *Film Criticism*, 14:3 (Spring), 39–54.

Nochlin, L. (1971) 'Why have there been no great women artists?' in Gornick and Moran (eds), *Woman in Sexist Society: Studies on Power and Powerlessness*, New York: Basic Books.

Offen, K. (1988) 'Defining Feminism', *Signs*, 14 (11).

Offermanns, D. (1985) 'Producer Van Heijningen joins Dutch Masters', *Screen International*, 495:6 (4 May), 278.

O'Grady, L. (1994) 'Olympia's Maid: Reclaiming Black Female Subjectivity' in Frueh et al. (eds), *New Feminist Criticism*, New York: Icon Editions.

O'Pray, M. (1986) 'Confronting the Media', in Finch (ed.), *ICA Video and Library Guide*, London: Institute of Contemporary Art.

O'Pray, M. (1992) 'Fatal Knowledge', *Sight and Sound*, 1:11 (March), 10–11.

Ortner, S. (1974) 'Is female to male as nature is to culture?', in Rosaldo and Lamphere (eds), *Woman, Culture and Society*, Stanford CA: Stanford University Press.

Pajaczkowska, C. and Young, L. (1992) 'Racism, representation, psychoanalysis', in Donald and Rattansi (eds), *'Race', Culture and Difference*, London: Sage.

Parker, R. and Pollock, G. (eds) (1987) *Framing Feminism: Art and the Women's Movement 1970–1985*, London: Pandora.

Parkerson, M. (1993) 'Birth of a Nation: Towards Black Gay and Lesbian Imagery in Film and Video', in Gever, Greyson and Parmar (eds), *Queer Looks*, London: Routledge.

Parmar, P. (1993) 'That Moment of Emergence', in Gever et al. (eds), *Queer Looks*, London: Routledge.

Pateman, C. and Gross, E. (eds) (1986) *Feminist Challenges: Social and Political Theory*, Sydney: Allen and Unwin.

Peckham, M. (1969) *Art and Pornography*, New York: Basic Books.

Penley, C. (ed.) (1988) *Feminism and Film Theory*, London: Routledge.

Penley, C. (1989) *The Future of An Illusion: Film, Feminism and Psychoanalysis*, London: Routledge.

Penthouse (1985) 20:7 (July).

Penthouse (1995) 30:11.

Petchesky, R. (1981) 'Antiabortion, Antifeminism, and the Rise of the New Right', *Feminist Studies*, 7:2 (Summer), 206–46.

Petchesky, R. (1987) 'Fetal Images: The Power of Visual Culture in the Politics of Reproduction', *Feminist Studies*, 13:2 (Summer), 263–92.

Petrie, D. (1993) 'Introduction' in Petrie (ed.), *Cinema and the Realms of Enchantment*, London: British Film Institute.

Piercy, M. (1972) *Small Changes*, New York: Doubleday.

Plummer, K. (1990) *Documents of Life, 2nd edn.*, London: Unwin Hyman.

Pollock, G. (1989) *Vision and Difference: Femininity, Feminism and the Histories of Art*, London: Routledge.

Potter, S. (1984) 'Notes', *National Film Theatre Programmes*, May, pp. 2–8.

Potter, S. (1987) 'On Shows', in Parker and Pollock (eds), *Framing Feminism*, London: Pandora.

Potter, S. (1992) 'Remembering Michael Powell', *Sight and Sound*, 2:6 (October), 25.

Potter, S. (1994) *Orlando*, London: Faber and Faber.

Quart, B. (1984) '*Entre Nous/A Question of Silence*', *Cineaste*, 13:3, 45–7.

Rabinovitz, L. (1991) *Points of Resistance: Women, Power and Politics in New York Avant-garde Cinema 1943–71*, Urbana: University of Illinois.

Rich, A. (1976) *Of Woman Born*, New York: W. W. Norton.

Rich, A. (1980) 'Compulsory Heterosexuality and Lesbian Existence', *Signs*, 5:4, 631–60.

Rich, R. B. (1984) 'Lady Killers: It's Only a Movie, Guys', *Village Voice*, 7 (August), 51–4.

Rich, R. B. (1990) 'Anti-Porn: Soft Issue, Hard World', in Erens (ed.), *Issues in Feminist Film Criticism*, Bloomington: Indiana University Press.

Riley, D. (1984) *Am I that Name? Feminism and the Category of 'Woman' in History*, London: Macmillan.

Riviere, J. (1986) 'Womanliness as a Masquerade', in Burgin, D. and Kaplan (eds), *Formations of Fantasy*, London: Methuen.

Roddick, N. (1983) '*Question of Silence*', *Films and Filming*, 342 (March), 33–4.

Rodowick, D. N. (1991) *The Difficulty of Difference: Psychoanalysis, Sexual Difference and Film Theory*, London: Routledge.

Root, J. (1986) 'Distributing "*A Question of Silence*": a cautionary tale', in Brunsdon (ed.), *Films for Women*, London: British Film Institute.

Rose, J. (1986) *Sexuality in the Field of Vision*, London: Verso.

Rosen, M. (1973) *Popcorn Venus: Women, Movies and the American Dream*, New York: Coward, McCann, Geoghegan.

Rowan, J. (1976) *Ordinary Ecstasy: Humanistic Psychology in Action*, London: Routledge, Kegan and Paul.

Rowbotham, S. (1973) *Woman's Consciousness, Man's World*, Harmondsworth: Penguin.

Rowbotham, S. (1989) *The Past is Before Us: Feminism in Action Since the 1960s*, Harmondsworth: Penguin.

Rowe, G. (1982) 'Three 1982 Film Festival Interviews', *Film News*, 12:6 (June), 10.

Ruddick, S. (1980) 'Maternal Thinking', *Feminist Studies*, 6:2 (Summer), 342–67.

Sarris, A. (1968) *The American Cinema: Directors and Directions 1929–1968*, New York: Dutton.

Sartre, J-P. (1966) *Being and Nothingness*, trans. H. Barnes, New York: Washington Square Press.

Sawtell, J. (1993) 'In a class of her own', *Morning Star*, 1 April, pp. 4–5.

Sayers, J. (1989) 'Melanie Klein and Mothering – a Feminist Perspective', *International Review of Psychoanalysis*, 16, 363–76.

Screen International (1984) 'Gorris'*Broken Mirrors*' set to repeat success of '*Silence*', 469 (27 October) 156–8.

Sedgwick, E. K. (1985) *Between Men: English Literature and Male Homosocial Desire*, New York: Columbia University Press.

Segal, H. (1979) *Klein*, London: Fontana.

Segal, L. and McIntosh, M. (eds) (1992) *Sex Exposed: Sexuality and the Pornography Debate*, London: Virago.

Shay, D. (1988) 'Double Vision', *Cinefex* 36 (November), 32–49.

Sherfey, M. (1976) 'A Theory on Female Sexuality', in Cox (ed.), *Female Psychology: The Emerging Self*, Chicago: Science Research Associates.

Showalter, E. (1977) *A Literature of Their Own: British Women Novelists from Brontë to Lessing*, Princeton, NJ: Princeton University Press.

Showalter, E. (ed.) (1986) *The New Feminist Criticism: Essays on Women, Literature and Theory*, New York: Pantheon.

Showalter, E. (1992) *Sexual Anarchy: Gender and Culture at the Fin de Siècle*, London: Virago.

Silver, B. R. (1992) 'What's Woolf Got To Do With It? or the Perils of Popularity', *Modern Fiction Studies*, 38:1 (Spring), 21–61.

Silverman, K. (1988) *The Acoustic Mirror: The Female Voice in Psychoanalysis and Cinema*, Bloomington: Indiana University Press.

Silverman, K. (1990) 'Dis-Embodying the Female Voice', in Erens (ed.), *Issues in Feminist Film Criticism*, Bloomington: Indiana University Press.

Situationist International Exhibition (1989), Institute of Contemporary Art.

Smelik, A. (1993) 'And the Mirror Cracked: Metaphors of Violence in the Films of Marleen Gorris', *Women's Studies International Forum*, 16:4, pp. 349–63.

Smith, B. (1977) *Toward a Black Feminist Criticism*, Brooklyn, NY: Out & Out Books.

Smith, D. (1987) *The Everyday World as Problematic: A Feminist Sociology*, Boston: North Eastern University Press.

Smith, V. (1994) 'Telling Family Secrets: Narrative and Ideology in *Suzanne, Suzanne* by Camille Billops and James V. Hatch', in Carson *et al.* (eds), *Multiple Voices in Feminist Film Criticism*, Minneapolis: University of Minnesota.

Snead. J. (1988) '"Black Independent Film": Britain and America', in Mercer (ed.), *Black Film, British Cinema*, London: Institute of Contemporary Art.

Snead, J. (1994) *White Screens Black Images*, London: Routledge.

Solanase, J. (1985) 'Sex Wars', *New Musical Express* (6 April), p. 18.

Sontag, S. (1966) 'The Pornographic Imagination', in *Styles of Radical Will*, Farrar, Straus and Giroux: New York.

South Bank Centre (1996) *Literature*, London: South Bank Centre.

Spelman, E. V. (1988) *Inessential Woman: Patterns of Exclusion in Feminist Thought*, Boston, MA.: Beacon.

Spence, J. and Holland, P. (eds) (1991) *Family Snaps: The Meanings of Domestic Photography*, London: Virago.

Spender, D. (1980) *Man Made Language*, London: Routledge & Kegan Paul.

Spero, N. (1987) *Nancy Spero*, London: Institute of Contemporary Arts.

Spivak, G. (1987) *In Other Worlds: Essays in Cultural Politics*, London: Methuen.

Stacey, J. (1990) 'Desperately Seeking Difference', in Erens (ed.), *Issues in Feminist Film Criticism*, Bloomington: Indiana University Press.

Stanley, L. (ed.) (1990) *Feminist Praxis: Research, Theory and Epistemology in Feminist Sociology*, London: Routledge.

Steady, F. (1981) *The Black Woman Cross-Culturally*, Cambridge, Mass: Schenkman.

Stimpson, M. (1993) 'Changing Role', *What's On In London*, 10 March, p. 23.

Stoneham, R. (1992) 'Sins of Commission', *Screen*, 33:2 (Summer), 127–44.

Suleiman, S. R. (1985) 'Writing and Motherhood', in *The (M)Other Tongue: Essays in Feminist Psychoanalytic Interpretation*, Ithaca: Cornell University Press.

Sulter, M. (ed.) (1990) *Passion: Discourses on Blackwomen's Creativity*, Hebden Bridge, West Yorks.: Urban Fox Press.

Suter, J. (1979) 'Feminine Discourse in *Christopher Strong*', *Camera Obscura*, 3/4, 135–50.

Swanson, G. and Moy-Thomas, L. (1981) 'An Interview with Sally Potter', *Undercut*, 1 (March/April), 41–4.

Tamblyn, C. (1994) 'The Hair of the Dog That Bit Us: Theory in Recent Feminist Art', in Freuh *et al.* (eds), *New Feminist Criticism*, New York: Icon Press.

Tanzania Media Women's Association (1991) *Sauti ya Siti*, Dar es Salaam: TMWA.

Tasker, Y. (1993) *Spectacular Bodies: Gender, Genre and the Action Cinema*, London: Routledge.

Taylor, C. (1988) 'We Don't Need Another Hero: Anti-Theses on Aesthetics', in Cham and Andrade-Watkins (eds), *Blackframes*, Cambridge: MIT Press.

Taylor, C. (1993) 'The Ironies of Palace-Subaltern Discourse', in Diawara (ed.), *Black American Cinema*, London: Routledge.

Thompson, E. P. (1978) *The Poverty of Theory and Other Essays*, London: Merlin Press.

Thompson, G. (1979) 'Television as Text: Open University"Case Study"Programmes' in Barrett et al. (eds), *Ideology and Cultural Production*, London: Croom Helm.

Touchette, C. (1994) 'Multicultural Strategies for Aesthetic Revolution in the Twenty-First Century', in Freuh *et al.* (eds), *New Feminist Criticism: Art Identity Action*, New York: Icon Editions.

Trinh, T. M-h (1991) *When The Moon Waxes Red: Representation, Gender and Cultural Politics*, London: Routledge.

Trinh, T. M-h (1994) 'A Minute Too Long', in Norrish (ed.), *Cinenova Catalogue of Films and Video Directed by Women*, London: Cinenova.

Trinh, T. M-h (1995) '"Who Is Speaking?" of Nation, Community and First-Person Interviews', in Pietropaolo and Testaferri (eds), *Feminisms in the Cinema*, Bloomington: Indiana University Press.

Tuchman, M. (1984) 'Fish Gotta Swim', *Monthly Film Bulletin* 51:605 (June), 192.

Walker, A. (1983) *The Color Purple*, London: The Women's Press.

Walker, A. (1984) *In Search of Our Mothers' Gardens*, London: The Women's Press.

Walker, A. (1989) *The Temple of My Familiar*, London: The Women's Press.

Wallace, M. (1990) 'Modernism, Postmodernism, and the Problem of the Visual in Afro-American Culture', in Ferguson *et al.* (eds), *Out There: Marginalization and Contemporary Culture*, Boston: MIT Press.

Wallace, M. (1992) 'Negative Images: Towards A Black Feminist Cultural Criticism', in Grossberg, Nelson, Treichler (eds), *Cultural Studies*, London: Routledge.

Wallace, M. (1993) 'Race, Gender and Psychoanalysis in Forties Film: *Lost Boundaries, Home of the Brave*, and *The Quiet One*, in Diawara (ed.), *Black American Cinema*, London: Routledge.

Wandor, M. (1981) *Understudies: Theatre and Sexual Politics*, London: Methuen.

Warner, M. (1993) 'The Uses of Enchantment', in Petrie (ed.), *Cinema and The Realms of Enchantment*, London: British Film Institute.

Washington, M. H. (1989) *Invented Lives: Narratives of Black Women 1860–1960*, London: Virago.

Watney, S. (1987) *Policing Desire: Pornography, AIDS and the Media*, Minneapolis: University of Minnesota.

Williams, L. (1988) 'A Jury of Their Peers: Marleen Gorris's *A Question of Silence*', in Kaplan (ed.), *Postmodernism and Its Discontents*, London: Verso.

Williams, L. (1992) 'Pornographies on/scene, or diff'rent strokes for diff'rent folks', in Segal and McIntosh (eds), *Sex Exposed: Sexuality and the Pornography Debate*, London: Virago.

Williams, L. (1993) 'Second Thoughts on *Hard Core*: American Obscenity Law and the Scapegoating of Deviance', in Gibson and Gibson (eds), *Dirty Looks: Women, Pornography, Power*, London: British Film Institute.

Williamson, J. (1983) 'Images of "Woman" – the Photographs of Cindy Sherman', *Screen*, 24:6, 102–6.

Williamson, J. (1988) 'Two Kinds of Otherness', in Mercer (ed.), *Black Film British Cinema*, London: Institute of Contemporary Arts.

Wilton, T. (1995) *Immortal Invisible: Lesbians and the Moving Image*, London: Routledge.

Winterson, J. (1995) *Art Objects: Essays on Ecstasy and Effrontery*, London: Jonathan Cape.

Wolf, N. (1990) *The Beauty Myth*, London: Chatto and Windus.

Wollen, P. (1969 and 1972) *Signs and Meaning in the Cinema*, London: Secker and Warburg.

Wollen, P. (1992) 'Delirious Projections', *Sight and Sound*, 2:4, 24–8.

Wollen, P. (1993) *Raiding the Icebox: Reflections on Twentieth Century Culture*, London: Verso.

Woolf, V. (1929) *A Room of One's Own*, London: Hogarth Press.

Woolf, V. (1953) *A Writer's Diary*, London: Hogarth Press.

Woolf, V. (1961) *The Death of the Moth and Other Essays*, Harmondsworth: Penguin.

Woolf, V. (1966–7) *Collected Essays* (ed.) L. Woolf, London: Chatto and Windus.

Woolf, V. (1976) *The Letters of Virginia Woolf: Volume 2 1912–1922* (ed.) N. Nicholson, New York: Harcourt Brace Jovanovich.

Woolf, V. (1978) 'The Cinema' in *The Captain's Death Bed and Other Essays*, New York: Harcourt Brace Jovanovich.

Woolf, V. (1992) *Orlando* (ed.) R. Bowlby, Oxford: Oxford University Press.

Yearwood, G. L. (1982) *Black Cinema Aesthetics: Issues in Independent Black Filmmaking*, Athens: Ohio University Center for Afro-American Studies.

Zalcock, B. (1994) 'Daring Directions', in Norrish (ed.), *Cinenova Catalogue of Films and Videos Directed by Women*, London: Cinenova.

FILMOGRAPHY

—◦◦—

KLUTE

Director: Alan J. PAKULA
Release year: 1971
Production company: Warner Bros Pictures
Synopsis: Detective searching for a missing friend becomes involved with a prostitute who gives him a lead to a man who is the murderer of that friend.
Cast:

Jane FONDA – Bree Daniel
Donald SUTHERLAND – John Klute
Charles CIOFFI – Cable
Roy SCHEIDER – Frank Ligourin
Dorothy TRISTAN – Arlyn Page
Rita GAM – Trina
Vivian NATHAN – Psychiatrist
Nathan GEORGE – Lt Trask
Morris STRASSBERG – Mr Goldfarb
Barry SNIDER – Berger
Richard SHULL – Sugarman
Betty MURRAY – Holly Gruneman
Jean STAPLETON – Goldfarb's Secretary
Robert MILLI – Tom Gruneman
Jane WHITE – Janie Dale
Shirley STOLER – Momma Reese

Credits:

Alan J. PAKULA – Director
Alan J. PAKULA – Producer
David LANGE – Co-producer
William C. GERRITY – Assistant Director

Andy K. LEWIS – Scriptwriter
Dave LEWIS – Scriptwriter
Gordon WILLIS – Photography
Carl LERNER – Editor
George JENKINS – Art Director
John MORTENSEN – Set Director
Michael SMALL – Music composed and conducted
Ann ROTH – Costume Designer
Arthur ECKSTEIN – Title Design
Chris NEWMAN – Sound

Running time: 114 mins.

VARIETY

Director: Bette GORDON
Release year: 1983
Production company: Variety Motion Pictures
                       Zweites Deutsches Fernsehen
                       Channel Four
                       Arnold Abelson
Synopsis: A woman takes a job in a sex cinema as a ticket seller. While developing a fantasy world for herself inspired by the cinema screen, she becomes involved with one of the patrons and begins to follow him to find out what is behind his mysterious activities.

Cast:

Sandy MCLEOD – Christine
Luis GUZMAN – Jose
Will PATTON – Mark
Nan GOLDIN – Nan
Richard DAVIDSON – Louis Tancredi
Lee TUCKER – Projectionist
Peter RIZZO – Driver
Mark BOONE Jnr – Business manager/porn customer
Spalding GRAY – Obscene phone voice

Credits:

Bette GORDON – Director
Renee SHAFRANSKY – Producer
Tim BURNS – Assistant Director
Kathy ACKER – Scriptwriter
Bette GORDON – Original story
Thomas DiCILLO – Photography
John FOSTER – Photography
Bette GORDON – Additional Photography

Ila von HASPERG – Editor
John LURIE – Music
Elyse GOLDBERG – Costumes
Optical House – Titles
Helen KAPLAN – Sound Recording
Magno Sound – Sound Re-recording

Running time: 100 mins.

DEAD RINGERS

Director: David CRONENBERG
Release year: 1988
Production company: Mantle Clinic II Ltd
                    Morgan Creek Productions
Synopsis: Identical twin gynaecologists, Beverly and Elliot Mantle, share everything, often interchanging places without anyone knowing. But their intense bond is fatally damaged when they both fall in love with the same internationally-known actress.
Cast:

Jeremy IRONS – Elliot and Beverly Mantle
Geneviève BUJOLD – Claire Niveau
Heidi von PALLESKE – Cary
Shirley DOUGLAS – Laura
Barbara GORDON – Danuta
Stephen LACK – Anders Wolleck
Nick NICHOLS – Leo
Lynn CORMACK – Arlene
Damir ANDREI – Birchall
Miriam NEWHOUSE – Mrs Brookman

Credits:

David CRONENBERG – Director
David CRONENBERG and Marc BOYMAN – Producers
Carol BAUM and Sylvio TABET – Executive Producers
David CRONENBERG and Norman SNIDER – Scriptwriters
        Based on the book *Twins* by Bari Wood and Jack Geasland.
Peter SUSCHITZKY – Cinematography
Bryan DAY – Sound
Ronald SANDERS – Editor
Howard SHORE – Music
Carol SPIER – Production Design

Running time: 115 mins.

A QUESTION OF SILENCE (*De Stilte Rond Christine M.*)

Director: Marleen GORRIS
Release year: 1982
Production company: Sigma Films
Synopsis: Feminist drama in which a woman psychiatrist is appointed by the Court to investigate the sanity of three women who have beaten to death a male boutique owner.
Cast:

> Edda BARENDS – Christine
> Nelly FRIJDA – Annie
> Henriëtte TOL – Andrea
> Cox HABBEMA – Dr Janine van den Bos
> Eddy BRUGMAN – Janine's husband
> Hans CROISET – Judge
> Eric PLOOVER – Court Official

Credits:

> Marleen GORRIS – Director
> Matthijs van HEIJNINGEN – Producer
> Conny BRAK – Assistant Director
> Marleen GORRIS – Scriptwriter
> Frans BROMET – Photography
> Hans BURGHARD – Lighting
> Hans van DONGEN – Editor
> Harry AMMERLAAN – Art Director
> Lodewijk de BOER – Music
> Jany HUBAR – Costumes
> Ullie ULLRICH – Make-up
> Victor DEKKER – Sound Recording

Running time: 96 mins.

BROKEN MIRRORS (*Gebroken Spiegels*)

Director: Marleen GORRIS
Release year: 1984
Production year: 1983
Production company: Sigma Films
Synopsis: Story of the life of two prostitutes Diane and Dora and of the abduction of a housewife Bea, who is murdered by slow starvation in a cold cellar.
Cast:

> Lineke RIJXMAN – Diane
> Henriëtte TOL – Dora

Edda BARENDS – Bea
Coby STUNNENBERG – Ellen
Carla HARDY – Irma
Marijke VEUGELERS – Francine
Arline RENFURM – Tessa
Anke Van't HOFF – Linda
Hedda TABET – Jacky
Elja PELGROM – Maria
Johan LEYSEN – Boss
Rolf LEENDEERTS – Doorman
Eddy BRUGMAN – Jean-Pierre
Beppie MELISSEN – His Wife
Wim WAMA – Andre

Credits:

Marleen GORRIS – Director
Matthijs van HEIJNINGEN – Producer
Hessel HAAK – Production Manager
Marleen GORRIS – Scriptwriter
Frans BROMET – Photography
Hans van DONGEN – Editor
Harry AMMERLAAN – Art Director
Harry WIESSENHAAN – Special Effects
Lodewijk de BOER – Music
Jany HUBAR – Costumes
Bernadette CORSTENS – Wardrobe
Winnie GALLIS – Make-up
Optical Arthouse – Titles and Opticals
Danniel DANNIEL – Sound

Running time: 116 mins.

THE LAST ISLAND

Director: Marleen GORRIS
Release year: 1990
Production company: First Floor Features
Synopsis: An aeroplane crashes on a desert island and seven people survive
– two women, five men and a dog.
Cast:

Paul FREEMAN – Sean
Patricia HAYES – Mrs Godame
Shelagh MCLEOD – Joanna
Kenneth COLLEY – Nick
March HEMBROW – Frank

Marc BERMAN – Pierre
Ian TRACEY – Jack

Credits:

Marleen GORRIS – Director
Laurens GEELS and Dick MAAS – Producer
Marc FELPERLAAN – Director of Photography
Casper POOTJES – Stills Photography
Bert FLANTIJA – Sound Engineer
Benthe FORRER – Script/Continuity
Harry AMMERLAAN – Art Director
Boudewijn TARENSKEEN – Music
Tamara JONGSMA – Costume
Winnie GALLIS – Make-up
Bickersaction – Special effects

Running time: 90 mins.

ANTONIA'S LINE

Director: Marleen GORRIS
Release year: 1995
Production company: Antonia's Line International
Synopsis: A family saga in which widow Antonia returns to her family's
farm in a Dutch village. Here she lives with her daughter and
granddaughter.

Cast:

Willeke van AMMELROOY – Antonia
Els DOTTERMANS – Daniëlle
Dora van der GROEN – Allegonde
Veerle van OVERLOOP – Thérèse
Esther VRIESENDORP – Thérèse at thirteen years old
Carolien SPOOR – Thérèse at six years old
Thyrza RAVESTEIJN – Sarah
Mil SEGHERS – Crooked Finger
Jan DECLEIR – Boer Bas
Elsie De BRAUW – Lara

Credits:

Marleen GORRIS – Director
Marleen GORRIS – Scriptwriter
Hans de WEERS – Producer
Antonino LOMBARDO and Judy COUNIHAN – Co-Producers
Willy STASSEN – Director of Photography
Harry AMMERLAAN – Art Director
Jany TEMIME – Costume Designer

Jan SEWELL – Make-up
Ilona SEKASZ – Music
Michiel REICHWEIN and Wim LOUWRIER – Editors

Running time: 93 mins.

DAUGHTERS OF THE DUST

Director: Julie DASH
Release year: 1991
Production company: Geechee Girls in association with American Playhouse
Synopsis: A film about the Gullah – descendants of the African slaves who
inhabited the beautiful offshore islands of South Carolina and
Georgia. The film shows the richness of their traditions and
culture, their oral sagas and the dilemma they faced at the turn
of the twentieth century – whether to remain in their environment with their traditions and culture or to uproot themselves
and go north for jobs and other opportunities.

Cast:

Alva ROGERS – Eula Peazant
Adisa ANDERSON – Eli Peazant
Kaycee MOORE – Haagar Peazant
Barbara-O – Yellow Mary Peazant
Cora Lee DAY – Nana Peazant
Trula HOOSIER – Trula
Umar ABDURRAHAMN – Bilal Muhammed
Cheryl Lynn BRUCE – Viola Peazant
Tommy HICKS – Mr Snead
Kai-Lynn WARREN – Unborn Child

Credits:

Julie DASH – Director
Lindsay LAW – Executive Producer
Julie DASH and Arthur JAFA – Producers
Julie DASH – Screenplay
Arthur JAFA – Director of Photography
Amy CAREY and Joseph BURTON – Editors
Kerry MARSHALL – Production Designer
John BARNES – Music

Running time: 112 mins.

ORLANDO

Director: Sally POTTER
Release year: 1992
Production company: British Screen Finance
Lenfilm
Mikado Films
Rio Films
Sigma Films
Adventure Pictures
Synopsis: An interpretation of Virginia Woolf's novel in which the young aristocrat Orlando journeys from 1600 to the present and, by changing sex along the way, shakes off his biological and cultural destiny.

Cast:

Tilda SWINTON – Orlando
Billy ZANE – Shelmerdine
Quentin CRISP – Queen Elizabeth I
Heathcote WILLIAMS – Nick Greene
Dudley SUTTON – King James I
Lothaire BLUTEAU – The Khan
Charlotte VALANDREY – Sasha
Anna FARNWORTH – Clorinda
John WOOD – Archduke Harry
Thom HOFFMAN – William of Orange
Jimmy SOMMERVILLE – Falsetto/Angel

Credits:

Sally POTTER – Director
Christopher SHEPPARD – Producer
Sally POTTER – Scriptwriter
Virginia WOOLF – Author of *Orlando*
Alexei RODIONOV – Photography
Herve SCHNEID – Editor
Bob LAST – Music Producer
Sandy POWELL – Costume Designer
Morag ROSS – Make-up

Running time: 93 mins.

INDEX

Wings of Desire, 32
Winterson, Jeanette, 155, 160
With Child, 180
Wolf, Naomi, 8
Wollen, Peter, 25, 96, 154
Wollstonecraft, Mary, 5
Wolpe, A., 26
'woman-centred perspective', 189
'Womanliness as a Masquerade' (Riviere),
    162
women
    Asian women's representation, 188
    Black *see* Black women
    dehumanisation of, 43
    denial of women's speech, 45
    destructive misrepresentation by
        patriarchy, 196
    empowerment of, 190
    experiential knowledge, 5
    fetishization, 31
    growth in employment, 196
    independent, 63
    literary differences, 100
    objectification of, 11, 29, 40
    as sex objects, 181
    silenced and marginalised, 29
    subordination, 31
    women's subcultures, 99, 100
Women Against Rape, 183
Women and the Cinema (Kay and Peary), 17
Women and Film (Kaplan), 28, 29
Women and Film magazine, 12, 98–9
Women in Film and Television [Australia],
    198
Women in Film Noir (Kaplan), 29
Women Technicians in Communication
    [Santo Domingo], 198
Women's and Gay Theatre Festivals
    (Almost Free Theatre), 180
Women's Alternative Media Unit
    [Santiago], 198
Women's Arts Movement, 180
'Women's Cinema as Counter Cinema'
    (Johnston and Cook), 28
Women's Film, TV and Video Network, 181
'Women's Genres' (Kuhn), 27
women's groups, 188–9
'Women's Images of Men' exhibition
    (Institute of Contemporary Arts), 8,
    180

women's liberation, 6
women's liberation movement, 97
Women's Liberation Workshop, 18
Women's Media Resource Project, 181
Women's Monitoring Network, 181
women's movement, 8, 10
    concern with images, 19
    critique of representation, 26
women's oppression, 197
    causes of, 6
    feminism's attack on, 5
    sexuality and, 6
Women's Pictures: Feminism and Cinema
    (Kuhn), 5, 26–7, 28, 144
women's publishing, 196
women's refuges, 196
The Women's Review of Books, 147
women's rights legislation (United States),
    97
The Women's Room (French), 24
Women's Strike for Equality (1970), 97
women's studies, 4, 36, 181–2, 189, 190
    as pioneering in the field of
        international new technologies, 199
women's workshops/galleries, 11
Wood, Bari, 62
Woolf, Leonard, 145, 152
Woolf, Virginia, 5, 37, 38, 143, 144, 145,
    147, 149, 153–7, 159–64, 166,
    169–72, 175, 177, 178
work, feminist theory and, 5
Working Papers in Cultural Studies
    (Birmingham Centre for
    Contemporary Cultural Studies), 20
workshops, 182–3
Workshops Declaration, 182
A Writer's Diary (Woolf), 145
Writing in Light (South Bank Centre), 90
Wuthering Heights, 91
Wuthering Heights (Brontë), 172

The Year Left journal, 30
Yearning (hooks), 31–2, 35, 128
Yearwood, Gladstone, 119
Young, L., 35

Zalcock, Bev, 181
Zami (Lorde), 120, 123, 137–8
A Zed and Two Noughts, 65
Zeitgeist, 171